Start Here:

Python Programming

Made Fun and Easier

by

Jody Scott Ginther

Published by
Alien Cat Studios ®

Quantum-Sight ™ (Educational Division)
1712 W Stevens #D
Bozeman, MT 59715

ISBN 9780989384704

Library of Congress Control Number: 2013907954

Printed in the United States of America
First Printing May 2013

DEDICATION

To my two sons, who helped me understand the deeper meaning of:

"Never give up!"

The next page is intentionally left blank just to bother people.

You will never know...

CONTENTS

ACKNOWLEDGMENTS

It is not possible to acknowledge by name everyone who has influenced me in writing this course. So, I will have to offer a generic "thank you" and acknowledge those unknown people who influence me along the way. I would like to acknowledge the people at Python.org for their unwavering support for Python programmers. I would also like to acknowledge those throughout the Python community who may have had a part in providing or influencing some of the code used in this course.

The next page is intentionally left blank just to bother people.

You will always wonder.

Introduction

Who Should Read This Book?

- ANYONE WHO WANTS TO LEARN PROGRAMMING IN PYTHON
- THOSE SOULS MASTERING THE ART OF INDEPENDENT LEARNING
- PROGRAMMING TEACHERS WITH A SENSE OF HUMOR
- PEOPLE WHO ARE CURIOUS
- PEOPLE WHO ARE BORED AND HAVE NOTHING BETTER TO DO
- YOU

The unexpected popularity of my mini-book on Python programming combined with constant requests to write a more in depth course; inspired me to write this one. The first book, "Start Here: Python Programming Made Simple for the Beginner" was a free introduction to Python programming. I had no idea that over 10,000 copies of this short e-book would spread worldwide in the first two months from one virtually unknown website. This opened my eyes to the need for programming books and courses that teach Python in an interesting or at least "different" way.

This book includes an updated, and re-written course that includes all the contents of the first book. So, it is unnecessary to read that book first. You can begin here. Content changes and improvements have been made to each chapter and we go deeper into the world of Python in this course. I use the term "course" rather than "book" because I have added some self-study exams, exercises, and quizzes. The intent is to use this as a programming course for classrooms; and a resource for those who prefer independent-study. When you finish this book, you will be able to do some programming in Python, make simple games, package them, and be well down the road to being a great programmer.

Why isn't this course free like the first mini-book? My wife likes to eat, so I guess I should feed her once in awhile. Unfortunately my time for free projects is limited.

The author, (that's me if you haven't guessed already), believes the theory that visual learning, humor, emotional learning, interactive or conversational communication, and action, (experiential learning), are some of the best ways for most people to quickly learn something. I attempt to be as brief as possible to transform the reader into a competent programmer as fast as possible. This means I did skip things about history, comparisons to other programming languages you probably don't know anyway, and anything else that may slow you down, (other than humor and visual elements to help you remember things and reduce boredom; yours and mine).

Sincerely Me,
Jody S. Ginther

Who's The Author?

WHO CARES? ***"I just want to get into programming quickly!"*** Then skip this part. The author, (Jody S. Ginther), chose to include only a few useless details about himself that you probably don't care about anyway, *(yeah it's a man with a girl's name, kind of like "Jackie" Chan).* If you must know a little about him; he has taught internationally at major universities for over 17 years, (Jody not Jackie Chan). He has a wide range of interests and has taught computers, programming, math, business, science, languages, communications, and martial arts. He has and continually researches effective learning methods to speed up the learning process. His hobbies include; programming, learning new things, directing, writing, art, playing drums, guitar, piano, singing, making movies, cartoons, and acting. Anyway, enough meaningless drivel about that guy, the focus in this course is not on useless information about that one, but is all about:

turning you into a programmer as quickly as possible.

(Empty white space for no apparent reason)

How To Use This Course

Even if you read my previous short e-book; "Start Here: Python Programming Made Simple" you should still begin at lesson one in this course. One reason is because it is always good to reinforce and review even if you already read most of this information. But most importantly, new information and expanded explanations have been added that may be important to you.

If you are an experienced programmer jump around at will to the parts you don't know; need to review; use this as a reference; or just read everything anyway for its entertainment value.

If you are new to programming this is the course to begin with. Although the lessons in this course have been made simple to understand; keep in mind that any programming does not seem very simple when you are new to it. But, just as any skills or talents, anything you practice enough will become easier and more simple as you become a master. A **master** *is someone who has done some skill so many times; it looks easy and has become easy for them to perform and teach it skillfully.*

Don't just read the book unless you plan to read a lesson one time through and go back to do it the second time through. Just as speaking any language can only truly be learned by speaking it; learning a programming language can only be mastered by doing it. Each code example is intended for you to do, not just to read. You will be surprised that things you thought looked too simple to bother typing, need to be practiced. The elimination of a space or a mild typo will destroy your program. You must practice as much as possible until you are a code perfectionist. This will save you countless hours of debugging or fixing your code and will radically lower your level of stress.

In this course, self-testing proficiency exams and quizzes are provided to help you understand how well you know the information that has been covered to that point. Depending on your style of learning, **you could approach these lessons in different ways**:

1. The best way for most people is to do each lesson, type, (don't copy and paste), all code as you follow along. *Why?* To re-enforce what you learn by doing it, and because the most common errors in programming come from typing and copying mistakes. If you don't completely understand the lesson, repeat it until you do before going on.
2. If you are the kind of person who gets bored easily and need an overview before you will remember things; use this approach: Read the lessons, do copy and paste code where you can, and fly through the book to get an overview. Return to the beginning and do the lessons slowly and type all the code for practice and mastery. Repeat the lessons you need until you master them.

Programming is learned best by doing it until you got it. Some people find that having an overview of the entire course and coming back to practice is a better approach. If you have a teacher or instructor for this course, then you should trust their experience and judgment. They will have specific objectives and a specific time frame planned for you. In this case you have the following choices:

1. Listen to your instructor.
2. Fail the class.
3. Learn it your own way and gamble with your grades.

The exercises provided should be repeated and altered at will until you reach a point of confidence and understanding. Don't just copy the code in the book, **play with it.**

Keep in mind that one of the primary purposes of this course is to give you some confidence in doing some simple programming while giving you an overview of Python.

You can dive into the deeper depths of every topic within this course as you feel ready to do so. To reach more advanced levels of programming see python.org's website; visit Python communities; advanced books; Python 3x or newer code exchanges; online resources, resources in Index C of this course, Python's documentation, python.org and www.toonzcat.com .

Other Uses for this course:

Of course, there are other uses for a book or course if you have a creative mind. My wife thinks books are where you put the hot frying pan so it doesn't burn the table. I once had an interesting experience when I taught my first class in China that opened my eyes to other creative uses for a book:

Setting: *One of the most famous Universities in China. Sometime after the Qing Dynasty. Daytime.*

I had just eaten some, not so safe local food, giving me a new definition to the term "fast food." I desperately searched for a bathroom on my way to class. Surprise one happened when I opened the door of the stall. I expected to see a friendly toilet staring back at me; in its place was a porcelain lined hole in the floor. But this was a desperate situation; I had no time to contemplate neither the reasoning behind someone stealing the toilet nor the philosophy behind lining the hole in the floor with porcelain. With some relief everything quickly came out OK. Then came surprise number two. I looked around for toilet paper. It was at that memorable moment in my life when I discovered a difference in our two cultures. In China, you are expected to bring your own toilet paper. Caught with my pants down, I looked at the time and saw I was about to be late for my first class. I frantically looked around the cubical for alternatives.

I entered the classroom as the bell was ringing, just in time! I went to the podium, cleared my voice, and declared; "For this lesson we will go directly to chapter two; chapter one has been chosen to serve a higher purpose."

Why the Strange Format?

Because strange, surprise, out of place, new, different, humorous, emotional, artistic, ugly, and downright weird experiences help us to learn faster. Oh, and of course the old tried and true method of seemingly useless repetition. Did I mention repetition? Our attention span is not much different than a child's in this respect. Sure, we have been beaten, threatened, and brainwashed into sitting like motion-less zombies in a classroom desk to pretend we are paying attention. In fact, those who move too much in some cultures are branded "hyperactive" and even drugged, (sorry "medicated"), to get them to sit still and stop interrupting those who are pretending to pay attention around them. When, in reality, we all have varying degrees of success in these vain attempts to continually focus. This depends upon many factors such as; level of interest, emotions, the amount of sleep we had last night, and how many distractions there are in the room that may be more interesting. From the beauty in the corner to the fly buzzing around someone's head, our mind occasionally longs for something, anything, other than the teacher or the subject of the class to focus on. We even tend to exaggerate the significance of these distractions to prolong our escape from these zombie impersonations expected of us.

A short story for understanding the moral of this section;

Cartoons by Jody S. Ginther ©2013

A *little* bee flies into the window in a family home. The family members may or may not notice, but will generally react with mild amusement or fear. They will continue watching TV, terminate the bee, let it out a window, or calmly lock it in grandma's *room.*

The same bee flies into a public classroom. Now we have a major event! Girls screaming, people laughing, irrational ducks, leans, objects being thrown, and other acts of total anarchy. Chaos escalates until the bee is no longer in the room or is viciously murdered after being beaten half to death by a mad mob during it's futile attempt to escape.

The same event occurred. But, as you can see how in the second instance; the importance of the bee was magnified in the minds of our fellow zombies, as a desperate, welcome escape from their required payment of time and energy to attention.

Even the importance of a simple insect can radically increase as our minds become desperate to fly around real, imagined, and internal realities as a welcome escape from focusing on one topic too long.

So, what's my point?

Ok...I'll get to it;

Faster learning methods, *(in this case visual and unique, with tried and sometimes true methods),* provide my excuse for not formatting this course in a *boring, or I should I say; "traditionally correct"* format. Let's face it; unless you have one of the few whose brains that are wired differently, things like math and programming can be boring. Furthermore, it is more fun for the author, to present this stuff in a different way.

Tips for Faster Learning:

- You will learn faster if something is interesting to you. *Change* is important to maintain interest.

- The higher the emotions are when you receive the new information, the easier it will be to remember. I call this "emotional learning." Think of funny, interesting or emotional things while learning.

- Visualization improves retention.

- Physically *doing* something improves retention. So, type all the examples multiple times if necessary.

- Repetition and practice. Repeat, repeat, and then repeat.

- Verbalizing what you learned causes deeper understanding, (or deeper delusions).

- Pacing of the information is important. Know when to take breaks and what intervals to review and reinforce new information. Know yourself. Some of the lessons are very short and some are very long. If they are too long split them into smaller parts.

- Simultaneously stimulating not only both hemispheres of the brain, but different regions of the brain improves learning. Classical piano music such as Bach's Goldberg Variations, or Mozart in the

BACKGROUND WHILE STUDYING CAN HELP. THE MUSIC MUST BE GENTLE, QUIET, AND NOT DISTRACTING. I FIND SOLO PIANO OR GUITAR WORKS BEST.

- **ALPHA BRAIN WAVE STATES; A RELAXED STATE OF MIND CAN HELP YOU LEARN FASTER. WHEN YOU FIRST WAKE UP OR ARE ABOUT TO SLEEP, YOUR BRAIN CAN RETAIN INFORMATION BETTER. GENERALLY, THIS IS BECAUSE YOUR BRAIN IS IN AN ALPHA STATE. WE HAVE ALL EXPERIENCED HEARING SOME SONG IN THE MORNING AND EVEN IF WE HATE THE SONG, IT IS STUCK IN OUR HEAD ALL DAY. WE EVEN GET DISGUSTED WHEN WE CATCH OURSELVES HUMMING IT. The first things you do in the morning and the last things you do before sleeping can more easily be retained.**

- **TEACH WHAT YOU KNOW. THIS FORCES DEEPER UNDERSTANDING.
IF YOU CAN, FIND SOMEONE WHO KNOWS LESS THAN YOU TO EXPLAIN IT TO. WHEN YOU HAVE TO EXPLAIN SOMETHING, THIS REINFORCES THE INFORMATION. STUDIES HAVE SHOWN THAT TEACHING WHAT YOU KNOW IS ONE OF THE FASTEST WAYS TO RETAIN INFORMATION. THOSE YOU TEACH MAY ALSO POSE QUESTIONS YOU NEVER THOUGHT OF AND EXPAND YOUR OWN UNDERSTANDING BY FORCING YOU TO THINK ABOUT IT FROM DIFFERENT ANGLES.**

I won't go into the research and verification of these learning methods. You will just have to believe me or go do some research yourself. This course is about programming so we won't spend much time on the research end of faster learning. Just try these methods and you will see a difference in your ability to retain new information. Believe it or not.

I also find it is useful to read and record information into an mp3 file to use for passive learning. You can listen to the new vocabulary and concepts while driving, walking, exercising, etc.

Lesson 1: The Beginner's Tour

WHAT YOU WILL LEARN:

- **WHAT'S A PROGRAMMING LANGUAGE**
- **WHAT'S PYTHON AND WHY LEARN IT?**
- **IDLE AND THE SHELL**
- **IDLE COLORS**
- **WHAT ARE BLOCKS OF CODE?**
- **REVIEW**

WHAT'S A PROGRAMMING LANGUAGE?

All languages begin with an understanding of some new terms. We will begin with some essential words that you should know before we get started. If you know these, skip over them. If not, take a moment to learn them.

A programming language is a language you can use to communicate with a computer.

What are programs? ***Programs*** *are algorithms and source code packaged together to achieve some objective(s).* Programs do something for you. As programmers, we should think in terms of how to solve problems with good decision making logic to reach the results we want. What's an algorithm or a source code? ***Algorithms*** *are sets of instructions that tell the computer what to do.* Algorithms tell the computer how to reach a goal or objective. Ok, an algorithm is a set of instructions; then what is source code? The ***"source code"*** *is referring to all the instructions written in a particular language.* All the words, commands, secret symbols, and other stuff we typed or didn't' type into our program is the source code.

For example; in our programs we will write the instructions, (algorithms), in Python source code. You could think of a program as a book with a specific story and purpose; algorithms as the sentences and paragraphs; and source code as all the words, letters and symbols used in that particular book. In our "books," (programs), we will write our source code in the Python language rather than common English.

Note: Project files for this course are available at www.toonzcat.com

***Programming** is the art and science of making the computer do what you want it to do by creating programs.* Computers are stupid and don't understand English. So, we have to use computer languages to translate what we say into Computerish. Actually, the language computers speak is referred to as a binary language. Binary language is a language based on two words; "on" and "off" represented by the numbers 0 and 1. Humans have trouble communicating in binary.

So, new computer languages where invented to make it easier for human brains to understand and be able to communicate with the computer.

WHY SO MANY COMPUTER LANGUAGES?

Different languages were designed for different purposes. Some are better at math, some are better at controlling computer hardware, and some are better for the internet. Python is a general purpose language. It can be used for many different purposes. Different computer languages are like different tools to a carpenter. You can still build a house with a hand saw and a hammer; but sometimes an electric saw and a staple gun would be better for a particular job. The world of programming is the same. You can survive using only one programming language, but you may get the job done faster and easier by having more than one tool to do the job.

WHAT'S PYTHON AND WHY LEARN IT?

Yes, it's a snake but Python is also the name of a computer language. Python is one of the easier computer languages to learn, yet it is very powerful. No programming language is truly "easy," for everyone in the beginning. Mastering anything takes time and effort. When Python has become easy to you; you have become a true Python master.

Python is known as a scripting language, (uses scripts), and is a high level language. A ***high level language** is a computer language that is closer to human language and easier for us to use than low level or machine languages.* High level languages also take care of many tasks like manipulating the memory of the computer for you. ***Low level languages** are used when the programmer wants more direct control* *over the machine he is using.*

This chart gives you a brief over-view of the levels of programming languages.

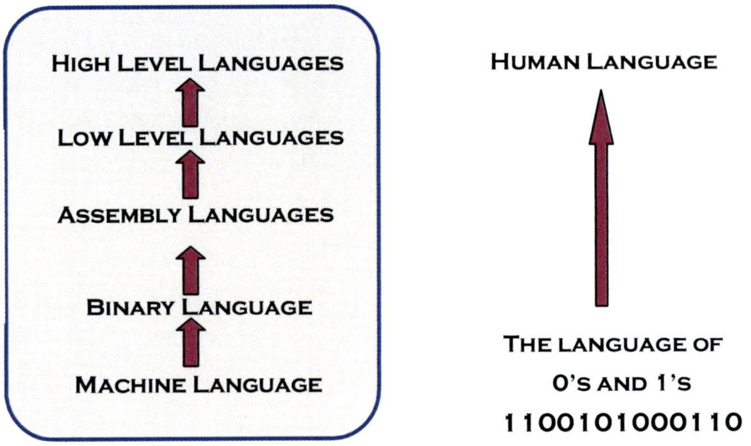

Interpreters and *compilers* both translate high level language code into low level binary code so the "machine" can understand it. However, they do the same job in different ways. *Why two different approaches?* Using a compiled language will generally result in faster running code. While using an interpreted language will generally result in less time for the developer to write and debug the code.

Here are some general comparisons:

Compiler:

- translates entire code into an executable
- saves code as it compiles it
- provides a list of errors after everything is translated
- takes longer to process code and find errors
- final code runs, (executes), faster

Interpreter:

- takes statements one-by-one to translate and execute
- does not save interpreted code
- stops translation when an error is detected and displays the error
- faster in processing code and generally for the developer to find errors.
- final code may run, (execute) slower

Compiled Languages:

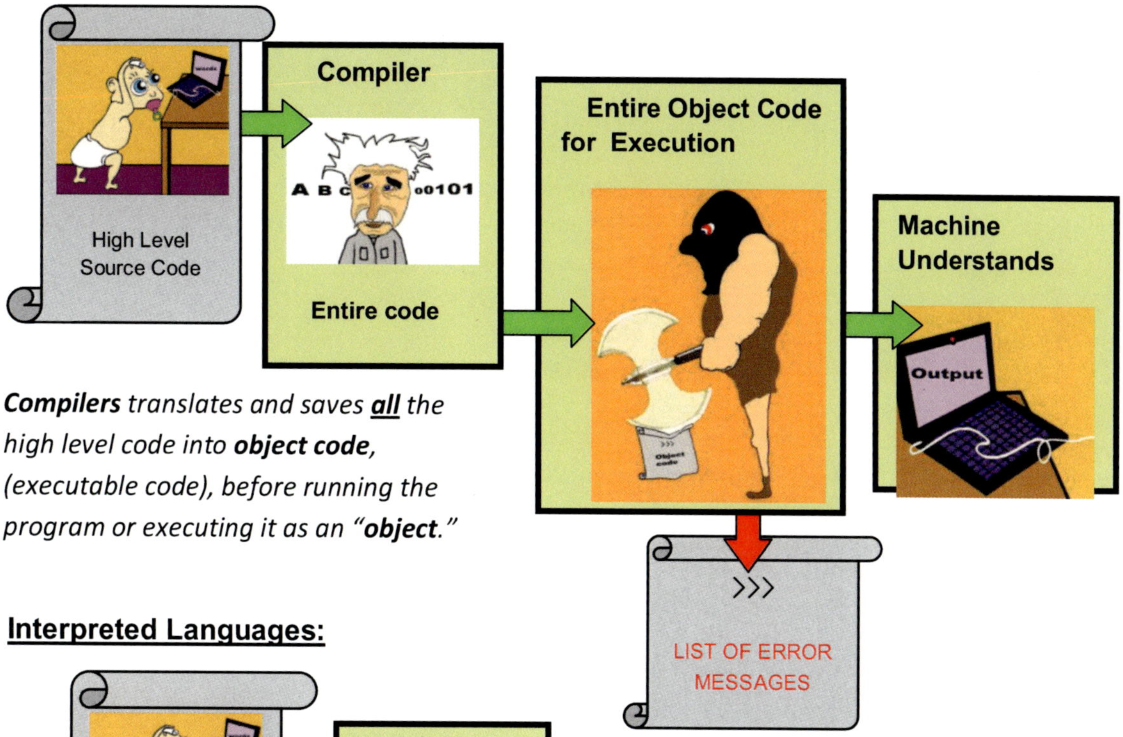

Compilers *translates and saves* ***all*** *the high level code into* ***object code****, (executable code), before running the program or executing it as an "****object****."*

Interpreted Languages:

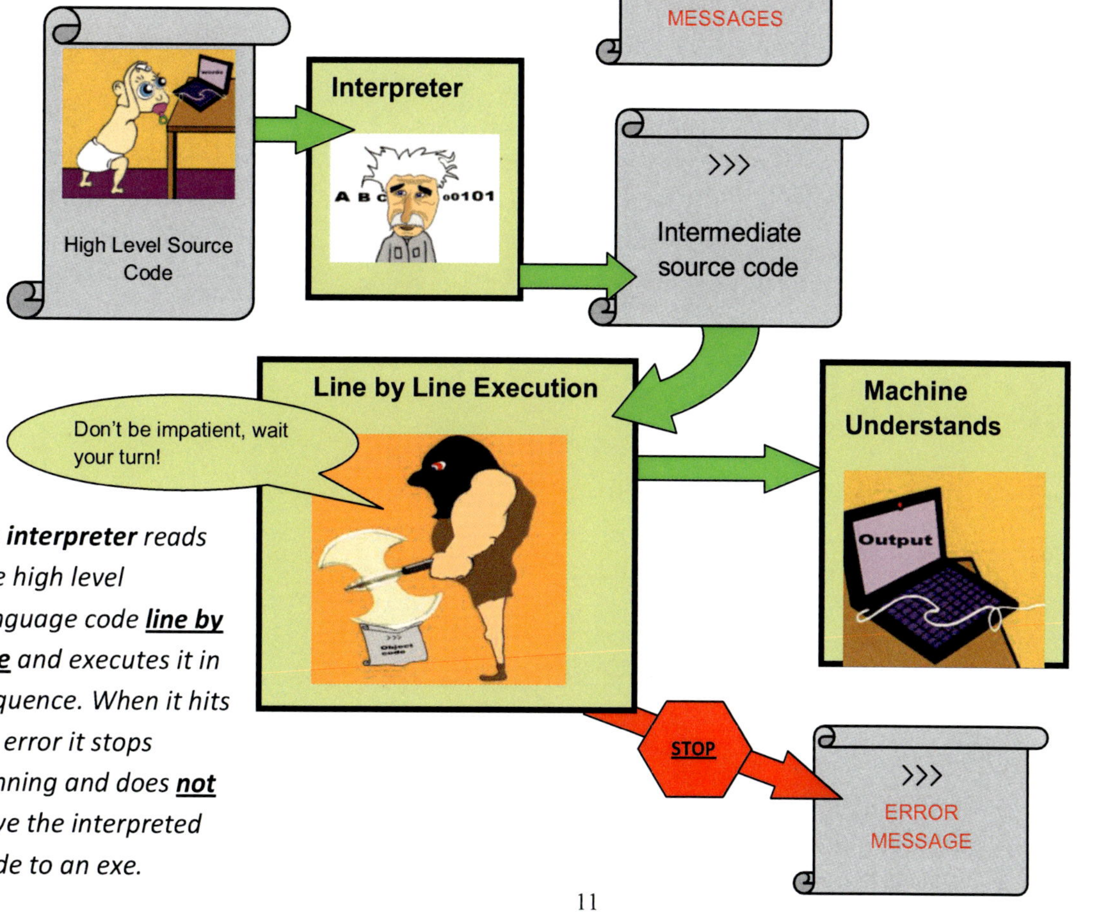

An ***interpreter*** *reads the high level language code* ***line by line*** *and executes it in sequence. When it hits an error it stops running and does* ***not*** *save the interpreted code to an exe.*

Python is an interpreted language. It does not need to be "compiled" before running it.

So what does this mean for you? It means you save a step and some time. You don't have to send your code through a compiler before you can run it and test it. Python even allows you to run small amounts of code in an "*interactive*" or instant manner as you write it.

Python simplifies some tasks in programming and is more readable to humans than many programming languages. Since code can be packages into moveable "*modules*" it can also save time by allowing you to reuse clones of code modules rather than rewriting them from scratch.

So, what is Python used for? Python is use for anything from games and data base programs to web applications. It is used from the New York Stock Exchange to NASA.

Python is considered a valuable tool and is used by many programmers throughout the world. Best of all, Python is easier to learn than most programming languages and is open source! So, let's get started!

Note: To read the history of Pythons development, refer to documentation at Python. org.

Getting and installing Python

Python is free. Download it from python.org. I used Python 3.2 for most of this course and played a little with 3.3. As you read this, a newer version may be available. I suggest choosing the latest stable version for your operating system. When using additional stuff like PyGame make sure it is compatible with the version of Python you are using. I primarily used Python 3.2 because it was thoroughly tested and compatible with the other software I used in these lessons. There were major changes made from Python 3 on, so backwards compatibility is limited. This course is not intended to be used with earlier versions of Python. Follow any special installation instructions you may need and check for the latest versions at:

http://www.python.org/download/

IDLE and the Shell

First, you can start Python in Windows by clicking on **Start>Programs>Python 3.x>IDLE**. Go ahead, try it...I'll wait here. ***IDLE** is software that helps you to communicate with the computer.* It is on the outside of the main program, just as a snail's shell is on the outside of the snail. Whack on a snail's shell and he will get the message;

IDLE works in a similar way; enter commands into IDLE and it will translate and send the message to your machine.

IDLE acts as your *interpreter* and translates what you say into a language that the computer can understand. If you really want to know, IDLE stands for **I**neractive **D**eve**L**opment **E**nvironment. Why did they choose the L in the middle of the word, "development?" I have no idea and it's not important for the purposes of this book, so let's move on and get over it.

There are two windows to work from in IDLE. There is the **Edit Window** and the **Shell Window**. The Python Shell window will say, "Python Shell" at the top of the window, while the Edit window will say, "Untitled" and have a "run" command listed on the top menu bar. If Python starts in the Shell Window and you want to use the Edit Window, just choose **File<New Window** and it will open an Edit Window. If you want to use the Shell Window from the Edit Window go to the "Run" menu at the top of the window and choose "Python Shell."

The ***Python Shell*** *is an interactive interpreter.* This means that when you press the enter key, it checks your source code and may give you some feedback. If you see (>>>), this is the first command prompt. It is letting you know the interpreter is patiently waiting for you to type something. If you see (…), this is the secondary prompt waiting for you to type something more.

The Python Shell looks like this:

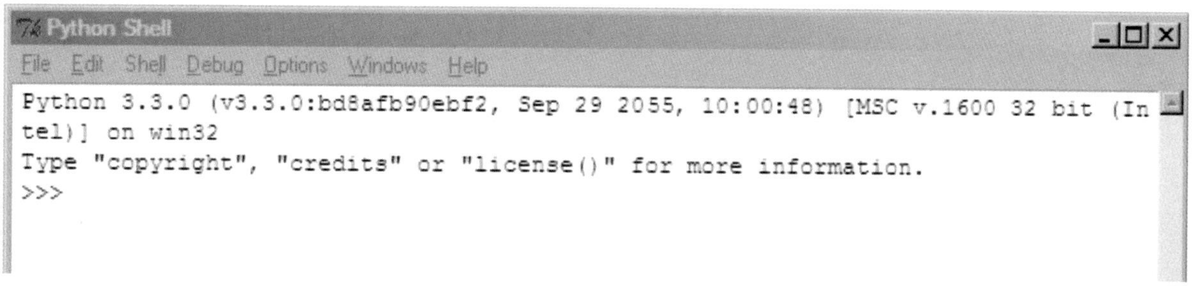

The Python Editor looks like this:

There are other editors that you can use for programming but to keep things simple in this book we will use IDLE for nearly everything. Besides, it's already packaged with Python. Remember that if you choose to use another text editor; you should stick to specific or simple text editors. Editors like notepad rather than one that will mess up your code by adding textual elements or applying unwanted formatting, (like Microsoft's Word program). We will discuss other useful editors later in the course.

Why are there two windows in IDLE and how do I use them? Python allows you to work in *script mode* or in *interactive mode*. What's the difference?

Script Mode *is great for writing programs you can save and run later. It is generally used for the final product*. You are running Script mode when you are in the Edit window.

Interactive mode *is for testing and trying small ideas quickly.* You are running in interactive mode when you are in the Shell window. Most people use both of these together. Script mode for working on their main program and interactive mode for trying new ideas; in the same way you would use a piece of scratch paper.

A third function of IDLE is that it is also a debugger. You can find the debugger button at the top of the Shell window. What's a debugger? It's a program to help you find bugs. No not the one crawling up your leg or living in your hair; but the bugs, or problems, that are in the code we are working on. Why are computer problems called bugs? Computer history tells us that one of the first major computer crashes was caused by an actual bug getting toasted on the circuit board of a computer; hence they named problems in programming computers as bugs. We will go deeper into that story later.

IDLE Colors

Did you notice that IDLE changes the colors of your text? *What's the meaning?* Let's look at a list of some of the most common syntax colors and their meanings in IDLE.

Common Python syntax colors:

Keywords	orange
Strings	green
Comments	red
Definitions	blue
Misc. Words	black

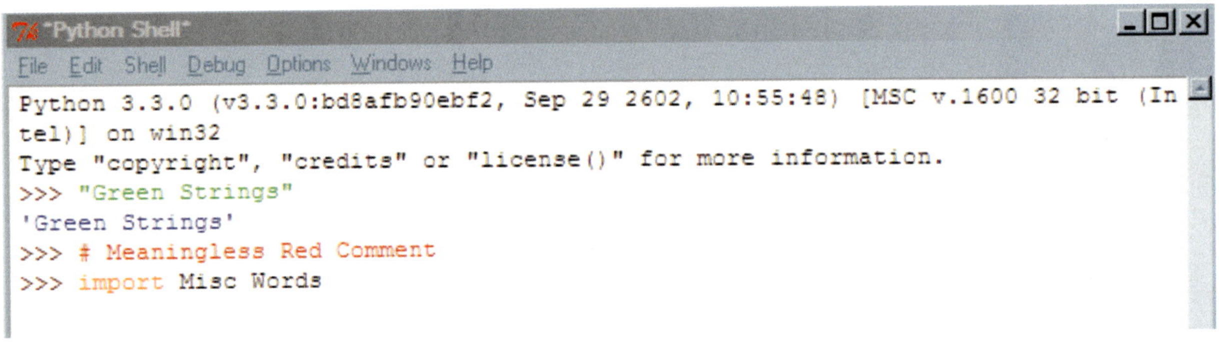

You needn't memorize these at this point, but knowing the meaning of the colors can help you see clearly where you typed something wrong.

If you were trying to type a string and it's not green, you probably forgot the quotation marks or did something else the computer didn't like. Don't worry, I will tell you what a string is later. The colors can also be changed according to your personal preferences and may vary in different editors.

WHAT ARE BLOCKS OF CODE?

While we are looking at the windows, how is your text arranged? The text is arranged in *lines, groups, and blocks*. A ***block** is just a group of code that goes together*. Like a city block, it can be divided into smaller groups like houses on the block, cars on the block, people, dogs, lions, cockroaches, etc. living on that block. This concept is important to tell the computer how to read and follow your code. To a computer, arranging your code with the proper grouping of lines and blocks is like a map that says; "first do this, second do that, or repeat this part. " It can also give directions like a map within your program by saying;

> "After doing this block go to block x and do... that."

Blocks are one way we dictate the running order in programming. You can have blocks in blocks just as you can have groups in groups. You may have a group of students under 100 years old. But, within that group you may have another group called "girls." Inside of that group you may have another group or block called "the names of girls with green hair."

Blocks make it easy to keep things or instructions in our code together in their correct group. This helps us refer to them and to direct the computer to use that group of instructions, in the order we want the computer to read them. Blocks are defined by the number of spaces used to indent each line of code. In the following examples I will use dots to show you clearly how many spaces would be in the code. In this lesson; "**...**" refers to three spaces. Remember to use spaces, not dots, when you type your code into Python.

***Note:** The color code in the following examples is <u>not</u> a part of IDLE's color scheme. These colors are used to emphasize what parts of a block belong together.

```
2 spaces   ..students under a hundred years old   (Block 1)
4 spaces   ....girls   (Block 2)
8 spaces   ........girls with green hair   (Block 3)
```

<u>**The number of times we indent**</u> helps the computer know ***how we are grouping the information.*** (Hang in there, a few more ideas and you will make your first game).

Here are some visual examples:

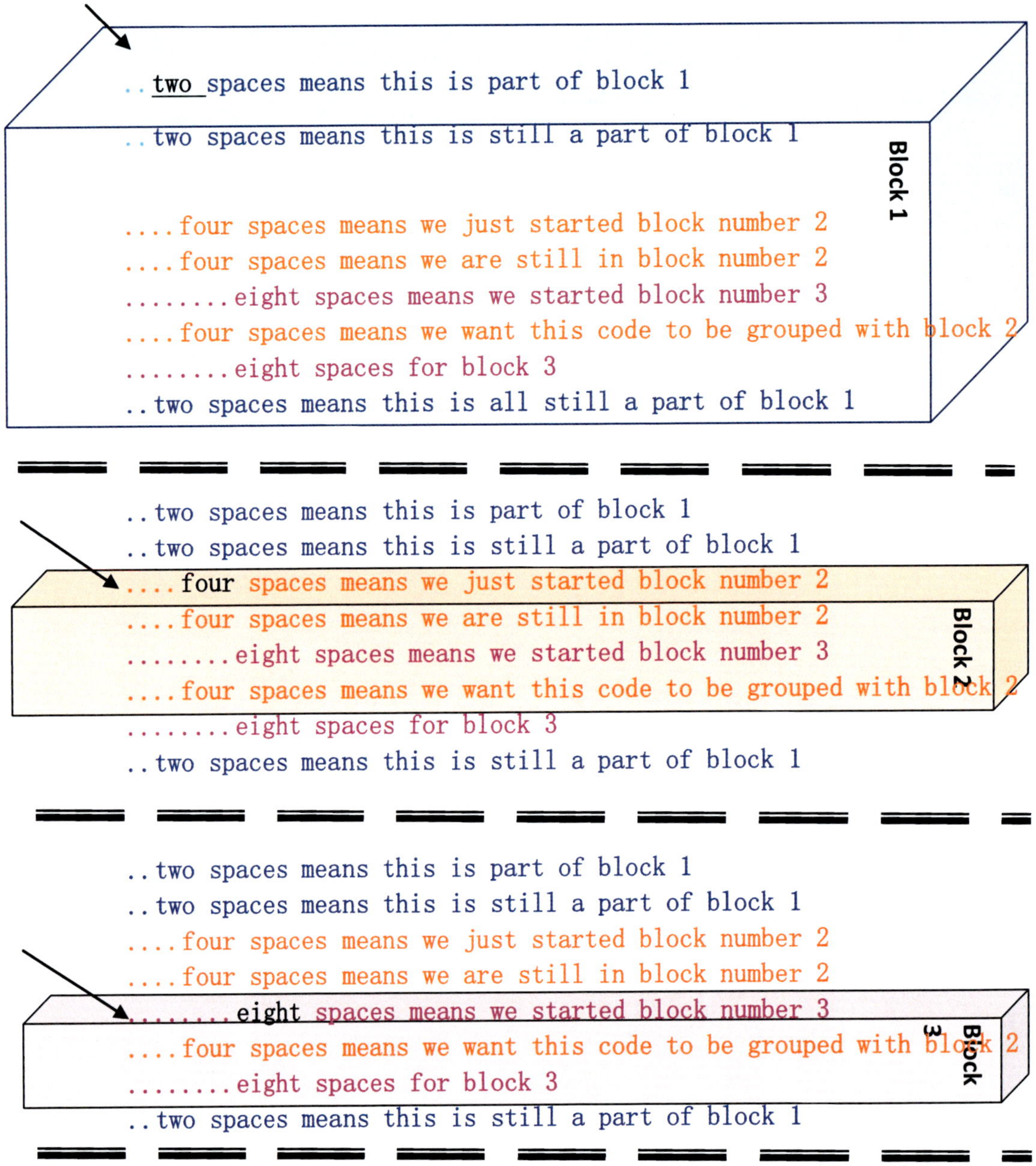

Whatever the number of spaces you choose, keep it consistent so you don't get confused.
Why do we care about blocks and grouping programming statements? Ah, I'm glad you asked, but I won't tell you until later.

Each block of code can reside and work within another block of code.

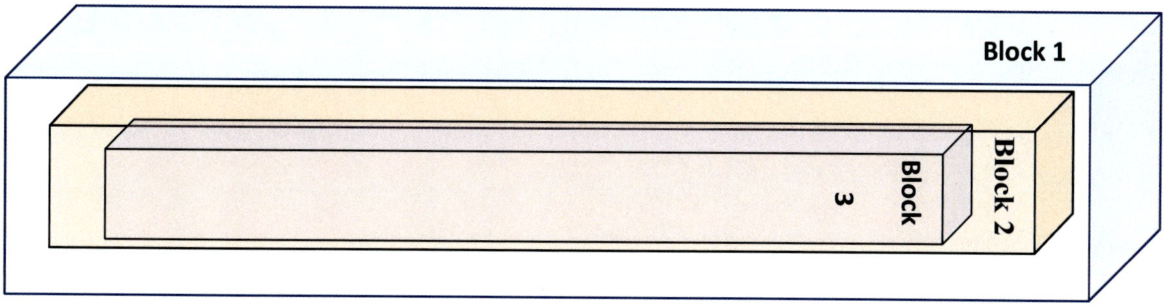

REVIEW: *(Yes, you should know these terms.)*

Before we get to the fun parts we have to speak the same language. Even things like going to the bathroom require special vocabulary like; "Toilette Paper!" "Open the window!" "Did I really eat that?"

Quiz 1:

Answer the following questions on a separate piece of paper or in a document if you prefer. Check your answers on the next page.

1.1 Define the following terms:

1. Algorithms
2. Block
3. High Level Language
4. IDLE
5. Interactive Mode
6. Programming
7. Python Shell
8. Programs
9. Script Mode
10. Source Code

1.2 Questions:

1. What's the difference between an interpreter and a compiler?
2. Which one does Python use?
3. Why is indentation important?

VOCABULARY

Algorithms *are sets of instructions that tell the computer what to do.*

Block *is just a group of code that goes together.*

High level language *is a computer language that is closer to human language and easier for us to use than low level or machine languages.*

IDLE *is software, (an editor), that helps you to communicate with the computer.*

Interactive mode *is for testing and trying small ideas quickly.*

Low level languages *are used when the programmer wants more direct control over the machine he is using.*

Programming *is the art and science of making the computer do what you want it to do by creating programs.*

Programs *are algorithms and source code packaged together to achieve your objective(s).*

Python Shell *is an interactive interpreter.*

Script Mode *is great for writing programs you can save and run later. It is generally used for the final product.*

Source Code *includes all the algorithms or instructions written in a particular programming language*

Quiz 1 Answers:

1.1 Refer to the vocabulary terms chart above.

1.2

1. ***Compilers*** *translate* ***all*** *the high level code into* ***object code*** *before running the program. An* ***interpreter*** *reads the high level language code* ***line by line*** *and executes it in sequence.*

2. Python is an interpreted language, therefore it uses an interpreter and has no need for a compiler.

3. Indentation tells the computer how to group the code into blocks that will be run in a particular order.

Lesson 2: Let's Begin Programming!

WHAT YOU WILL LEARN:

- YOUR FIRST PROGRAM
- VARIABLES
- OPERATORS
- KEY WORDS (TO USE OR NOT TO USE)
- BOOLEAN DATA TYPES
- INTRODUCING STRINGS
- STRING PLACEHOLDERS AND ESCAPES

YOU'RE FIRST PROGRAM!

You are now a programmer, or will be shortly. Don't be intimidated by all the new geek words within each lesson. You will be speaking Geek as well as typing in Python faster than you think, (unless, of course, you are delusional.)

Ok, let's start playing…err… programming. Open your Python Shell window to type some things. Type the following code exactly as you see it. ***Then hit the enter key after each line.***

```
# the computer ignores comments near the # sign
“hey look a programmer”
“cool” + ‘cat’
wow
```

From this point on in your life, you have to be a fanatic about details and a perfectionist about typing. Every space, dot, symbol, upper or lower case, can have an impact on your source code. If something doesn't work, go back and look at your typing carefully.

Most errors by beginning programmers are in the syntax of their code. This is why it is important that you don't just copy and paste code, but you actually type it in for practice and perfection of your programming skills. Train your eye and your fingers, (or both eyes if you have two).

If you entered these correctly, it should look like this:

```
Python 3.3.0 (v3.3.0:bd8afb90ebf2, Sep 29 2055, 10:55:48) [MSC v.1600 32 bit (In
tel)] on win32
Type "copyright", "credits" or "license()" for more information.
>>> # The computer ignores your comments near the # sign
>>> "Hey look! A programmer!"
'Hey look! A programmer!'
>>> "cool" + 'cat'
'coolcat'
>>> wow
Traceback (most recent call last):
  File "<pyshell#3>", line 1, in <module>
    wow
NameError: name 'wow' is not defined
>>>
```

If you type the # key in front of some text, the computer ignores the text. This is useful for adding comments in your programs that will not be misunderstood as instructions by the computer; or if you just feel like being ignored. Ah, our first error message. Get used to these because they are the programmer's constant companion. In time, you will see them less and understand they do have a purpose other than raising your blood pressure.

We will be explaining more about this code shortly; for now I just wanted you to type something and get the feel of the shell.

VARIABLES

Have you ever asked; "When am I going to use this kind of math?" Now that you are a programmer you should remember some simple math concepts to make your life easier. Don't worry, I'll be brief. You don't have to remember complex math at this point, but higher levels of math will definitely increase your programming skills. For now, all you need to know is the world of math has animals called "*operators*" and "*variables*." In programming we use these same mathematical concepts and math-like logic when designing algorithms.

***Variables** are like little like boxes or containers to put different things in.* In math your teacher may have told you that 1 + *x* = some other number. The 1 is an ***integer**, (a complete number as opposed to part of a number like ½),* and the *x is a variable.* In programming, you get to name your variable anything you want. You can create an imaginary box with anything you want to put in it, and define/label that imaginary box, (or variable), by any name you choose.

This means a variable in programming can refer to or contain integers, strings, and some other data creatures you will be meeting as we continue on this path into the world of Python. Let's try it. Let's imagine a box of chocolate. We want to tell the computer that the box labeled "chocolate" has happiness and joy inside of it. To do this we use the = sign to define what our variable means for the computer to understand us.

In the Python shell window type:

Chocolate = **"happiness and joy"**

Hit the enter key.

Now, let's type the word without quotes;

Chocolate

Hit enter.

Your computer should reply, **'happiness and joy'**

You just *defined* a variable and then *called* it. This is very useful in programming. You will constantly be teaching the computer how to think as you write programs and will define things for it.

Variables** are chunks of data stored in the computers memory.* There are generally three types of data stored in variables. Variables can be in the form of ***integers or in a ***string*** as mentioned previously. Another type of data, called a ***float***, refers to the *non-whole numbers like decimals.* Remember to use the = sign to assign a variable. If you want the computer to think the variable *x* means 5 is in the variable box named "*x,*" then you type:

x=5

Now the computer holds a 5 in memory and when you type or call an x, it tells you '5' when you hit the enter key. *What if you want to name a variable now, but you want to assign a value or put something in it later?* One way is to assign the no value, or "None." You could do it this way:

x=None

You can then "overwrite" or replace the value "None" later. There are times when you write code but don't know what value will be placed in a variable. All you have to do to delete and replace the word "None" with the value, (or to overwrite it); is type it with the new value you want to assign to it, (in this case "23):

x=23 #(overwrites the old x value)

KEYWORDS: TO USE OR NOT TO USE?

You can name a variable almost anything and use symbols like the _ underscore. But there are some rules. You can't use special key words that Python understands as having special meanings. Don't use these words for variable names:

```
and     continue except    global   lambda    pass     while

as      def      False     if       None     raise with

assert  del      finally   import   nonlocal return yield
```

If you should accidentally, (or just out of rebellion), use these words something like this will happen:

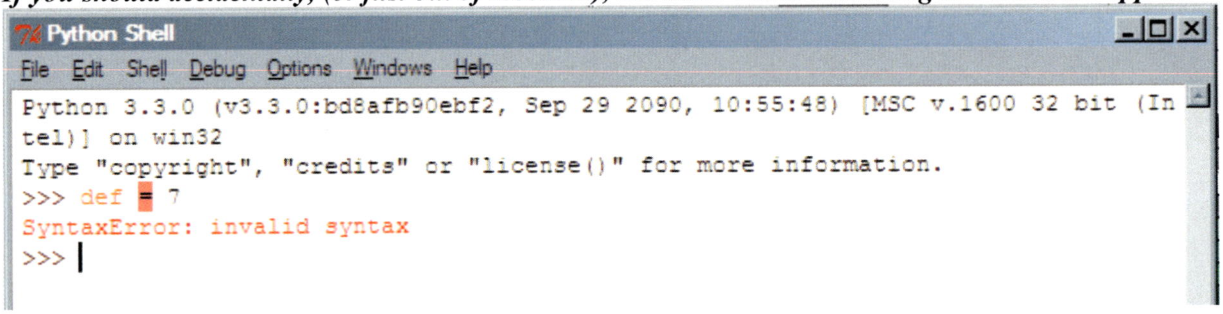

"`SyntaxError: invalid syntax...`" is Python's ways of saying, "*Hey, you don't know what you are talking about and neither do I! Speak Python!*" Don't take it personal, as a programmer you will get used to these insults. You will find your computer has an attitude. **Don't begin a variable name with a number**. The name "34th_apple" would not be accepted by Python. Underscores are allowed. There are also other illegal characters you can't use because they are used for other things in Python. Like the dollar sign, ($).

Python is case sensitive, so remember when you used capital letters. It also pays attention to blank spaces.

Other than these minor rules, you can name a variable anything you want. To sound more like cool geeks, we don't always call them "names," we sometimes call them "identifiers." Remember that ***identifiers*** *are just the names we give to our containers.*

```
people_list = [man, woman, child]
```

Operators

Operators *do something, like add, multiply, divide, subtract, or compare.*
Notice that we already used the = sign to assign an identifier. So, we can't use the equal sign as an operator. Instead we must use two equal signs, (==), to mean the; "equals" symbol used in normal mathematics. *What other useful things can be done with operators?* In the Python shell type:

```
"words words words words words"
```

Hit enter and type:

```
"words " *10
```

Hit enter.

Which is easier? If I knew this in primary school I could have really saved countless hours and gone home at the same time as the other kids. I could have just written:

"I will not run on the desks nor refer to my teacher as something I saw floating in the toilet." *** 1000**

Of course, at that time my teachers preferred to see my handwriting rather than a print-out. Operators are life saving tools for the programmer. A good programmer in Python rarely needs to type the same code more than once. As you guessed by now, the asterisk * symbol is used to express multiplication and to repeat things. You could use it to repeat a string or tuple for a specific number of times. Remember to add a space at the end of "words " before the closing quotation marks or your 10 words will look like one long one.

+ for addition
- for subtraction
/ for division
*** for multiplication**

These are the most common operators.

You can also use operators with strings of data. Try it. Make two strings with any words you want between quotation marks and add them together. ***Like this:***

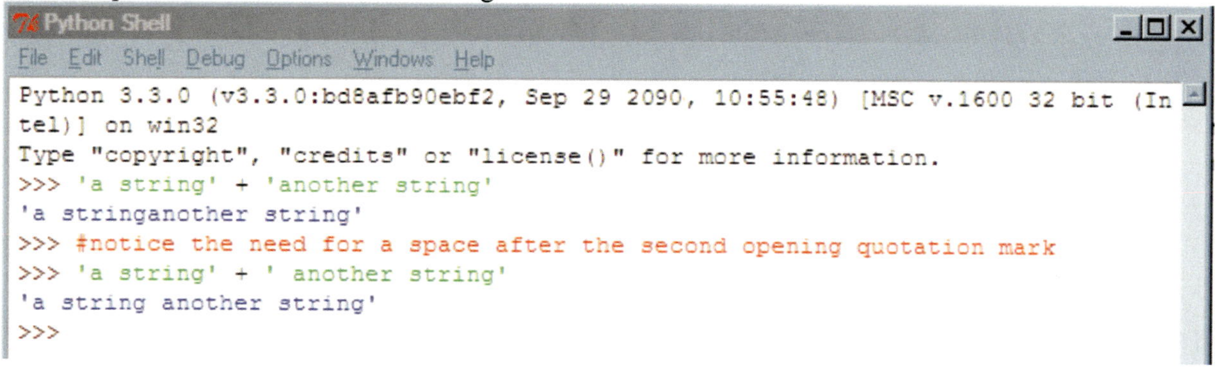

We also have ***comparison operators*** for…you guessed it; *for comparing things!*

Here are some of those:

> for greater than
< for less than
<= less than or equal to
>= greater than or equal to
= = equal to
! = not equal to

Remember that we already used the = symbol to define or tell the computer the meaning of our variables. So we don't confuse our little computer, we must use double equal signs "= =" to express the traditional meaning of "equals to."

Now try some of these until you get bored. Any math expression will do. But wait! Use only integers; no decimals at this point.

Due to the way a computer deals with ***floating point numbers,*** *(numbers with a decimal point)*; you won't always get the same results as a calculator. Use a **"."** in all floating point numbers to solve this problem, (1.0, 0.234).

For now, remember that Python is not your math teacher; although they may look similar. In math, 7.0 is still an integer because numbers like 0, 5, 177, are integers. But computers are not so clever, so in Python the number 7 is an integer but since 7.0 includes a decimal point; it's called a *floating point* number.

Logical Operators

The *words "**and, or,**" and **"not"*** are ***logical operators*.** Logical operators are for comparing and establishing relationships. *A **simple condition** is a comparison that only uses two values:*

9<19

*A **compound condition** is a comparison using more than two values:*

x < 10 and x>5

These logical operators generally mean the same thing in programming as they do in English.

BOOLEAN DATA TYPES

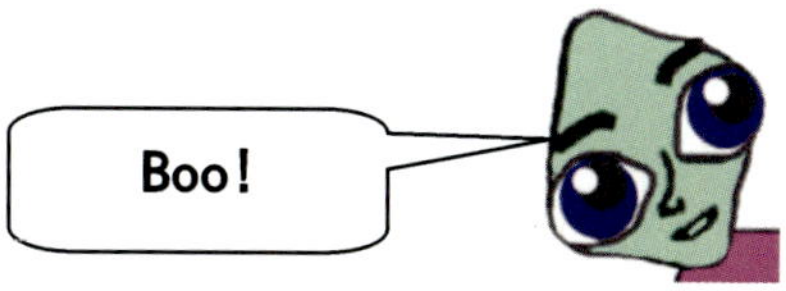

*What's a **Boolean**, some kind of scary alien?* No. You and the computer often need to know if something is true or not. *A **Boolean** data type is referring to two possible values; **True or False**.* A computer is an electric machine and really only understands two things; on and off. Binary is the computer language based on the use of 1 for on and 0 for off. Although reading 1001100011110000011110000 is easy for a computer, it is not so good for humans. As we mentioned earlier, this is why we use programming languages like Python to do the work of communicating with the computer on the machine level. But, we should still keep in mind that everything in our logic and programming will come down to two values we call "True" and "False." True is 1 and false is 0. To think like a computer, always relate your code to these values. ***A 0 in Python is false, while 1 or any other integer is true.***

Boolean expressions are sometimes called ***conditional expressions*** because they *are based on the condition that something is either true or false.*

But, what exactly is an *expression* in Python? Shorty you will also run into the word, "*statement*." You know what they are in English but in programming they have special meanings. *An **expression** is any combination of values, (numbers), that can evaluated into another single value, (number).* This is just a fancy way of saying; " In 3 + 2 =5 is an expression." *A **statement** can be instructions that evaluate into a single value or a expressed fact,* (just as in English). If you wrote a line in your game like: "If the spaceship hits an asteroid, they both explode." This would be a statement.

Now that you are a programmer, your whole life will be about the pursuit of truth, (or not). You will be converting every problem and task into true, false, and logical sequences.

Let's play with some of this new knowledge. Open IDLE and type the following, but feel free to play with your own ideas after you try these:

8>3
Hit enter.
Ah, the computer agrees, it says, "**True**."

3>8
Hit enter.
Hey! The computer just said, "**False**."

I told you the computer has an attitude! Finding Boolean values of "True or False" is vital to the programmer.

To see if and expression is true or false you can compare the values in the expression using "==":

7==7
>>> **True**

7==4
>>> **False**

INTRODUCING STRINGS

If you noticed I typed the words "hey look a programmer" in quotation marks. Later I used; ' ' single quotation marks and got the same exciting result. When we hit enter, the computer just repeated what we typed back to us. It printed the characters as output on the screen. *A sequence of characters, words, or sentences like this one is called a **string**. When we use single or double quote symbols to tell the computer what is in our string, we call these quotation symbols "**delimiters**." We tell the computer that we are entering or ending a string by using single or double quotation marks.* The computer don't care which kind you use as long as you are consistent in pairing them. We can now say we have *declared* or "***delimited***" the string, (a fancy way of saying we put it in quotation marks). You did what to that string? Yes, you delimited it and there is nothing to be ashamed of. In IDLE **strings are green** and **the output is blue**. The **error message is red.**

You can also add strings together using a math operator. We will talk more about that in a moment. Putting the string "cool" with 'cat' produced **'coolcat'**. If I want a space between them when they are added together, I should add one in my string; **"cool "+"cat" or "cool"+ " cat"** would generate **'cool cat'**, because in the first one I added a space after "cool" and in the second one I added a space before "cat."

What happened when I typed, "wow?" The computer said;

```
"Blah blah blah…is not defined. "
```

This is the computer's way of saying; "huh? I don't understand." Python attempts to give you an idea of what went wrong. When I typed the word, I did not include it inside quotation marks to tell the computer that I was entering a string. So, the computer went, "Huh?" "Not defined" means that you did not tell the computer the meaning of "wow". You did not *delimit it* nor did you *define* it for the computer by putting it into quotation marks.

STRING PLACEHOLDERS AND ESCAPES

There are times in programming that you need to have an empty space in a string to place something in later. It is like leaving an empty blank in a sentence to fill in later.

Let's say you are making a game and your character has to pick up and object.
You are not sure of which object at this point so you need to leave that part blank in your code. You will need to express something like; "Fred enters the swamp and picks up a ____ to eat later." We left a blank where we will place a word or value later. *A symbol in our code that indicates a blank value is called a **placeholder**. The position of the placeholder in a string can be indicated by using %s instead of a blank line. You then use % to tell the computer what value(s) you want to put in that placeholder.*

Let's have a look at the code:

```
Python 3.3.0 (v3.3.0:bd8afb90ebf2, Sep 29 2029  10:55:48) [MSC v.1600 32 bit (Intel)] on win32
Type "copyright", "credits" or "license()" for more information.
>>> mystring = 'Fred enters the swamp and picks up a %s to eat later.'
>>> food1= 'python'
>>> food2= 'swamp apples' #Defining what valuse could go in the place holder
>>> print(mystring % food1) #Choosing a value and checking it
Fred enters the swamp and picks up a python to eat later.
>>> #It works!
>>>
```

We can reuse our string and add more values. We can also add multiple placeholders, (%s), in the same string as follows:

```
Python 3.3.0 (v3.3.0:bd8afb90ebf2, Sep 29 2032, 10:55:48) [MSC v.1600 32 bit (Intel)] on wi
n32
Type "copyright", "credits" or "license()" for more information.
>>> mystring= 'Fred enters the swamp and picks up a %s and a %s to eat later.'
>>> food1= 'python'
>>> food2= 'swamp apple'
>>> print(mystring % (food1, food2)) #Remember to use double parenthesis
Fred enters the swamp and picks up a python and a swamp apple to eat later.
>>> #We are free to change, add more values, or reuse the old ones
>>> food3= 'chocolate covered garlic'
>>> food4= 'peanuts' #Now we have four choices
>>> print(mystring % (food3, food1)) #Choosing two
Fred enters the swamp and picks up a chocolate covered garlic and a python to eat later.
>>>
```

Sometimes you may want to use punctuation marks that Python sees as having another meaning. As you have seen, programmers assign other meanings to traditional characters.

True and totally useless story: I once asked two students to tell their meaning of the word; "love." One student rolled up her eyes, cooed and softly whispered, "Wonderful."
The next student stood up, violently swung a fist in the air and yelled; "Pain! Death! Misery!"
The same word; but two people had two very different meanings.

Just as two different people can see different meanings in the same word; Python must also be told which meaning we want to use if we have more than one.

Now to escape! There are escape characters in Python to tell the computer to ignore the Python code meaning of the character and see it as normal punctuation.

*The **escape** character tells Python to stop or continue to read the code through the eyes of Python.* In this case we will use a pair of backslash, (\"x"\), escape characters to stop and then to continue Python thinking.

```
Python 3.3.0 (v3.3.0:bd8afb90ebf2, Sep 29 1600, 10:55:48) [MSC v.1600 32 bit (In
tel)] on win32
Type "copyright", "credits" or "license()" for more information.
>>> print("\"Escape!\"")
"Escape!"
>>>
```

Without the escape characters we would only see the word without the quotation marks in our output.

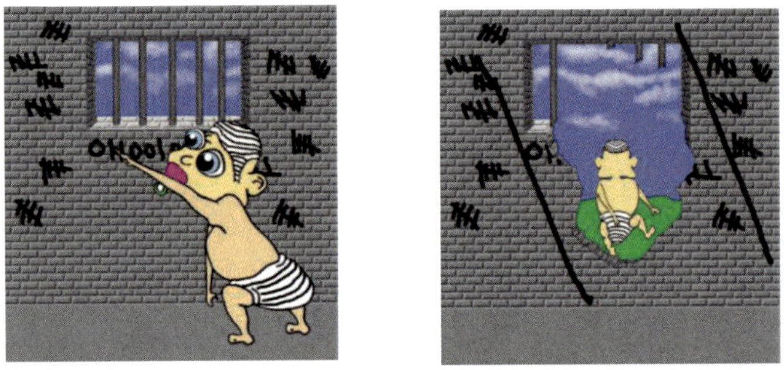

Remembering the escape characters can be very useful.

A single backslash " \ " can be placed at the end of a line of code as a *continuation character*. This tells the computer to treat the continued line as a single line:

```
>>>stuff = "This is a very very very long string that I typed here \
to make my point."
>>>print (stuff)
This is a very very very long string that I typed here to make my point.
```

To break a line of text and start another line use **"\n\"**:

```
>>>stuff = "This is a very very very long string that I typed here \n\
to make my point, but in this case I want two lines."
>>>print (stuff)
This is a very very very long string that I typed here
to make my point, but in this case I wanted two lines.
```

If you ever find yourself in a situation where you need to use a lot of backslashes, (probably won't happen until you get deeper into programming), you may have to tell Python to store all your backslashes as they appear. Otherwise the backslash will have a different meaning to Python and it will eliminate some of them as in the examples above.

You may need to do this if you want to output a DOS path in Windows. Messing with the backslashes in C:\program files\put it here\folder\ would not be a good thing. For this we use an "r'' to indicate our string is a *raw string literal.* Yeh, I know, just a weird way to say, "read and store it literally/as it is written." What's a "***string literal***?" A string literal is just fancy way to say; "*text or values between quotation marks for Python to ignore*."

Review:

Quiz 2:

Answer the following questions on a separate piece of paper or in a document if you prefer. Check your answers on the next page.

2.1 Define the following terms and check your answers on the next page:

1. Boolean
2. Comparison operators
3. Compound condition
4. Delimiters
5. Float
6. Floating point numbers
7. Identifiers
8. Integer
9. Logical operators
10. Operators
11. Simple condition
12. String (not the one your cat plays with)
13. Variables

2.2 Practice Exercises

1. Print to output the following sentence, including the punctuation marks:
2. " This is a @#%$ sentence!, (Pardon the foul language)."

3. Create a string with a place holder and output the string with the value "7" in that placeholder.

4. What will you see if you type in "3>1" and hit enter?

5. What do I use to tell Python that I want multiple lines of code treated as a single
   a. line?

VOCABULARY

Boolean *data type is referring to two possible values;* ***True or False****.*
Comparison operators *are for comparing things, (<, >, ==, !=, etc.).*
Compound condition *is a comparison using more than two values, (x < 10 and x>5)*
Conditional expressions *(also called Boolean expressions), are based on the condition that something is either true or false.*
Delimiters *defining quotation marks to tell the computer we are entering a string.*
Escape *character tells Python to stop or continue to read the code through the eyes of Python*
Float *non-whole numbers like decimals..*
Floating point numbers *numbers with a decimal point*
Identifiers *are names*
Integer *a complete number as opposed to part of a number like ½*
Logical operators *the words "**and, or,**" and "**not**"*
Operators *do something, like add, multiply, divide, subtract, or compare.*
Placeholder *(%s) a symbol in our code that indicates a blank value*
Simple condition *is a comparison that only uses two values, (9<10)*
String *a sequence of characters, words, or sentences in quotation marks.*
Variables *are like little like boxes or containers to put different things in.*

2.2 Practice Exercises (Answers)

1.
```
>>> print("\"This is a @#%$ sentence!, (Pardon the foul language).\"")
"This is a @#%$ sentence!, (Pardon the foul language)."
```

2. *Anything similar to:*
```
>>> mystring= 'I think I ate %s pizzas today.'
>>> pizzas = '7'
>>> print(mystring % pizzas)
I think I ate 7 pizzas today.
```

3.
```
>>> True
```

4. Use a continuation character, (a single backslash, \), in your code.

Lesson 3: Your First Game!

WHAT YOU WILL LEARN:

- SAVING YOUR PROGRAM
- THE MEANING OF THE CODE
- CONDITIONAL STATEMENTS
- LOOP FOR A "WHILE" STATEMENTS
- GETTING LOOPY (MORE ON LOOPS)

SAVING YOUR FIRST PROGRAM

To help you understand your first game you will write a smaller program first. Now you will work in the editor window and learn how to save your file. Open the *editor window*, ***not*** the *shell window*, and type:

```
#My first program
print( 'How many eggs can you eat?' )
amount=input()
print( 'Wow you can really eat,  ' +amount)
```

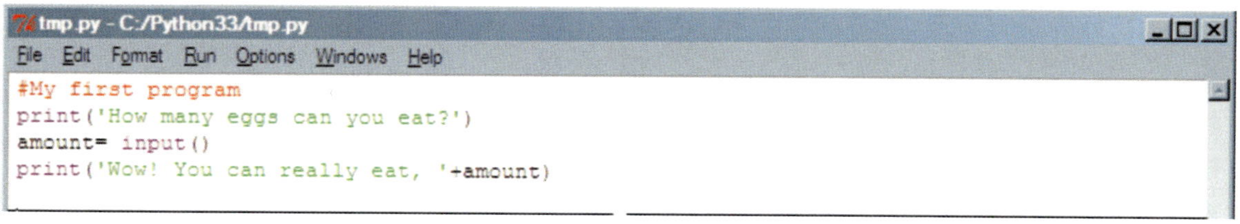

Save your program and give it a name, but add .py after the name you choose. Then close Python. Reopen IDLE and go to *file,* then *recent files,* and choose your program name.
Go to the run button at the top of the edit window and choose "Run module."
When it asks you, "How many eggs can you eat?" type a number or a word. *I typed "1000 green ones".*

It should respond and look something like this:

```
Python Shell
File  Edit  Shell  Debug  Options  Windows  Help
Python 3.3.0 (v3.3.0:bd8afb90ebf2, Sep 29 2048, 10:55:48) [MSC v.1600 32 bit (Intel)] o
n win32
Type "copyright", "credits" or "license()" for more information.
>>> ================================ RESTART ================================
>>>
How many eggs can you eat?
1000 green ones
Wow! You can really eat, 1000 green ones
>>>
```

If your program didn't work, go back and make sure everything is typed exactly as I typed it, and make sure you typed in the right windows. Before we go on to your first mini game I will explain more about the program you just made.

The Meaning of the Code

```
#My first program
```

This first line of your program was just for you. Remember that the computer ignores comments that begin with the # sign.

```
print( ‘How many eggs can you eat?’ )
```

This line was to tell the computer the words you wanted it to show or print on the computer screen.

```
amount=input()
```

The above like was to do two things. We made up the name of a variable and called it “amount.” We also used the **input**() command to tell the computer that the computer user would put some data into amount variable/box.

```
print( ‘Wow you can really eat,   ‘ +amount)
```

This line was to tell the computer to print these words on the computer screen but to add our variable. Our variable was called amount and now contains in memory whatever you typed for the input.

Change the lines above and make up your own mini programs to practice and see what happens. When you are ready, go on to the next part and make your first mini game.

CONDITIONAL STATEMENTS

As a programmer you will often find yourself needing to use ***conditionals***, *(statements based on a condition)*. If you eat 2000 candy bars: you will get sick. This kind of conditional statement is called an "if" statement.

We will use the if and the elif statements to make your first simple game. Let's name your game; "Fred; The Middle Aged Alien Chicken."

To start programming I will make a note of the name of my game at the top of the window as a reminder, using the "#" key.

Enter the following code and then we can play and explain it:

```
#Fred the Middle Aged Alien Chicken

print('How old is Fred the alien chicken?')
number= 17
guess= int(input('Enter a number: '))
if guess== number:
    print('Yes! Fred is a middle aged alien chicken at 17!')
elif guess < number:
    print('No! That is too young to be a middle aged alien chicken!')
elif guess > number:
    print('No way! That is too old to be a middle aged alien chicken!')
```

Make sure you are in the right window and that you type everything exactly as you see above. Then click on *run* and *run module* to try it. Enter a number and it will give you a reply. Enter another number and ...ahh!! it just repeats what you entered! You close the game and run it again to try again. So, at this point, you can only make one guess before the game replies and stops working. Don't worry; we will fix that in a moment when you learn about loops. For now, I will explain the code we have so far:

```
#Fred The Middle Aged Chicken
```

Again the # sign makes this information to ignore for the computer, but a reminder or information for us humans and aliens who know how to read.

```
print ( 'How old is Fred the alien chicken?' )
```

This tells the computer to print the string of characters inside the ('') to the screen.

```
number=17
```

This tells the computer that the variable we called "number" will mean "17."

```
guess=int(input( 'Enter a number: ' ))
```

This tells the computer that the variable we call "guess" will mean; we want an integer input from the computer user. A string of characters, 'Enter a number: ' , to make the request inside the inner set of parenthesis. *What's with the parenthesis in parenthesis?* This tells the computer what to do first. Just as in math, the parenthesis are done from the inner to the outer ones; the inner pair first, followed by the outer pair. Here, the string ('Enter the number') will be seen by the computer before the (input()) is expected. The inner parenthesis in (input()) has the meaning of (input (something here)). So, the computer displayed, "Enter a number" and waited for us to input an integer before going on.

```
if guess==number:
```

This was to tell the computer that if the variable we called "guess" really is equal to the integer typed in the input : (then) do... The : sign means "then" in Python.

```
print( 'Yes!, Fred is a middle aged alien chicken at 17!' )
```

This tells the computer to print or put the string inside the ('') on the computer screen.
Notice that this and all the print commands are indented the same amount. This will become important soon when we explain how to create blocks of code that tell the computer what goes together. We will do this to teach about loops and how to fix the little problem of our game only allowing one guess before it goes stupid and just repeats what we type again.

```
elif guess<number:
```

Here's a new one. *What's an elif?* No, not that. It means "or else if..." Here, we are telling the computer that in the past a guess was made and we told it what to do; but if what we said may happen, does not happen; here is something else to do. So, (elif), the "guess" variable, is less than the "number" variable we told the computer meant "17." Read that again if you didn't get it. Think of Python as an old man with the ability to think like Einstein but the slurred vocabulary of a drunken two year old. Not to criticize it; this is one of the ingenious aspects of Python. Saying little with a powerful meaning can help us make powerful programs by writing less code within a very short time.

```
print( 'No that is not too young to be a middle aged alien chicken' )
```

Here we indent and tell the computer to print a string to the screen again.

```
elif guess>number:
```

This is a repeat of the elif above, but changing the meaning to; "if the guess is greater than the number then..."

```
print( 'No way, that is too old to be a middle aged alien chicken' )
```

Again, we indented and told the computer to print a string of characters.

Remember pages ago when we talked about blocks? You were younger then, but maybe you remember. Well, we need to review that stuff and expand on the meaning to be able to teach you about loops. Only then will you know how to fix our games problem of stopping after one guess.

LOOP FOR A "WHILE" STATEMENTS

If you haven't guessed it, *a **loop** is when the computer goes back and repeats something in a cycle until something breaks it out of that cycle.* The ***while statement*** *tells the computer to continue looping while some condition is continuing to happen; while it is still true.*

As long as some condition is true in a while statement, a block of statements or code will be repeated. It will break out of that loop when the condition is no longer true for that block of code.

Let's fix our game. Change your code to look like this:

```
*tmp.py - C:/Python33/tmp.py*
File Edit Format Run Options Windows Help
#Fred the Middle Aged Alien Chicken

print('How old is Fred the alien chicken?')
number= 17
run= 17 #Type this new line to define run.
while run: #Type this while statement here..note the empty spaces and indentation
    guess= int(input('Enter a number: '))
    if guess== number:
        print('Yes! Fred is a middle aged alien chicken at 17!') #Notice indentation
        run= False #This will make the loop stop and end the game
    elif guess < number: #Notice indentation
        print('No! That is too young to be a middle aged alien chicken!')
    elif guess > number:
        print('No way! That is too old to be a middle aged alien chicken!')

print('Game Over')
```

Most of this code was already explained, so we will just look at the changes and the new things. You didn't need to type any of the red comments for your code to work. These were just there to help you. The spaces are also ignored by the computer and are placed in code to make it easier for humans to read. The indentations are important changes. We will discuss those in a moment. Now, if you try the game, you can continue guessing until you guess correctly. The game will only end when you guess the correct answer. Play around with the game and the code before moving on.

The code:

```
run=17
```

Here we named another variable called "run," and told the computer that it also means "17."

```
while run:
```

The *while statement is known as a looping statement. It tells the computer to repeat the next block of code as long as it continues to be true.* Notice the empty line after the line of code with the while statement. In this example, I used a blank lines before and after the block of code that the while statement applies to. This entire block will continue to repeat forever until the run variable becomes false. So, the meaning of this would be to repeat the next block of code while the run variable is true; "then, (:), do this..." Here we can add if or elif statements to tell the computer when our run variable is true or when our run variable becomes false. If the run variable becomes false, our while run loop is no longer true and will stop looping/repeating.

```
    guess=int(input( 'Enter a number: ' ))
```

Here we created another variable called "guess." We told the computer that when we use this word we mean the integer input that a person will type when he sees the string; (**'Enter a number: '**), on the computer screen.

```
    if guess==number:
```

This means that if the guess, (input), really equals, (==), the number, (17), then, (:)...

```
        print( 'Yes! Fred is a middle aged...' )
        run= False
```

These two statements are indented equally to tell the computer to run them if the guess ==number happens. This tells the computer that if this happens and the person inputs the number 17, then do the following indented things/lines of code. If this happens first print the string in parenthesis to the screen, then make the meaning of our run variable; "**False**." This causes the while statement to now be false and the computer knows to stop repeating this loop and jump out of this set of indented lines, (or this block of code), and continue on the next block, (indicated by less indentation). That would make it jump to the print statement with the string ('Game over').

If the number 17 is not guessed, (our input), this would make the while statement continue to be true. So, the computer should continue and repeat the while block again by going to the next line in the block:

```
elif guess < number:
```

This means, "or else if the guess is less than 17 then, (:)...

```
    print( 'No, that is too young...' )
```

Print the string in parenthesis to the computer screen.

```
elif guess > number:

# Or else if the guess is greater than 17 then...

    print( 'No, that is too old...' )

# Print the string in parenthesis to the computer screen.
```

```
print( 'Game over' )
```

This statement will not run as long as the computer is looping the while block of code, because we let the computer know this is outside the while block by not indenting it. It will only run when our while block become false because 17 was the input.

Whew! Now you can understand how Python can save you time. Look at how many English words it just took to explain what we were doing. Then look again at how short the Python blocks of code are:

```
*tmp.py - C:/Python33/tmp.py*
File Edit Format Run Options Windows Help
#Fred the Middle Aged Alien Chicken

print('How old is Fred the alien chicken?')
number= 17
run= 17 #Type this new line to define run.
while run: #Type this while statement here..note the empty spaces and indentation
    guess= int(input('Enter a number: '))
    if guess== number:
        print('Yes! Fred is a middle aged alien chicken at 17!') #Notice indentation
        run= False #This will make the loop stop and end the game
    elif guess < number: #Notice indentation
        print('No! That is too young to be a middle aged alien chicken!')
    elif guess > number:
        print('No way! That is too old to be a middle aged alien chicken!')

print('Game Over')
```

GETTING LOOPY (MORE ON LOOPS)

Learning to think like a loop thinks is very important to understanding what will happen in the algorithms you write. Let's look at some simple while loop psychology to understand the looping process.

What will the following code do? *(Don't try it yet, just think about it.)*

```
x = 0
while x < 12:
   print(x)
```

**Remember that to type all of this in and run it you need to open a new window in IDLE. Don't try to use the Shell window because you will not be testing and running it line by line.*

If you didn't listen and actually ran this, you found that it will loop eternally and you have to kill it by closing the window. The better way to kill an eternal loop is to hold down the **control key and hit the "c"** key at the same time. Now that you know a better way to kill it, you can give it a try.

Why? Well, in the print function we told Python to print x, which is = to 0; and we told the loop to continue while x or 0 is less than 12. Zero will always be less than twelve so the loop will repeat forever until the user interferes to kill it.

Ok, now you know. *Try this one:*

```
x = 0
while x < 12:
        print(x)
        x = x + 3
```

Before running it, what do you think will happen?

(Don't move on to the next page until you have a theory.)

Your output should be:

0
3
6
9

So, what exactly is happening here?

```
x = 0 # we defined x as being 0
 while x < 12: # we told Python to loop as long as x is less than 12
      print(x) # we told Python to print x every loop as long as the above
                  conditions are being met.
       x = x + 3
```

This last statement is redefining what x is every loop. The first loop it prints 0 then goes to this x = x +3 statement so now: x = 3 for the next loop.

<u>Original Code:</u>

```
x = 0

while x < 12:
```

<u>Running through the loop the FIRST TIME:</u>

```
x = 0
while 0 < 12:    Yes, 0 < 12 is TRUE so continue...

     print(0)
                                        prints 0

     0 = 0 + 3    is 3 so...
...now make x = 3 for the second run through the loop:
```

This loop will repeat and run again until x is no longer less than twelve.

<u>Running through the loop the SECOND TIME:</u>

Running through the loop the **SECOND TIME:**

x = 3
while 3 < 12:   Yes, 3 < 12 is TRUE so continue...

↓

print(3)

prints 3

↓

3 = 3 + 3   is 6 so...

now make x = 6 for the second run through the loop:

Running through the loop the **THIRD TIME:**

x = 6
while 6 < 12:   Yes, 6 < 12 is TRUE so continue...

↓

print(6)

prints 6

↓

6 = 6 + 3   is 9 so...

now make x = 9 for the second run through the loop:

Running through the loop the **FOURTH TIME:**

x = 9
while 9 < 12:   Yes, 9 < 12 is TRUE so continue...

↓

print(9)

prints 9

↓

9 = 9 + 3   is 12 so...

now make x = 12 for the second run through the loop:

Running through the loop the **FIFTH and FINAL TIME:**

Running through the loop the FIFTH and FINAL TIME:

```
x = 12
while 12< 12:
```

FALSE! 12 IS NOT < 12 SO BREAK LOOP!!!

Wow! If we looped that much we would be dizzy. Fortunately, the computer can handle it and all that looping just results in a simple output for us humans:

```
0
3
6
9
```

There are different ways to exit a while loop. One way is to just add the word "***break***" and the loop will end at that point. Another common way to end a loop is to define when it is true and when it is false.

```
while done = = false:
    for...(here I would enter my code block)
        if...(this will repeat in the loop until it becomes true)
            done = true (when done is true, we exit the loop, and are done with it)
```

Are you ready for a quiz? If not; go back and loop until you go it; if you think so; go on to the next page.

REVIEW

Quiz 3:

Answer the following questions on a separate piece of paper or in a document if you prefer. Check your answers at the end of this lesson.

3.1 Define the following:

1. If statement
2. Loop
3. While statement

3.2 *Answer the following questions*:

1. Give two examples of conditional statements.

2. *Correct the following portion of code (without referring to the text):*

```
number = 17
run = 17
while run:
guess = int(input(Enter a number:)
if guess = number:
print 'Yes.'
run = False
elif guess < number
```

CHALLENGE:

Write a while loop that does a countdown from ten to one and then prints, "Go!"
*Check the end of this lesson to see one possible solution. *Hint: The "break" statement can be used to break out of a loop.*

VOCABULARY

If Statement *a conditional statement/ a statement based on a condition.*	
Loop *when the computer goes back and repeats something in a cycle until something breaks it out of that cycle.*	
While statement *tells the computer to continue looping while some condition is continuing to happen; usually while it is still true.*	

3.2 *Answers*:

1. "if" and "elif," (you could also include "else").
2. *Obsessive attention to details and syntax must be developed as early as possible to be a great programmer. It is better to spend time developing these skills than in debugging messed up code after you write it. Prevention is better than repair but both skills need to be developed.*

Code:	*Errors:*
`number = 17`	
`run = 17`	
`while run:`	
`guess = int(input(Enter a number:)`	***indent, 'quotation marks', parenthesis))***
`if guess = number:`	***indent***
`print 'Yes.'`	***indent, quotation marks around 'Yes'***
`run = False`	
`elif guess < number`	***indent, missing colon : after "number"***

```
*tmp.py - C:/Python33/tmp.py*
File Edit Format Run Options Windows Help
#Fred The Middle Aged Alien Chicken

print('How old is Fred the Alien Chicken?')
number= 17
run= 17 #Type in this new line here but you don't need to type in these red comments.
while run: #Type this while statement here..note the empty spaces and indentation

        guess= int(input('Enter a number: ')) #Indent here
        if guess== number:
            print('Yes! Fred is a middle aged alien chicken at 17!') #Indent
            run= False #This will make the loop stop and end the game
        elif guess < number: #Notice indentation
            print('No way! That is too young to be a middle aged alien chicken!') #Indent
        elif guess > number:
            print('No way! That is too old to be a middle aged alien chicken!')

print('Game Over!')
```

Challenge *(one possible answer, (you figure out the correct indentation)):*

`x = 10    while x <=10:    print(x)    if x < 1:    print("Go!")    break    x = x-1`

Lesson 4: Basic Python Parts

WHAT YOU WILL LEARN:

- **LISTS**
- **SLICES**
- **TUPLES**

LISTS

*A **list** is a sequence of elements.* A list is referred to as an "*array*" in some programming languages. You could make a list of the family members in your home:

Family = ['Dad', 'Mom', 'Brother', 'Sister', 'Me', 'Cat', 'Cockroaches']

Each element in the list has a position of reference. In other words, they are numbered for indexing or referring to them later. *The elements within the brackets are often called the "**index.**"* But, instead of calling the first element in the list; "1," programmers begin with "0." So, now you won't be confused if you see a programmer counting how many cups of coffee he had tonight by beginning with; "0, 1, 2, 3..." Lists can store numbers, strings, both, and they can store other lists.

They may look like this:

Numbers:	theAlist=[2, 4, 6, 8]
Strings:	theBlist=['words', 'abc', 'fuglet']
Both:	theClist=['abc', 4, 'words', 7]
Other Lists:	AllLists=[theAlist, theBlist, theClist]

We can edit lists. But, the word "*edit*" is too common for a programmer to use, so let's use the word "*mutable.*"

Later you will learn about tuples. Tuples are immutable. Huh? ***Mutable** means we can edit it.* ***Immutable** means we can't edit it.* So the secret meaning is that lists can be edited; but strings and tuples can't be edited, (*directly*).

www.Toonzcat.com

Maybe you would like to edit your list of family members. Remember our list:

Family =	["Dad",	"Mom",	"Brother",	"Sister",	"Me",	"Cat",	"Cockroaches"]	
Index position:	**0**	**1**	**2**	**3**	**4**	**5**	**6**	**7**

Let's say you bought a mouse and he ate the family cockroaches. It was a sad event but life goes on and now you must edit your list of family members. You need to replace "Cockroaches" with "psycho mouse."

To replace an item in a list you need to understand what is in a particular index position. Index position references begin before an item and at the comma after the item in the list. Since "Cockraoches" is in the 6th position of our "Family" list, (remember you count from 0), we do this:

Family[6]= "Psycho Mouse"

Give it a try. First, define what is in your list by typing:
Family = ["Dad", "Mom", "Brother", "Sister", "Me", "Cat", "Cockroaches"]

Then, type:
Family[6]= "Psycho Mouse"

Test it by typing:

```
print(Family)
```

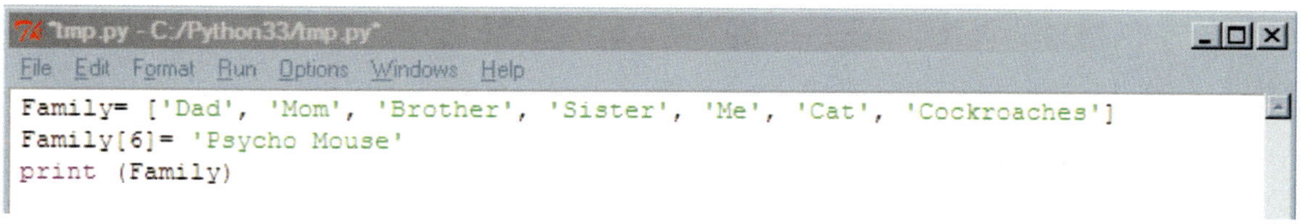

Now run your program.

```
Python Shell
File Edit Shell Debug Options Windows Help
Python 3.3.0 (v3.3.0:bd8afb90ebf2, Sep 29 2012, 10:55:48) [MSC v.1600 32 bit (In
tel)] on win32
Type "copyright", "credits" or "license()" for more information.
>>> ================================ RESTART ================================
>>>
['Dad', 'Mom', 'Brother', 'Sister', 'Me', 'Cat', 'Psycho Mouse']
>>>
```

What happens if I want to add something to my list? *Adding something to a list is referred to as **appending** the list.*

Let's say that our Cat and Psycho Mouse got married and had a baby. We will call it, "Cathouse." Now we have a new member of our family and we must append the list.
We add this line before our print statement:

```
Family.append( "Catouse" )
```

```
*tmp.py - C:/Python33/tmp.py*
File Edit Format Run Options Windows Help
Family= ['Dad', 'Mom', 'Brother', 'Sister', 'Me', 'Cat', 'Cockroaches']
Family[6]= 'Psycho Mouse'
Family.append('Cathouse')
print (Family)
```

Run it:

```
Python Shell
File Edit Shell Debug Options Windows Help
Python 3.3.0 (v3.3.0:bd8afb90ebf2, Sep 29 2012, 10:55:48) [MSC v.1600 32 bit (In
tel)] on win32
Type "copyright", "credits" or "license()" for more information.
>>> ================================ RESTART ================================
>>>
['Dad', 'Mom', 'Brother', 'Sister', 'Me', 'Cat', 'Psycho Mouse', 'Cathouse']
>>>
```

How do I remove an item? I'm glad you asked. Let's say that Psycho Mouse gets angry and eats the Cat. To remove "Cat" from the Family list we use del for delete and give the index position:

```
del Family[5]
```

```
*tmp.py - C:/Python33/tmp.py*
File Edit Format Run Options Windows Help
Family= ['Dad', 'Mom', 'Brother', 'Sister', 'Me', 'Cat', 'Cockroaches']
Family[6]= 'Psycho Mouse'
Family.append('Cathouse')
del Family[5]
print (Family)
```

Run it to confirm the removal of the cat:

```
Python Shell
File Edit Shell Debug Options Windows Help
Python 3.3.0 (v3.3.0:bd8afb90ebf2, Sep 29 2012, 10:55:48) [MSC v.1600 32 bit (In
tel)] on win32
Type "copyright", "credits" or "license()" for more information.
>>> ================================ RESTART ================================
>>>
['Dad', 'Mom', 'Brother', 'Sister', 'Me', 'Psycho Mouse', 'Cathouse']
>>>
```

Just to complicate our lives, our sister marries a guy and now another family has become part of our family. Fortunately, adding two lists together is easier than combining two families. First we define what is in the second list. Let's add this list second family list under our Family list:

```
Family2=[ "a guy", "dog", "father", "mother" ]
```

Then to add the two lists change the print statement to:

```
print(Family+Family2)
```

```
tmp.py - C:/Python33/tmp.py*
File Edit Format Run Options Windows Help
Family= ['Dad', 'Mom', 'Brother', 'Sister', 'Me', 'Cat', 'Cockroaches']
Family2= ['a guy', 'dog', 'Father', 'Mother']
Family[6]= 'Psycho Mouse'
Family.append('Cathouse')
del Family[5]
print (Family + Family2)
```

Run it to output a combination of the two lists:

```
Python Shell
File Edit Shell Debug Options Windows Help
Python 3.3.0 (v3.3.0:bd8afb90ebf2, Sep 29 2012, 10:55:48) [MSC v.1600 32 bit (In
tel)] on win32
Type "copyright", "credits" or "license()" for more information.
>>> ================================ RESTART ================================
>>>
['Dad', 'Mom', 'Brother', 'Sister', 'Me', 'Psycho Mouse', 'Cathouse', 'a guy', '
dog', 'Father', 'Mother']
>>>
```

SLICES

Remember how we used an index to cut one part of a list out to exchange it or delete it? Wouldn't it be great if you could choose any part of the list or a string; one character; half of an index; all of the list; or any part you want to copy or work with? You can! *A slice is cutting a list into smaller parts. A* ***slice*** *is a subset of a list or a string.* Just as you can choose what piece of pie you want to cut and how big you want to cut it; you can cut a slice from a list or a string starting and ending where you want it.

Let's cut up a string pie. Don't worry; you don't need to eat it. The strings always get caught between your teeth anyway, (but they are good fiber). Remember that we use a 0 for our first index position. But, when talking about slices of pie or strings you have to use two reference points. You need an index or reference point for the first cut and one for the final cut of the slice. So, our index points are on each side of the characters in our string.

If we want to slice out the "**s**" we have to tell the computer the ***beginning and ending index for the slice, [0:1].***

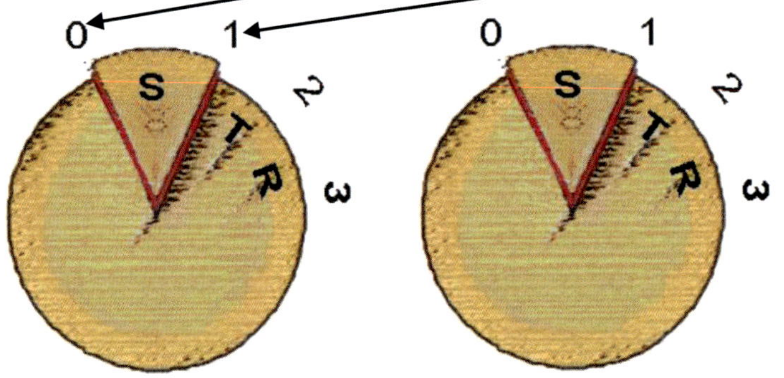

It is probably easier to think about it this way:

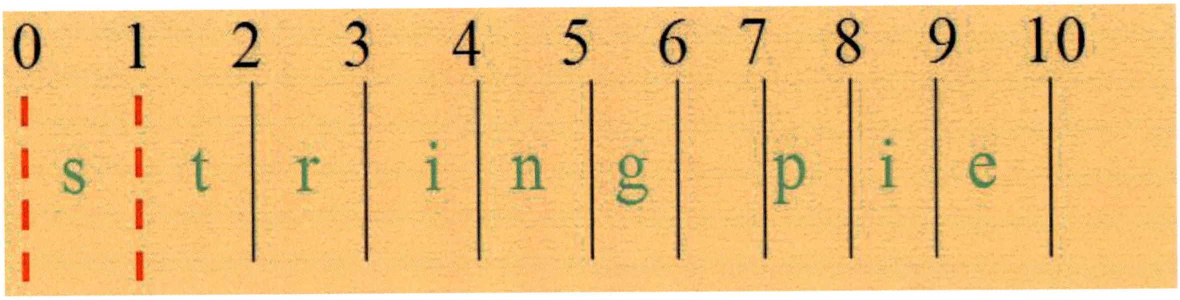

Try this:

```
piece= "string pie"
print(piece [2:5])
```

Run it:

```
Python 3.3.0 (v3.3.0:bd8afb90ebf2, Sep 29 2012, 10:55:48) [MSC v.1600 32 bit (In
tel)] on win32
Type "copyright", "credits" or "license()" for more information.
>>> ================================ RESTART ================================
>>>
rin
>>>
```

I'm not sure what a "rin" tastes like but we successfully sliced a piece of our string from index position 2 to 5!

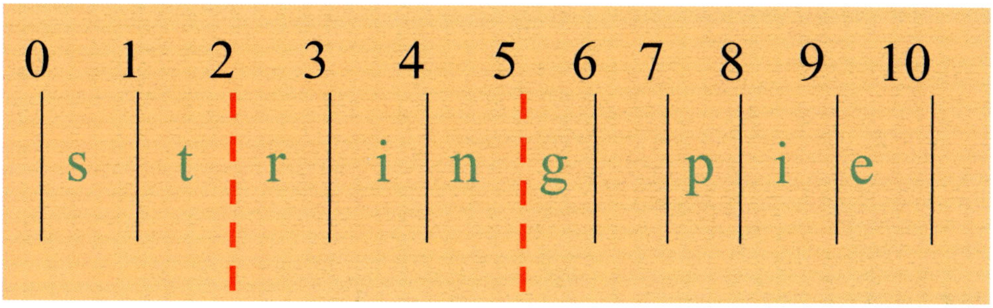

You try a few to practice. First choose the letters you want to cut out of the string. Then choose the beginning and ending cut for your slice of the string. Practice until you are confident in choosing the index positions and getting the slice you want.

There is another way to refer to index positions in a slice if you want to use it. You can think backwards! There are practical uses for this in more advanced programming.

For now, I will only introduce you to it and you can play with it. In this index system, index positions use negative numbers.

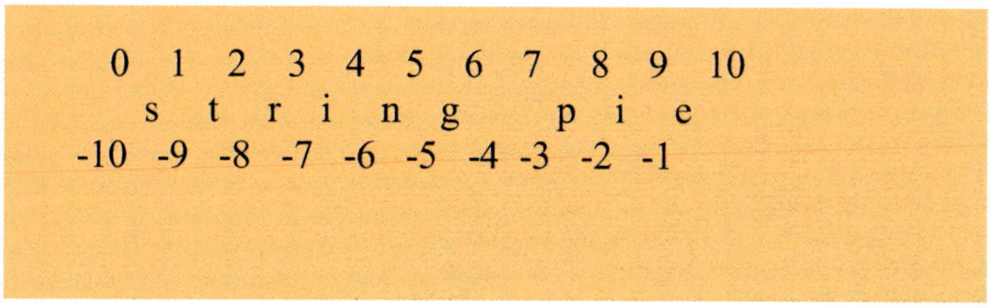

Try it:

```
*tmp.py - C:/Python33/tmp.py*
File Edit Format Run Options Windows Help
piece= "string pie"
print(piece [-9:-2])
```

Run it:

```
Python Shell
File Edit Shell Debug Options Windows Help
Python 3.3.0 (v3.3.0:bd8afb90ebf2, Sep 29 2012, 10:55:48) [MSC v.1600 32 bit (In
tel)] on win32
Type "copyright", "credits" or "license()" for more information.
>>> ================================ RESTART ================================
>>>
tring p
>>>
```

A "tring p" probably tastes better than a "rin," but I'm only guessing. When you program you will find that making a copy of part or all of what you have typed before will save you a lot of time. Slicing strings is a useful talent.

<u>Practice 4.1 Do this:</u>

Look at what we have done so far, and take a guess about what you think will happen before doing the following:

1. What do you think happens if you create a string and you print [:3] of that string?
2. What happens if you create a string and you print [3:] of that string?

Come on! Take a guess. Try it before looking at the answer at the end of the lesson.. Learning by doing it and thinking about it makes things easier to remember.

Here are a couple more slicing operations you can play with:

```
>>> string1='pronounce'
>>> string2= 'deepfat'
>>> newstring = string1 + string2
>>> print(newstring)
pronouncedeepfat
```

In the previous example you can see how easy it is to create a new string variable that contains the combined data of other variables.

```
>>> newstring = string1[:3] + string2[4:]

>>> print(newstring)
```

If you put a space here [4:], rather than [4:], it will not work.

In the above example you can see how easy it is to create a new string that is a combination of parts of other strings. These same slice operations work for lists. *What is the difference when slicing lists or strings?* With strings each character and empty space is indexed as separate data. Lists are *compound data types* where each chunk of data is indexed according to the location of the commas you used to designate each item of data. In other words, with strings you would count index positions before and after each character or empty space; with lists you would count index positions before the first item as 0 and at each comma after each item in the list.

<u>*String index positions*</u>:

```
     s    t    r    i    n    g
  0    1    2    3    4    5    6
```

<u>*List index positions*</u>:

Mylist = ['pickles', 'catchup', 'hamburger', 'bread', '20', 4, 1000]
0 1 2 3 4 5 6 7

Strings and lists also differ in the fact that strings are ***immutable***, *(cannot directly edit them)*, while you can change and edit items in lists. *Try this:*

```
>>> list1 = ['up', 'down', 300, '40']

>>> list1[2]=list1[2]+77

>>> print(list1)

['up', 'down', 377, '40']
```

But what happens if you add something to an item that is not an integer?

```
>>> list1[1]=list1[1]+ 'erk'

>>> print(list1)

['up', 'downerk', 377, '40']
```

You can also ***append***, (add something to the end), a list:

```
>>> mylist = ['up', 'downerk', 377, '40']

>>> mylist.append('kitten')

>>> print(mylist)

['up', 'downerk', 377, '40', 'kitten']
```

What else can you do to edit lists? I'm glad you asked!

<u>You can:</u>

<u>Replace items</u> in a list:

```
>>> mylist = ['box','pen', 4, '100', 'hat', 'horse']

>>> mylist[0:3] = ['rug', 2, 'pencil']

>>> print(mylist)

['rug', 2, 'pencil', '100', 'hat', 'horse']
```

<u>Remove items</u>:

```
>>> mylist[0:2] = []

>>> print(mylist)

['pencil', '100', 'hat', 'horse']
```

<u>Insert items</u>:

```
>>> mylist[3:3] = ['onions', 'carrot', 44]

>>> print(mylist)
```

Insert a copy of itself:

```
>>> mylist [:0] = mylist

>>> print(mylist)

['pencil', '100', 'hat', 'onions', 'carrot', 44, 'horse', 'pencil', '100', 'hat',
'onions', 'carrot', 44, 'horse']
```

Or in a copy to another location within the list:

```
>>> mylist [2:2] = mylist

>>> print(mylist)

['pencil', '100', 'pencil', '100', 'hat', 'onions', 'carrot', 44, 'horse',
'pencil', '100', 'hat', 'onions', 'carrot', 44, 'horse', 'hat', 'onions',
'carrot', 44, 'horse', 'pencil', '100', 'hat', 'onions', 'carrot', 44, 'horse']
```

Let's find out how many items are in our list:

```
>>> len(mylist)
```

Let's clear the list:

```
>>> mylist[:] = []

>>> print(mylist)

[]
```

You can now understand why lists will be one of your most valuable tools for manipulation of data. Play and practice with these until you are confident.

TUPLES

Let's talk tuples! *A **tuple** is like a list but can't be edited or changed, (immutable), in its original form.* If we really want to be able to modify tuple, we must convert it to a list by using the list(tuplename) first. We generally use parenthesis, ( ), rather than brackets, [ ], to tell Python we are defining a tuple. If it is very obvious to Python that it is a tuple, parenthesis can be skipped.

This is a *string*:

```
Family3 =  'creatures'
```

This is a *tuple*:

```
Family3 = ( 'a guy' ,  'dog' ,  'cat' )
```

This is a *list*:

```
Family3 = [ 'a guy' ,  'dog' ,  'cat' ]
```

Tuples are not easily changed so why would we use them?

As we mentioned; a program can run a tuple with more efficiency than a list. Unless the program is very small, tuples are faster. So, if you don't need to change your list data, it's generally better to use a tuple. Tuples can contain many *things you may not want to change or "read only" code.* These ***constants*** in your program may be; music, a sequence of sound files, a sequence of images, etc. You can assign an individual item to a variable or you could assign a group of items in a sequence to a tuple. Tuples can also be ***nested**, (placed), inside* of other tuples; called up as *functions*; and can hold any data type. For some applications, tuples are used much more often than lists. We will be getting into functions later. For now, just understand the basic principles and the importance of tuples and lists.

Manipulating data with strings, lists, and tuples is going to be a major part of your daily routine as a programmer. It would be best for you to think of your own scenarios where you might need these skills and practice more before going on.

If that sounds boring then continue on, don't let me stop you. You can always return to this lesson if you feel you missed something. You will be using these skills continually from now on, so you will eventually master them in the context of your work.

So, what are some the other differences between tuples lists and strings? Check out what methods are available for each of these and get more information by typing: dir(list), dir(string), help(list), help(string). You will understand more about what you see when you study methods in future lessons. For now, just remember how to find more help and information within Python on these very important data types.

REVIEW

Quiz 4:

Answer the following questions on a separate piece of paper or in a document if you prefer. Check your answers on the next page.

4.1 Define the following terms:

1. Immutable
2. List
3. Mutable
4. Nested
5. Slice
6. Tuple
7. constants

4.2 Questions:

1. What is the most important difference between a tuple and a list?
2. If "mooplug" is a string, what is at index position 0?
3. How do we modify a tuple?
4. How do we remove an item from a list?
5. Show an example of appending a list called, "girls."

4.3 Activity:

1. Practice making lists, appending them, and removing items until you are confident with indexing references.
2. Make some tuples and convert them so you can edit them.

VOCABULARY

Immutable *means we can't edit it.*	
List *a sequence of elements*	
Constants *are read only data*	
Mutable *means we can edit it.*	
Nested*, (placed), inside*	
Slice *a subset of a list*	
Tuple *like a list but can't be edited or changed in its original form.*	

4.2 *Answers:*

1. Tuples are immutable while lists are mutable.
2. "m" is in index position 0.
3. Convert it to a list?
4. Use "**del** Listname[index position]".
5. girls.append(**"girl2"**)

4.3 Activity

Answers will vary. Refer back to the lesson examples if you don't fully understand.

Practice 4.1 Answers:

1. [:3] produces everything in your list up to index position 3.
2. [3:] produces everything in your list after index position 3.

Remember to type the syntax correctly.

```
>>> mystring = 'astring'
>>> print(mystring [3:])
ring
>>> print(mystring [:3])
ast
```

Lesson 5: Functions

WHAT YOU WILL LEARN:

- WHAT'S A FUNCTION
- MAKING YOUR OWN FUNCTIONS
- ARGUMENTS AND PARAMETERS
- DOCSTRINGS AND SUITES
- GLOBAL AND LOCAL SCOPE

WHAT'S A FUNCTION?

*Again; a **function** is a re-usable mini program inside of your program.* One of the greatest things about functions is that you never have to repeatedly type code, ***if you need to repeat it, let a function do it.*** You have already been using functions throughout this book. The "`print()`" *function call* for the print function is the one you have used most.

Calling a function:

Cartoons by Jody S. Ginther ©2010

A ***function call*** *is the code you type to turn on or access a function.*

MAKING YOUR OWN FUNCTIONS?

It is common in writing code to use the same code many times. If we assign this code to a function, we only need to call that function again rather than retype the code. To define the meaning of a function for the computer we use the def statement.

***The def statement** is made up of:*

the keyword, def

*our function **name***

*followed by **parenthesis** where you can add parameters or arguments*

*a **colon***

*and finally the **def-block.***

```
def thename ():
   Here we put the details of our definition block.
   We can put other functions or code here.
```

Let's try it. Below is the code for a new game based on our Alien Chicken game. The purpose of this game is to show you that by making and using your own functions, you can save a lot of time rather than retyping things. We have a two part introduction to this game. The second part will be repeated until the game is over. So, this part will be defined as a function and called up when we need it.

Type this:

```
tmp.py - C:/Python33/tmp.py
File Edit Format Run Options Windows Help
#Hamburger Game

print('You are hungry for a hamburger but you have no money.')
print('You decide to go for a walk to get your mind off of it.')
print("You just can't think of anything else.") #Why was it better to use double quotes here?

def IntroTwo():
    print('You pause a moment, but you are still hungry for a hamburger.')
    print('You decide to continue your walk.')
    print('As you are walking, you see 2 coins and 4 diamonds on the ground.')
    print('Which do you choose?')

IntroTwo ()

coins= 2
diamonds= 4
run= 2

while run:
    guess= int(input('the 2 or the 4      '))
    if guess== coins:
        print('Yeah! You can buy a hamburger with your coins!!')
        run= False
    if guess== diamonds:
        print("YOU CAN'T EAT DIAMONDS!!!")
        IntroTwo()

print('Game Over! Your Full!')
```

Here is the result if you make the wrong guess a couple of times, and finally get it right:

```
Python Shell
File Edit Shell Debug Options Windows Help
Python 3.3.0 (v3.3.0:bd8afb90ebf2, Sep 29 2012, 10:55:48) [MSC v.1600 32 bit (In
tel)] on win32
Type "copyright", "credits" or "license()" for more information.
>>> ================================ RESTART ================================
>>>
You are hungry for a hamburger but you have no money.
You decide to go for a walk to get your mind off of it.
You just can't think of anything else.
You pause a moment, but you are still hungry for a hamburger.
You decide to continue your walk.
As you are walking, you see 2 coins and 4 diamonds on the ground.
Which do you choose?
the 2 or the 4     4
YOU CAN'T EAT DIAMONDS!!!
You pause a moment, but you are still hungry for a hamburger.
You decide to continue your walk.
As you are walking, you see 2 coins and 4 diamonds on the ground.
Which do you choose?
the 2 or the 4     4
YOU CAN'T EAT DIAMONDS!!!
You pause a moment, but you are still hungry for a hamburger.
You decide to continue your walk.
As you are walking, you see 2 coins and 4 diamonds on the ground.
Which do you choose?
the 2 or the 4     2
Yeah! You can buy a hamburger with your coins!!
Game Over! Your Full!
>>>
```

This game will repeat our function, "IntroTwo," until you answer correctly.

**Challenge: How can you re-write the code so you can reduce the number of print statements?*

Let's have a brief look at the code:

```
#Hambuger Game

print ("You are hungry for a hamburger but you have no money.")
print ("You decide to go for a walk to get your mind off of it.")
print ("You just can't think of anything else.")
```

We are repeating the print statement to output each statement as a separate line on the computer screen. Yes, there are easier ways to do this, but you probably need typing practice and repetition for now.

```
def IntroTwo ():
   print (" You pause a moment, but you are still hungry for a hamburger.")
   print ("You decide to continue your walk. ")
   print ("As you are walking, you see 2 coins and 4 diamonds on the ground.")
   print ("Which do you choose?")

IntroTwo ( )
```

The brackets, ( ), in a def *statement give us an optional place to add* ***parameters.*** In our Hamburger Game we had no additional arguments so the parentheses were left empty.

```
 coins=2
  diamonds=4
  run=2
while run:

     guess= int(input('the 2 or the 4     '))
     if guess == coins:
         print ('Yeah! You can buy a hamburger with your coins!!')
         run = False
     if guess==diamonds:
         print ("YOU CAN'T EAT DIAMONDS!!!")
         IntroTwo()
print (' Game Over! Your Full!!')
```

The code here is a repeat of the code we used in our Middle Aged Chicken game. If you don't remember the purpose of each line of code refer to the previous explanations in Lesson 3. The main difference here is that we added our function, IntroTwo().

ARGUMENTS AND PARAMETERS

String arguments:

*Additional data we put within the parenthesis of a function is referred to as the function's " **arguments.**"*

In our first function we did not use any arguments and we did not use a return statement.
Generally we will add a return statement that optionally returns some data and exits the function. If no parameters are defined or no return statement is used, Python will return a value of "None."

Functions generally use data that comes from other places in our source code, processes it, and returns it. This means we may have to create some empty variables or containers for this data to be stored. These variables will only be seen within the function. The "*scope*" of a function will be explained in detail in a later section. For now, let's look some details on how to make functions.

Construction:

1. *The **def** statement- function name*
2. *A list of parameters within parenthesis, (optional)*
3. *A colon.*
4. *Of course our code block is indented.*
5. *The first line of a function is generally a docstring or documentation string giving us some information or comments.*
6. *Next is our processing code block or "**suite**" as it is sometimes referred to in Python. (A "**suite**" is just another way to refer to an indented block of code.)*
7. *Last is our return statement.*

Syntax:

```
def name(parameters):
        "docstring"
        suite, or code block
        return [expression]
```

When we name a function, choose its parameters, and design its block of code; we say we have "*defined*" the function.

Jody Ginther ©2013

The "*parameters*" are like the instructions to variables or containers waiting for some data to be put in them. The "*arguments*" are the data or values that will be "*passed*" to, (*entered into*), these containers.

To use the function we must *"call"* it.

For example:

I define a function with two parameters waiting for data:

```
def function_name(parameter1, parameter2):
        "docstring"
        suite, or code block
        return [expression]
```

Later, I call that function and enter, (or pass), the arguments:

```
def function_name( "argument1" ,  "argument2" )
```

Function arguments and parameters are generally referred to as:

- *Default*
- *Positional*
- *Keyword*
- *Variable-length (arbitrary)*

Note: Arguments can be required or optional.

DEFAULT VALUES

We can make some optional entry parameters for a function with default values in case the user doesn't enter these values. To define the default values we would use the assignment operator (=) you are already familiar with. ***Assignment** is just referring to an instruction that "assigns" a meaning or relationship of one thing to another.* Remember something like; "This homework has been assigned to you." You and the homework now have a meaningful relationship. When using a default value it should be an immutable constant.

Take a look at the following function and its behavior:

```
Python 3.3.0 (v3.3.0:bd8afb90ebf2, Sep 29 2012, 10:55:48) [MSC v.1600 32 bit (In
tel)] on win32
Type "copyright", "credits" or "license()" for more information.
>>> def what(words, times= 1):
        print(words * times)


>>> what('cool')
cool
>>> what('cool', 3)
coolcoolcool
>>> what('cool ', 3)
cool cool cool
>>> what()
Traceback (most recent call last):
  File "<pyshell#6>", line 1, in <module>
    what()
TypeError: what() missing 1 required positional argument: 'words'
>>>
```

What's up?

In the "what" function we defined one parameter as "words" and one parameter as "times" with a default value of "1." We called our function and entered "cool" as the first argument. Our function multiplied this value to the default value of times, which is 1 and printed one "cool."

We then entered both arguments "cool" and the number "3" and our function multiplied the value "cool" to the value we entered as our second argument, (3). "Cool" was printed three times. However, you can see that we need to indicate an empty space if we want to separate words.

Finally, we ran the function without passing any arguments and got an error message. In this case our function has one *required* parameter because it has no default value.

Warning: *You can't have an argument without a default value following an argument with a default value.*

Python will remind you if you try:

```
Python 3.3.0 (v3.3.0:bd8afb90ebf2, Sep 29 2012, 10:55:48) [MSC v.1600 32 bit (In
tel)] on win32
Type "copyright", "credits" or "license()" for more information.
>>> def what(times= 3, words):
        print(words * times)

SyntaxError: non-default argument follows default argument
>>>
```

Positional Parameters

Positional refers to when parameter values are assigned according to their relative position. In other words; the argument values entered will be assigned to the parameter values in the same order they are listed:

```
Python Shell
File Edit Shell Debug Options Windows Help
Python 3.3.0 (v3.3.0:bd8afb90ebf2, Sep 29 2012, 10:55:48) [MSC v.1600 32 bit (In
tel)] on win32
Type "copyright", "credits" or "license()" for more information.
>>> def eeek (value1, value2, value3):
        print(value1, value2, value3)


>>> eek(1, 2, 3)
Traceback (most recent call last):
  File "<pyshell#3>", line 1, in <module>
    eek(1, 2, 3)
NameError: name 'eek' is not defined
>>> eeek(1, 2, 3)
1 2 3
>>>
```

Watch for typos! Our arguments 1, 2, and 3 were assigned in that order to value1, value2, and value3. We can manipulate the order for output after these values have been assigned, but they will still be assigned according to their position:

```
>>> def eek(value1, value2, value3):
        print(value1, value3, value2)


>>> eek(1, 2, 3)
1 3 2
>>>
```

Keyword Arguments

In keyword arguments, the values are assigned according to the parameter name you used when you defined your function. This works like dictionary entries where there is a keyword and an assigned definition, (or in this case a value). You can assign the values in any order you want, (you are not limited by positional assignment).

```
>>> def oog(value1=0, value2=0):
        print(value1 - value2)

>>> oog(value1=20, value2=5)
15
>>> oog(value2=7, value1=30)
23
```

You can see in this example that we first called our function and passed arguments in the order we defined them in our parameters; then we passed arguments ignoring the order in our function definition. No problem! This is the freedom of keyword arguments!

Variable-Length (Arbitrary) Arguments

Since you are now old enough, it is time to introduce you to "*args" and "**kwargs."
If you want to create a function to accept a list of arguments of an unknown length, you must use *args and **kwargs.

> *args refers to a variable-length list of arguments.
>
> **kwargs refers to a variable-length dictionary-like list of arguments, where keywords will be used and associated to values in pairs.

The terms "*args*" and "*kwargs*" are just traditional syntax conventions in programming. In reality, you could call them anything you want. The power is in the single * and double ** asterisks. The asterisk creates a tuple of whatever length is necessary to contain the arguments entered.

These **arbitrary arguments** are listed **after** the positional or "formal" arguments in your function parameters.

Syntax for using *args in a function:

```
def function_name(formal, *args):
        "docstring"
        suite, or code block
        return [expression]
```

Example (try it):

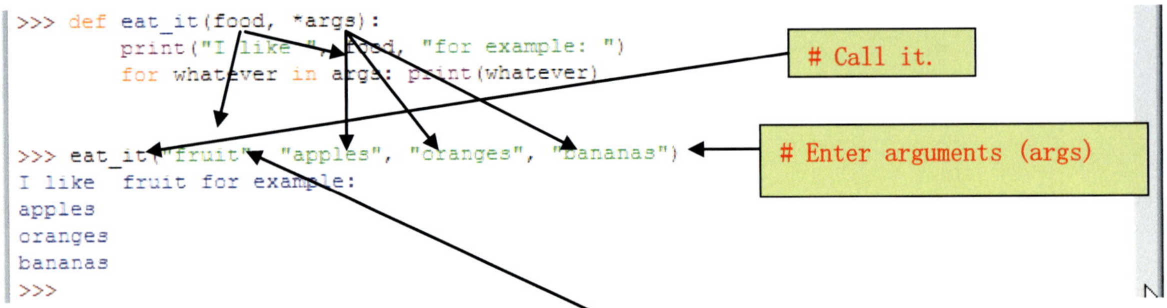

When you call the function "*eat_it*" you can enter one argument for "*food*" and as many examples or "**args*" arguments as you have time to enter. The syntax is the same for ***kwargs*. In these examples we are not using the return statement because we have not explored it yet. To keep things simple we are using the print function. We will have a closer look at ***Kwargs* in the next lesson when we look at dictionaries.

Did you get an error message? A common error here is to call the function, *(type "eat_it"),* without returning to the prompt ">>>" first, *(hit enter a couple of times),* when you are working in the interactive shell. The most common errors are typos, spaces, and punctuation errors.

Docstrings and Suites

What's a docstring? A *docstring* is a *document string* used within source code similar to a comment. *The difference is that a docstring is retained throughout the runtime of the program making it available for the program to see* these lines to use as ***metadata***, *(data about data)*. Data about data is necessary when you want to record some valuable information or notes within your program. It is also used for the creation of an interactive help system. We will look at metadata details in Lesson 21 when you learn how to package your games and programs.

Docstrings *document the purpose of something.* In a function it would be a short note to tell other programmers what that function does and may include exceptions and additional notes needed to use the function.

We will look at the conventional syntax for doctrings in detail later in Lesson 19 on styles of writing code. Briefly:

- Don't use blank lines before or after a docstring
- If the docstring is too long to fit on one line put the closing triple quotes on a separate line:

```
"""This is a short one."""
```

```
        """This is what to do if your document string is
        going to be on multiple lines
    """
```

Let's make a function that will print three values we put into it. We will also add a long docstring to see how it works:

```
>>> def eek (value1, value2, value3):
        """This is a long document sting that we are adding to this function to
demonstrate the way it should look in Python
"""
        print(value1, value2, value3)


>>> eek(3, 7, 9)
3 7 9
>>>
```

Review:
1. We called our function. 2. We entered arguments. 3. Our function printed the arguments.

Remember that a "*suite*" in Python just means a particular block of code. The suite in our function is the block of code associated with the *defined name*, ("eek" in this case), and the function's *parameters,* ("value1, value2, value3").

Return Statements

Let's have a closer look at the return statement. The return statement can pass an expression back to the caller and/or exit the function. If there is no data to pass, it will return, "none" meaning; "nothing to pass." An easier way to think about this is "return" exits the function and returns what you tell it to, (or nothing), and then returns to continue reading the code outside the function.

Try this:

```
>>> def biggest(value1, value2):
        if value1 < value2:
                return value2
        else:
                return value1


>>> print(biggest(3, 2))
3
>>> print(biggest(1, 7))
7
>>>
```

You just created a function that can compare two values and return the largest. How do you think this would be used in a game? Comparing physical strength of each character? What other practical examples can you think of to apply this comparison function?

Methods Vs. Functions

***Methods** are functions that belong to certain objects.* This means that methods often alter their objects in some way. Later, you will learn about how to place methods, *(special functions)*, within something called a "*class*." Methods use dots to distinguish them from normal functions:

```
objectname.methodname
```

Methods also require that their first parameter be "self." *Don't worry about total understanding at this point. More examples and details will be given later when we talk about methods within classes. For now, take note of some differences, lay awake at night, and wonder.*

Function:	***Method:***
`def my_function():`	`def my_method (self):`

Python uses methods for some things and functions for others. Why? One reason is traditional use and history. Functions were intended to be more generic for use with objects that didn't have methods, (like tuples). Sometimes using functions requires less code than when using methods. Each case is different your coding style and experience will guide you. You probably noticed that functions often have underscores, ("_") in their names.

Just Do It:

Sometimes the best way to understand what something does in programming is to just try it. Try the following in the Python shell and see what happens:

```
creatures = [ 'man' ,  'woman' ,  'child' ,  'wombat' ,' alien' ]
[creature.lower() for creature in creatures]
[creature.upper() for creature in creatures]
```

GLOBAL AND LOCAL SCOPE

or Local?

When you create a function, sometimes you want to control what part of your code the function will work in. You may want your function to work within a certain block of code or you may want it to be applied to all of your code. This is the same with variables. You may want them accessed anywhere in the program or just within a particular block of code. Previously, we controlled what block of code a statement influenced by proper indentation. With a function, we can add a statement to clarify its *region of influence or the **scope** of the function*. A function can't be seen by the computer outside its scope or region of influence. If you want it to work at the top level of your program you must tell Python that it's a global function. *A **global statement** tells Python to be able to use the function everywhere in the program; (to always see it as being in the outer block of code).*

The syntax of this kind of global statement is:

```
x = 7
def FunctionName ():
        global x
```

```
x = 7
def FunctionName ():
        global x
        local_1= 9
```

The Global variable; "x" is accessed outside the block. The next variable we called, "local_1=9" is a local variable accessed only within the "FunctionName" block. Python is reading from the inside out, (more on that in a moment).

Let's look at limited scope another way:

The above illustration has three variables and three functions. The variables created under the functions `def fun1()` and `def fun2()` are like dogs within a fence. Any variables you create are limited to roam within the fence, (within their local block of code). The variable `dog1` has no effect on anything outside the scope of his fence. Neither does the variable `dog2`. However, the bird variable, like a bird, can move or work anywhere within the program. Adding the keyword "global" to one of our dogs would be like opening the fence and allowing him to roam outside his normal area. In this example, ***the indentation and location of each function has defined its scope or region of influenced***. Functions will behave this way unless you use a *global or local statement* to specify their scope.

Remember if you don't tell Python a function call is global, Python will assume it's local.

Another interesting thing about Python compared to other computer languages is the way it approaches global and local variables. The default action of many languages is to assume a global scope to a variable unless it is specifically declared. Python is the opposite. Python assumes a local scope if none is specifically declared

Some languages being from the outside working inward, using global scope variables to find the information; while Python works in-to-out to select the default information. Python begins locally and works outwardly like an expanding spiral. The reasoning behind this approach is the fact that creating too many global variables is a bad habit that will often increase your number of conflicts. Python teaches you reduce these kinds of problems.

To understand let's look closer at Python's looping behavior:

```
>>> words= "More words outside of the function block."
>>> def some_function():
        words= "Inside of the function block."
        print(words)


>>> some_function()
Inside of the function block.
```

In this first example you can see there are two variables with the same name; "words." By reading inside to outside to determine priorities; Python chose the variable "words" within the function to print.

```
>>> words= "More words outside of the function block."
>>> def some_functionb():
        global words
        print(words)
        words= "Even more words inside."


>>> some_functionb()
More words outside of the function block.
>>>
```

In this second example you can see that if you attach "global" to the first "words" variable within the function; Python will chose the global "words" outside the function block to print.

You will learn much more about functions in later lessons. For this lesson we are keeping things simple. Before writing complex functions you should remember that Python has many functions built in; has many within its standard library; and many are available in the modules you may choose to use. You may find one that already does the job for you rather than taking the time to write one. It's a good idea to become familiar with what is already out there before using your valuable time to create functions you didn't need to write. But, this is a judgment call. If it takes less time to write one than to find what you need; then write it. Python functions can be stored as objects that can be used later as arguments within other functions. This is just a fancy way to say you can keep and copy functions to be like building blocks to use within more complex functions later. We will cover some built-in functions in the Lesson 7, "More Python Parts."

**To see the list of built-in functions type "dir (_builtins_)" in IDLE, (without the quotation marks).*

REVIEW

Quiz 5:

5.1 Define the following terms and check your answers on the next page:

1. Function
2. Function call
3. Global statement
4. Scope
5. Docstring
6. Methods
7. Suite
8. Metadata

5.2 Answer the following questions:

1. What is the syntax for making a function?
2. Fix this docstring:

```
""This is what to do if your document string is
  going to be on multiple lines"
```

3. What is the syntax for a global function?

5.3 Activity:

Construct and call a function that will return the average value of three integers.

VOCABULARY

Function *a re-usable mini program inside of your program*
Function call *the code you type to turn on a function.*
Global statement *tells Python to be able to use the function everywhere in the program*
Docstring *a document string to document information about a function or object*
Methods *functions that belong to certain objects.*
Suites *are another name for indented and grouped code blocks in Python.*
Metadata *is data about data.*
Scope *region of influence*

5.2 Answer the following questions:

1. def name(parameters):
        "docstring"
        suite, or code block
        return [expression]

2. *Corrected:*

No extra space here → """This is what to do if your document string

Indentation → is going to be on multiple lines

"""

*Quotation marks **location** and they should be **triple**; not double quotation marks.*

3. x = 7
   def FunctionName ():
        global x

5.3 Activity:

Answers will vary.

```
>>> def average(val1, val2, val3):
        """This is a function to average three integers."""
        return (val1 + val2 + val3) /3

>>> average(3, 22, 77)
34.0
>>>
```

Lesson 6: Basic Modules, Tkinter, and Dictionaries

WHAT YOU WILL LEARN:

- **OOP AND MODULE BASICS**
- **ENOUGH WORDS! LET'S GET GRAPHIC!**
- **DICTIONARIES (NOT THE ENGLISH KIND)**

OOP AND MODULE BASICS

What's an OOP? An OOP is an "***Object Oriented Programming***" language like Python. *What does that mean?* In an effort to shorten the time it takes for programming, programmers decided that it would be really great if they could divide large programs into smaller pieces. Then, make these pieces to be self-contained mini-programs that could be combined according to the needs of the programmer. These pieces are often referred to as ***objects***. ***Objects** are little chunks of code you can move around*. Strings, tuples, functions, dictionaries, modules, etc. are all objects. Object oriented programming allows programmers to reuse code as much as possible. One way to do this is to use and create modules.

Modules** are programs that can be activated in Python and provide you with more tools and functions to get things done more easily. They are moveable **groups** of code.* Modules are a way of grouping data like functions, methods, classes, executable code, and other objects. Sometimes modules are referred to as "libraries***." Modules can be mini- programs you can use or borrow stuff from, (like libraries you can borrow books from). You can import definitions into other modules or into your main module.

Modules give you the power to easily share chunks of useable code with others or move the code around. You can move it to other programs or within the same program easily. You can save your module as a text-file with a **".py"** extension to store it or share it. You will learn how to package modules later in Lesson 21.

You can check Python's standard library and the internet for module sharing sites to see what modules are available before writing them from scratch. Check the Resources Index and Chapter 21 when you are ready to find modules specific to your needs.

You can import an entire module or parts of the module. Of course, importing only the necessary parts will make your code run faster and more efficiently. Limiting what you import can also reduce the chances of conflicts due to the possibility of your module having functions or other code with the same names as functions within the modules you are importing.

Python has some built-in modules, some you can import from the standard library and others that must be added. You will have to import and get familiar with every module you choose to use. To have a look at what is in the module you can use the "`dir()` " statement. To see built-in statements you need to use "`dir(built-ins).`"

Try this and see what happens:

```
>>> import tkinter
>>> dir(tkinter)
```

Wow! This; "`dir`" lists the currently defined names of variables, functions, modules, etc. but not ones that are built-in.

Now try this one:

```
>>> import builtins
>>> dir(builtins)
```

To display the built-ins you use; "`dir(built-ins).`" Don't panic at the overload of information. You will learn to make use of it later. For now, we continue our tour.

It will be necessary to get familiar with the available objects within any modules you have decided to use. To call specific functions and objects will require the use of the "*dot*" operator, (period). So, an example to use a module function would be:

```
nameOfModule.functionName(arguments)
```

Enough Words! Let's Get Graphic!

"See Science as Art; And Art as Science"

Leonardo Da Vinci

(Note: If you would like to spend nearly five hours hearing the very thoughts of Leonardo from his personal notebooks, check out the audio book at www.AlienCatStudios.com (Yeah, I know...shameless advertising, but I really feel everyone could benefit by spending nearly five hours in DaVinci's mind).

Graphics and computer sciences have become one in modern times. We are visual creatures and understand things better when we see them. Whether it is the graphics in computer games; or graphical windows to make using the program easier; we need visual elements in software. Back in the dinosaur days, I remember staring at a black computer screen that only displayed a white, blinking, underscore. In those days; when we were not hiding from a tyrannosaurus rex or going to our club to find a date; we only had a boring black and white screen to stare at.

It worked! Rex felt if Dos-like interfaces could hide behind Graphical User Interfaces; maybe dinosaurs could too!

Jody S. Ginther, 2013

With the delusion of an advancing civilization came Graphical User Interfaces, new music, and new ways to go to a club for a date! So, for the sake of mindlessly fulfilling the desires of the masses; we must also consider using graphical interfaces for our software.

This is where the Tkinter module comes in. First, we must tell Python that we want to use a module by using the "import" command. The import command is placed at the beginning or top of our source code. ***Tkinter** is a module for creating simple graphics for interfaces*, or a graphical way for you and your computer to communicate. Many additional functions for Tkinter can be downloaded and added to Python. I will just introduce you to some simple functions available that are normally within the standard download of Python. In this way, you can use what you have and not worry about downloading or installing modules. *We will get to that in Lesson 21.Tkinter, GUI's, advantages and disadvantages, will be covered in more detail in Lessons 10 and 11.*

For this lesson, some higher level typing challenges will now begin...watch every dot and space!
*Enough talk, let's get started. Enter this in your **Edit** window, (**not** the shell):*

tmp.py - C:/Python33/tmp.py

File Edit Format Run Options Windows Help

```
from tkinter import*

class Application(Frame):
    def say_Yeh(self):
        print("Yeh! Your button just did something!")

    def createWidgets(self):
        self.QUITBUTTON= Button(self)
        self.QUITBUTTON['text']= 'QUIT BUTTON'
        self.QUITBUTTON['fg']= 'red'
        self.QUITBUTTON['command']= self.quit

        self.QUITBUTTON.pack({'side': 'left'})

        self.do_something= Button(self)
        self.do_something['text']= 'CLICK TO DO SOMETHING BUTTON',
        self.do_something['command']= self.say_Yeh

        self.do_something.pack({'side': 'left'})

    def __init__(self, master= None):
        Frame.__init__(self, master)
        self.pack()
        self.createWidgets()

root= Tk()
app= Application(master=root)
app.mainloop()
root.destroy()
```

*Note that these are double underscores.

Now click on *run* then click *run module*, save it, and *WOW!*
A button appeared! Or at least it should have appeared. If it didn't appear you either have to check your code or check your eyes. Whenever code that you think is correct disappoints you; go back and make sure every detail of the code was typed correctly. The red complaints will sometimes help you find mistakes. Once every dot, parenthesis, underscore, indentation, and letter is correct; your program will run and the awesome buttons will appear. Check everything and keep troubleshooting until it works. Don't get frustrated. As a programmer you will spend much of your time solving problems with code.

Your work should look like this:

Click on the; "CLICK TO DO SOMETHING BUTTON."
The result should look like this:

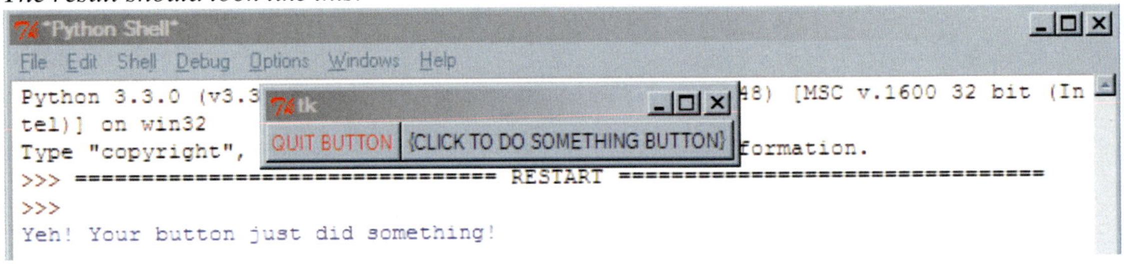

When you are happy click the; "QUIT BUTTON." The "QUIT BUTTON" is boring. It just quits the program we just made. The explanations for the code on this will be brief. My objective here is to introduce you to some visual aspects of Python. After you understand the basics of Python you will be ready to go deeper into modules and graphics.

Code explanation:

```
from tkinter import *
```

This imports the parts of the tkinter module we will be using.

```
class Application(Frame):
```

Calls a *constructor* for the parent class called," Frame." Huh? Sorry that was geek talk, let's translate that to English. This line of code is bringing in, (calling), the code that makes or constructs a frame. The frame is just a rectangle like a picture frame. We establish it as a parent. A parent and child relationship is used in programming and in 3D animation to describe how you want things to work. For example; your arm bones are parents to your hand bones. If you move your arm, your hand will also move. However, you can move your hand without moving your arm. Move a parent object and the child moves with it. The child object can move by itself without moving the parent.

```
    def say_Yeh(self):
        print("Yeh! Your button just did something!")
```

These lines of code define the name, (say_Yeh), and a string that we want to print to the computer screen.

```
def createWidgets(self):
        self.QUITBUTTON = Button(self)
        self.QUITBUTTON["text"] = "QUIT BUTTON"
        self.QUITBUTTON["fg"]   = "red"
        self.QUITBUTTON["command"] =  self.quit
        self.QUITBUTTON.pack({"side": "left"})
```

These lines define the name and the details of our “Quit” button. The self statement will be covered later.

```
    self.do_something = Button(self)
        self.do_something["text"] = "CLICK TO DO SOMETHING BUTTON",
        self.do_something["command" ] = self.say_Yeh
        self.do_something.pack({"side": "left"})
```

These lines define the name and details of our “CLICK TO DO SOMETHING” button.

```
    def __init__(self, master=None):
        Frame.__init__(self, master)
        self.pack()
        self.createWidgets()
```

These are instructions to determine how things within our frame will behave. The first line means our application must “inherit” from Tkinter’s Frame class. The “init method” is a constructor; while the “master” defines the parent. The second line calls the constructor for the parent class, (frame). The last lines bring our widget to the screen so we can see it.

```
root = Tk()
app = Application(master=root)
```

The main program will start here. This creates a top level window with a title bar to be our “root widget.” The top level window is normally called the “root.” Only create one root widget for an application. After creating your root you can make other widgets. The second line is bringing in one instance of the application class with the root as the parent.

```
app.mainloop() #starts main loop, waiting for (keyboard/mouse)input
root.destroy()
```

These lines are to instruct the computer to create a loop, (`mainloop`), to execute and wait for some specific keyboard event to happen. In this case it is waiting for the click of a button on our widget. The "`destroy`" method is waiting for some event to happen in the root that will allow it to exit the loop and close the window.

Yes, I know we rushed over these explanations. For now, stop whining and just copy the code. After you have studied more on functions, classes, and other stuff, you can return here to read the code again. For now, this is just a quick glance at GUI stuff.

To be a master of widgets and graphics requires much more information and practice than can be provided in a basic course. In some cases, you will not truly understand code until you have used it. Just as you can only get good at basketball by playing basketball. You will never get great at basketball by sitting on the bed reading books about it. So, relax and do programming to learn it. This was a brief introduction to the Tkinter module but you will see more of it in lesson 11. There is a whole Tkinter world to explore.

The modules and aspects of Python that you choose to master first will depend upon your objectives. If your objective is to write computer games; you will have to master graphics at a higher level than you will need for simple applications. If you are going to work with stock market forecasting; math and data manipulation modules would be more important to you. Think about your goals and objective and chose the appropriate modules. There are standard library modules, third party modules, and modules of your own creation. The internet is loaded with modules for nearly every purpose a programmer may need. Set you goals, and choose accordingly.

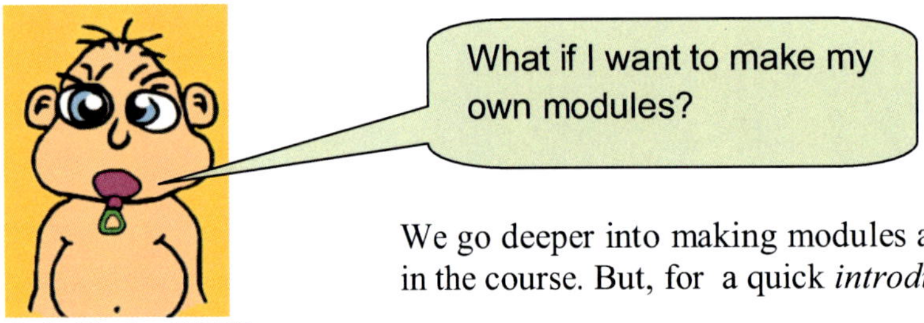

Jody Ginther ©2012

We go deeper into making modules and packages later in the course. But, for a quick *introduction*:

What do you want it to do? First, you have to decide what the purpose of your module is and what functions, methods, and classes you want in it. You should write a module when you have a lot of code you will be re-using. This group of useful related functions and classes would all be placed within your module. It will be saved as a .py file in Python's file directory. Any .py file can be used as a module. Modules you make yourself are often referred to as "*user-defined modules.*"

When you make a module and save it as a .py file, Python will generally make a .pyc version in the same directory. The .pyc version of your module will be *byte-compiled.* Byte-compiled files are platform independent and will work much faster, (take less processing time).

Just as any other module, when you import a module you have created you have a number of options. You can import the entire module into another module or program; or you can just import parts of it.

- To import the entire module you could use: import NameofModule.
- To import a function or other part of a module you would use: from NameofModule import NameofFunction.

You will learn more about modules in Lessons 10 and 21. You can also find many resources for getting modules and libraries in Index B.

DICTIONARIES (NOT THE ENGLISH KIND)

You can see that programmers need to arrange data many different ways to produce programs quickly. Python and object oriented languages allow many ways to organize your code to access and use it quickly. A dictionary is another way to organize your code. You can create custom dictionaries of code for a specific project or program. Your imagination is the only limitation to what kind of dictionaries you can create. Unlike a normal dictionary however, Python dictionaries don't have to organize the keywords and definitions in any particular order.

*We define the name we choose for our dictionary entry as the "**key**". We name the details or definition of our entry as the "**value.**" Programmers often refer to the key and its associated value as a "**key-value pair.**"*

Just as in a real dictionary, we find the definition, or value, we are looking for by looking up the keyword, or key. We can't look up the definition to find the key.

```
Python Shell
File Edit Shell Debug Options Windows Help
Python 3.3.0 (v3.3.0:bd8afb90ebf2, Sep 29 1600, 10:55:48) [MSC v.1600 32 bit (In
tel)] on win32
Type "copyright", "credits" or "license()" for more information.
>>> mydictionary= {'chocolate':'happiness', 'moon':'something to howl at'}
```

First, we must make a name for our dictionary. In this case I just called it, "mydictionary." We then create a key-value pair for each entry. This dictionary only has two entries, but you can enter as many as you want. Be careful. Note that the entire dictionary is bracketed with {}, the keys and the values are separated by colons, :, and they are enclosed in single or double quotation marks, " ". If your dictionary does not work, check your syntax. *How do we find or access our dictionary entries?*

To call an entry from our dictionary:

```
>>> mydictionary= {'chocolate':'happiness', 'moon':'something to howl at'}
>>> mydictionary['moon']
'something to howl at'
>>>
```

The syntax to call a dictionary entry is:

dictionaryname ['keyword']

You can only use immutable objects for keys, but you can use immutable and mutable objects for values. Dictionaries are sometimes referred to as "*associative arrays*" in other programming languages.

Sequences, (like lists and tuples), are accessed by index locations or numbers; while dictionaries are accessed by keys. **Mutable objects**, (like lists), **can't be** used as **keys**.

*Dictionaries are sometimes referred to as "**mappings**" because their keys are "mapped" to data objects.* The data in a dictionary is arranged in ***key:value*** pairs separated by commas. You create a dictionary by placing your *key: value* pairs within braces {}. Since you can't use the index position to reference an item in a dictionary, you use `dictionaryname[ 'itemname' ]` to refer to a particular item.

```
Python Shell
File Edit Shell Debug Options Windows Help
Python 3.3.0 (v3.3.0:bd8afb90ebf2, Sep 29 1212, 10:55:48) [MSC v.1600 32 bit (In
tel)] on win32
Type "copyright", "credits" or "license()" for more information.
>>> weapons= {'guns':3, 'eggs':7, 'snowballs':14} #defining dictionary entries
>>> print(weapons['eggs']) # referring to the key item to get its value
7
>>>
```

Here we named a dictionary; "weapons" and entered three key value pairs.

Dictionary keys must be unique to a particular dictionary. If you add a key you have already used, it will replace or overwrite the old one with the new key: value pair. You may want to check and make sure you have not already used a key by typing `dictionaryname.key()`. This will give you an unsorted list of your keys. If you want them sorted alphabetically use `sorted(dictionaryname.keys())`. If you want to search for a specific key you can use `dictionaryname.get( 'item' )` and even add a second argument `dictionaryname.get( 'item' ,' not here' )` to output "not here" if it didn't find anything.

```
>>> erp= {'this':24, 'that':"", 'other':21}
>>> erp.get('mook')
>>> erp.get('moook', 'not here')
'not here'
>>> erp.get('this', 'not here')
24
>>> erp.get('that', 'not here')
''
>>> #If our key has an empty value we left to enter data later, .get will ouput the
empty quotation marks indication the key is there but has no value.  We entered the
second argument "not here" to tell us the key wasn't found. Notice that when we put
'mook' in .get to find it,we got no reply from Python,because it found nothing and
we did not enter the second argument 'not here.'
```

Create your own dictionary and practice accessing your code.

Some other common things to know about dictionaries:

- You can delete a key: value pair with `del dictionaryname[ 'item' ]`.
- You can add a key using the = sign: `dictionaryname[ 'item' ]=77`.
- You can also access contents with `dictionaryname.keys()` `dictionaryname.values()` and `dictionaryname.items()`
- You can clear all entries in the dictionary to start over with: `dictionaryname.clear()`.
- You can ***not*** use a tuple as a key ***if it contains a mutable object.***

Here's how:

```
Python Shell
File Edit Shell Debug Options Windows Help
Python 3.3.0 (v3.3.0:bd8afb90ebf2, Sep 29 2012, 10:55:48) [MSC v.1600 32 bit (In
tel)] on win32
Type "copyright", "credits" or "license()" for more information.
>>> foodpower= {'grapes':5, 'bread':2, 'tea':4, 'worms':1}
>>> del foodpower['worms']
>>> print(foodpower)
{'tea': 4, 'bread': 2, 'grapes': 5}
>>> foodpower['grasshoppers']= 3 # to add a key value pair
>>> print(foodpower) # to check
{'tea': 4, 'bread': 2, 'grapes': 5, 'grasshoppers': 3}
>>> foodpower.keys() # to have a look at the keys
dict_keys(['tea', 'bread', 'grapes', 'grasshoppers'])
>>> foodpower.values() # to have a look at the values
dict_values([4, 2, 5, 3])
>>> foodpower.items()
dict_items([('tea', 4), ('bread', 2), ('grapes', 5), ('grasshoppers', 3)])
>>> foodpower.clear() # to clear all the items
>>> print(foodpower) #checking
{}
>>>
```

When looping, you can use `dictionaryname.values()` and `dictionaryname.items()` to get a value; or both the value and the item. If you loop through dictionaries using a for loop, only keys will be ***iterated***,*(read by the computer).*

Let's convert an existing list into a dictionary. We could create a list of weapons with a reference to the level of damage they can do. Later we decide we want this list to be in the form of a dictionary. The syntax for our list is:

```
weapons=[('hand_laser', 'low'),('wide_laser', 'medium'),('sniper_laser', 'high')]
```

To convert our list to a dictionary we would use the ***"dict"*** contructor:

```
dictionaryName = dict(listname)
```

```
Python 3.3.0 (v3.3.0:bd8afb90ebf2, Sep 29 2012, 10:55:48) [MSC v.1600 32 bit (Intel)] on win32
Type "copyright", "credits" or "license()" for more information.
>>> weapons= [('hand_laser','low'),('wide_laser','medium'),('sniper_laser','high')]
>>> weapons_pwr= dict(weapons) #Name the new dictionary and use dict to turn the list into a dictionary
>>> print(weapons_pwr) #Checking to see if it worked
{'sniper_laser': 'high', 'hand_laser': 'low', 'wide_laser': 'medium'}
>>> #YES! We made a dictionary from our list!
```

You can see that dictionaries are a little too in-depth to cover in only one lesson. Don't worry, we will be returning to them often as we travel down the path to better programming. This course is to give you a quick over-view and get you practicing as fast as possible. Giving you experience asap.

*Remember when I left you hanging in Lesson 5 on **kwargs?* This lesson is where we have a deeper look at those things.

Syntax:

```
def function_name(formal, **kwargs):
      "docstring"
      suite, or code block
      return [expression]
```

Back when you were younger, (in lesson 5), we looked at making some functions with an unknown number of parameters just waiting for you to come along and enter your arguments. You survived and found success by using *kwargs. Now that you are older, you will now understand the need for setting up a function with an unknown number of argument "pairs." Let's say that you want to make a function that will output; what type of food; the names of each food; and the associated number that you ate today. Since Python dictionaries are not in alphabetical order like English dictionaries, we will also ask Python to sort the pairs in order according to the names of their keys. The keys would be the names of the food; while their associated values would be the number you ate today.

***Try this*:**

```
def eat_it(foodtype, **kwargs):
    print("How much ", foodtype, "did you eat?")
    keys= sorted(kwargs.keys())
    for fruitname in keys: print(fruitname, ":", kwargs[fruitname])

eat_it("fruit", apples= "8", oranges= "2", bananas= "1")
```

Constant argument

**kwargs arguments

#Call it and enter arguments.

You should get this:

```
>>>
How much  fruit did you eat?
apples : 8
bananas : 1
oranges : 2
>>>
```

*Our print order would be undefined if we did not use the sort statement. Since we used the sort statement our " **kwarg" entries were printed in alphabetical order.*

REVIEW

Quiz 6:

6.1 Define the following terms and check your answers on the next page:

1. OOP
2. Objects
3. Modules
4. Libraries
5. Tkinter
6. Dictionary (in Python)
7. Key
8. Value
9. Key-value Pair
10. Mappings

6.2 Answer the following questions:

1. What is an advantage of object oriented programming?
2. What do we call modules you have created yourself?
3. What is the syntax to call a dictionary entry?
4. What is the syntax for loading a module?
5. What is the syntax for loading part of a module?
6. When can a tuple ***not*** be used for a dictionary key?
7. What is the file extension to save a module in Python?

6.3 Activity:

Create a dictionary from a list.

VOCABULARY

OOP *stands for Object Oriented Programming.*	
Objects *are moveable chunks of code.*	
Modules *are programs that can be activated in Python and provide you with more tools and functions to get things done more easily. They are moveable groups of code.*	
Mappings *another name for dictionaries.*	
Libraries *another name for modules or collections of related code.*	
Tkinter *a Python module for making graphical interfaces*	
Dictionary *a way to organize and reference data in key-value pairs rather than by index numbers.*	
Key *the name we chose for our dictionary entry*	
Value *the details or definition for a dictionary entry/key*	
Key-value pair *a key and its associated value*	

6.2 Answers:

1. Moveable and reusable blocks of code.
2. User-defined modules.
3. dictionaryname ['keyword']
4. import NameofModule
5. from NameofModule import NameofFunction
6. When it contains a mutable object.
7. .py

6.3 Activity:
*To convert our list to a dictionary we would use the "**dict**" contructor:*

```
dictionaryName = dict(listname)
```

```
Python Shell
File Edit Shell Debug Options Windows Help
Python 3.3.0 (v3.3.0:bd8afb90ebf2, Sep 29 2012, 10:55:48) [MSC v.1600 32 bit (Intel)] on win32
Type "copyright", "credits" or "license()" for more information.
>>> weapons= [('hand_laser','low'),('wide_laser','medium'),('sniper_laser','high')]
>>> weapons_pwr= dict(weapons) #Name the new dictionary and use dict to turn the list into a dictionary
>>> print(weapons_pwr) #Checking to see if it worked
{'sniper_laser': 'high', 'hand_laser': 'low', 'wide_laser': 'medium'}
>>> #YES! We made a dictionary from our list!
```

Lesson 7: More Python Parts

WHAT YOU WILL LEARN:

- INTRO TO CLASSES
- NAME SPACES AND SCOPE
- BASICS OF CREATING CLASSES
- MORE ON METHODS
- MORE FUNCTIONS
- MORE KEYWORDS AND EXPRESSIONS

INTRO TO CLASSES

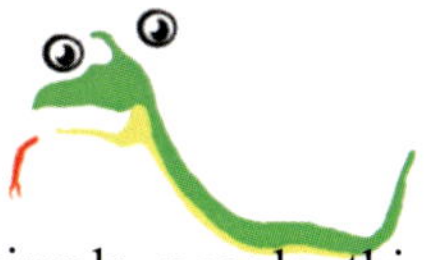

Just as we classify things in life; animals, people, things, etc. we classify kinds of data. Data types have different characteristics. The list class does not have all the same characteristics as the tuple class. A characteristic of the list class is that it is mutable; while a characteristic of the tuple class is that it is immutable.

Remember that objects are self-contained mini programs. A ***class*** *object is a template that will contain your methods, functions, and other data for that object*. This data type object could be a machine, person, or creature in a game. You could create a class container to represent all the details of that object. A class representing a car in the game may contain details like; maximum speed, fuel, sounds, etc. A class representing a character could include life, weapons, age, etc.

<u>A few other useful features of a class:</u>

- Class objects can have arbitrary amounts of data.
- An inheritance system can be used to create multiple base classes.
- Methods of one class can over-ride methods of other classes.

NAME SPACES AND SCOPE

To understand when to use a class and how they work, you need to understand *namespaces* and their *scope*. You can think of the *"**scope**" as their region of influence.* Remember that we talked about local and global scope of variables? *(Say; "Yes" or go back and review).* We used the concept of land with two individual yards or blocks of property within it. We had a bird with global scope and a couple of dogs limited to their yards, or local scopes. The namespace concept is a little like that. But, in this example comparing namespaces to reserved parking places in various parking lots seems to make things easier to understand.

First of all, what's in a name? Any object in Python can have a name or more than one name. But, sometimes two objects are called by the same name and are different things, (like two people with the same given name are different things...er people). So the computer don't get confused, there are *spaces reserved for names, called **namespaces***. This is like making a map to the name of each object. This is why *the assignment of the namespace to a particular name is called **mapping***. Namespaces can be preserved for different lengths of time in memory, just as parking spaces can be temporary, one hour parking, or reserved spaces with a name on it for permanent parking. Your module's namespace is reserved on loading the module and it's functions get reserved namespaces to park when you call them.
You could have two red Porsche's going to park in a huge parking lot. If you just say, "Get the red Porsche." This might be a problem. So, parking lots have divisions within them, just as blocks of code have different name space reserved. There may be a huge parking lot where the outside area is for public use, an interior parking block preserved for VIP's , another for workers, etc. We must have a way to refer to any of these spaces at any given time.

When you give your module a name, that name becomes it's main namespace and every other block is referred to from there. When you are working on your module and have not named it, Python will reserve the name _main_ for your "main" block of code. So, Python, (like a worker in a parking lot), automatically supplied a reference space name to your code. Next, all classes, functions, and other objects get a namespace reserved for reference. *Python's **namespace** assignment works like a dictionary. It is sometimes referred to as "**mapping**" your namespace names to objects. The assignment of a name to an object is called **binding.*** Every block of code has a namespace.

Why is this important? Because now you can have two functions or other objects with the same name in different places in your code and they won't conflict with each other when run. *Why?* This is where scope comes in. Local or Global scope can tell the computer where to begin looking for the object you are referring to in your blocks of code. Just as in our parking lot example, you may need to know that your car is in Parking lot A, in row nine, in parking space four.

Let's say you have the two red Porsche's parked in two different parking lots. The two cars, *(like some of our functions)*, may both have the same name; "red Porsche." However, they are in different parking lots, *(modules)*. If one red Porsche is in the VIP parking lot, *(or module),* starting it, *(calling it),* and driving it around, *(using it),* will not interfere with what is happening in the Customer Parking lot where the other red Porsche is sitting quietly. Two functions with the same name can happily live in different modules without interfering with one another due to the local scope of their influence and their different namespaces.

In the last example, you would have two modules; "VIP" and "CustomerParking" each having a function called, "red_Porsche". You would import the modules and call the red_Porsche in the VIP parking space, (namespace) using dot notation in this way:

```
VIP.red_Porsche
```

Let's say you want to call a function called "fire_up(mylist)." This function lives in a module you saved earlier called "MyModule."

The safest way to do this without causing name conflicts would be to import your entire module and then call the function:

```
import MyModule
```

The syntax would then be to use the namespace for the module, a dot, and the name of the function so Python knows where to look:

```
import MyModule
ModuleName.my_function( )
```

For our function it would be:

```
import MyModule
MyModule.fire_up(mylist)
```

What if I don't want to type "MyModule?" This is when you could just import the part of the module you plan to use rather than the entire module, (from MyModule import fire_op(mylist). But, then your function will be added to your current namespace block. If you have another module by the same name in that namespace it will be over-written.

I mentioned earlier that namespaces are like limited parking. You could be allowed to park for fifteen minutes, one hour, or have permanent parking. Name spaces also have different lifetimes. Most are created when the function is called and deleted when the function returns a value or an error, (exception) or when you exit the interpreter. Like a car being assigned to a parking space when it arrives and losing that space when it moves. Built-in namespaces have permanent namespaces like permanent parking spots. These are never deleted.

Assignment of name spaces does not mean the functions or code blocks are copied and moved around. Assignment only binds names to objects creating a "map" for Python to find things.

Basics of Creating Classes

To create your own simple class you just begin by calling it a class:

```
>>>class NameofMyClass:
    pass
```

In creating your own class, you should capitalize the class name. Do not capitalize the word "class" when using it to define a class. The "pass" statement is a placeholder to tell Python to continue. You can call up a class in the same way you call a function. Classes may define methods, include docstrings, inherit things from other classes, and assign attributes.

Notice: **Class names should begin with an uppercase (capital) letter. You will not be arrested by the Python police and thrown into a snake pit if you don't; but it is the standard practice of Python programmers. For variables, and functions you are free to chose upper or lower case.*

***Attributes** are extra characteristics or pieces of information.* Once an attribute is assigned, it can even be accessed outside the class. Sometimes the extra information within a class is referred to as "*fields*." Creating a class is done to group and call related stuff as one object, or to be able to access individual attributes within that group. For example, you may need different vehicles in a game with different attributes and need to group them accordingly. First you should make lists of your vehicles attributes and turn these groups of attributes into classes in the game:

***Vehicle1** attributes:*

color = red
speed = fast
size = small
type = sports_car

***Vehicle2** attributes:*

color = brown
speed = slow
size = big
type = truck

Your actual class would look a little more like the following example:

```
class Vehicle1:
        def __init__():
        color = 'red'
        speed = 'fast'
        size = 'small'
        type = 'sports_car'
```

Don't worry, we will get to the unexplained code shortly. For now, just notice how to plan and create the general structure of a class and its attributes. You may also define things like "speed" or "size" by using numerical values and add more details to each of the attributes you have placed in this class.

To get information on the class and read the docstrings, use the following syntax:

help(NameofMyClass)

First, define a class:

```
>>> class PythonProgrammers():
        """This is a class of future programmers."""
        pass
```

Then use "help" to have a look at it:

```
>>> help(PythonProgrammers)
Help on class PythonProgrammers in module __main__:

class PythonProgrammers(builtins.object)
 |  This is a class of future programmers.
 |
 |  Data descriptors defined here:
 |
 |  __dict__
 |      dictionary for instance variables (if defined)
 |
 |  __weakref__
 |      list of weak references to the object (if defined)
```

Ok, so we got help, *but how helpful is it?* This gives us a good overview of our class. The first line mentions what module namespace our class is in. Then, the name of our class is displayed. The docstring normally contains some useful information about the class. Next *data descriptors* are defined. We are given a little information about the dictionaries and a *weak reference* list.

Data descriptors *are those that define both _get_( ), and _set_( ) for the object.*

Non-data descriptors *only define _get_( ) and are generally used for methods.*

A ***descriptor*** *is an object attribute that can over-ride default attribute behaviors*. ***Descriptors*** *modify default behavior within classes but not in other objects*. Default behavior for attribute access is to getting, setting, or deleting the attribute from an object's dictionary. *If any of the methods _get_( ), _set_( ), or _delete( ) are defined, the object is considered a* ***descriptor***.

A ***weak reference*** is applied using the weakref module. ***Weak references*** *provide a way to clean up the cache and free memory by not keeping objects "alive" beyond their current use.* Detailed understanding and expert usage of weak references is beyond the scope of a beginner's course. *(Hey, we have to leave something to learn later).*

Ok, back to the information and skills that you will be using shortly. To keep things simple, I will only introduce you to two more elements of creating classes at this point.

- These two elements are **self. (something)** and **def __init__.**

For example:

```
>>>class    NameofMyClass:
    def __init__(self, txtstring):
    self.txt=txtstring
```

In this example we named and defined our class; "NameofMyClass," and we created two methods within the class. The def __init__ , (initialize), method is sometimes referred to as a "***constructor***" because it indicates that *a new instance of an object has been made. You could think of the "**instance**" as; "this particular appearance of a class or object in your code."* Self is required as the first parameter because it refers to the instance where you called the method. In other words it is referring to itself as the instance it is now talking about. *Adding* **self** *to variables tells the computer that these particular variables only apply in this instance of the class.* You can change the variables in their next appearance, (instance), of the class if you want to, but for this *instance, (or appearance)*; the variable is behaving the way it was *defined this time.*

Finding your "self" parameter

You can call "self" to wake up and take action.

MORE ON METHODS

Operators and *methods* are different kinds of operations available for different kinds of data. You have already seen the logic operators from mathematics used between two or more operands. We also talked briefly about methods earlier but let's take a deeper look at them. ***Methods** are functions that are made to be used exclusively within a particular class or object. Methods belong to that particular object or class.*

In other words; if you make a function to work for that class, it is called a "method." Python uses a ***dot operator*** *to indicate the method following the name of the class.* As mentioned previously, the first argument of a method is often "*self.*" This is a reference argument for methods. This is Python's way of telling the interpreter that the assignment is to an *instance variable* rather than a *local variable.* The methods of a class must refer the "self" to find and access attributes within its own class.

What's the difference between and instance variable and a local variable?

A complete description is an intermediate to advanced topic beyond the scope of this beginner's course. But, since you asked, we will look at this briefly. Local variables and instance variables live in two different ***namespaces***, *(reserved spaces in memory).* As mentioned, designating *.self* makes it clear that this is an instance variable. You can think of an instance as a copy of the original that can be altered without altering the original.

Ok, don't be impatient. Now, we want a method to belong to a particular class or object so their will be no conflicts with those outside of that class or object. But, how do we know what methods we are going to need? Later, I will mention how <u>verbs</u> can suggest methods for a class; but you will have to wait for awhile before I even mention anything about that.

For now, let's look at how you actually write a method within a class:

```
class Frog:
    def jump(self):
        print('Frog jumped')
```

To make it.

Remember that methods require the first parameter to be "self." Yeah, I know; other than the "self" thing, this looks just like a normal function. But, *(I am sure you remember),* the syntax for <u>calling a method</u> uses a dot operator. *How does the code look, you ask?*

Like this:

```
1 Fred = Frog ( )
2 Fred.jump ( )      <---- To call it.

3 Frog jumped
```

Line 1: *We made a new object called "Fred" and assigned our "Frog" class to it, with parenthesis to indicate any parameters that might go along with it.*

Line 2: *We called the method in the Frog class. The anatomy of a method is:*

```
Objectname.methodname (parameters)
```

Line 3: *This is our output. Of course, in a real game we could add the code here to animate the jumping of Fred Frog rather than just printing words.*

More on Functions

Types of functions:

Ordinary functions *are the common type of functions that follow a mathematical model and return a value using the return statement.*

Procedural functions *have no parameters.* This kind of function *doesn't use the return* statement *and doesn't return a value.*

Built-in functions *are functions that come within Python.*

User-defined functions *are functions you make yourself.*

Built-In Functions Quick Tour

This is not a comprehensive study of all built-in functions. This lesson just introduces you to a few more functions and what you can do with them. You needn't try to memorize all of them; just become familiar with what can be done with them for future reference.

We will not repeat information on functions we have already covered like; frozenset(), input(), len(), print(), set(), and import().Try some of these to see what they do. *See Python's documentation for a complete list of functions and their uses.*

abs() No, not your stomach muscles. This one stands for *absolute value*. This function does just what is sounds like it would do; *it changes any number to it's absolute value*. The argument can be an integer or a floating point number. Like this:

```
>>> print(abs(77.7))
  77.7
  >>> print(abs(-80.3))
  80.3
```

bin() *This one converts integers to a binary string*. This is not very useful to you at this point, but it is really cool to play with if you want to see what the binary version of any integer looks like. To calculate binary is a bit of a pain on large numbers. With binary numbers one through ten are easy if you can see the pattern; but after that you need to use a formula.

For example:

```
1=01 (in binary)   6=110
2=10               7=111
3=11               8=1000
4=100              9=1001
5=101             10=1010
```

The formula for calculating larger binary numbers is:

Let the integer be x. Take x/2 and if the remainder is an odd number use "1"; if it is even use "0" and repeat /2 until you can no longer get a whole number.....Huhhh!?

Let's say we want to see the binary for the number 57:

57/2 =28	r = 1 that's odd so we use 1
28/2=14	r = 0 even........so we use 0
14/2=7	r = 0 even..................0
7/2=3	r = 1 odd..................1
3/2=1	r = 1 odd..................1
1/2=1	r = 1 odd..................1

This means the binary version of 57 is 111001.

Yuk! With the bin() *function you would just do it this way:*

```
>>> print(bin(57))
0b111001
```

Ahhhh! This is much nicer. The result is even a valid Python expression.

bool((x)) *Finding truth*! Remember that we said Boolean expressions are all about true or false? If (x) is false or missing this will return "False." Otherwise it returns True.bool, which is a class and a subclass of int. This bool class can't be subdivided into more classes; it will only result in "true" or "false," (0). The word "None" returns "False" while all other numbers return "True."

```
>>> print(bool(None))
  False
>>> print(bool(4))
  True
```

eval() No, it's not "evil" it represents; "evaluate." This function *evaluates simple expressions using a string for it's parameters*.

```
>>> eval(' 7*100' )
700
```

float() As you may have guessed this *one turns a number or a string into a floating point, (decimal)*. It expresses absolute value, so adding a "+" or "-" will have no effect on the end result.

```
>>> float('77')
77.0
>>> float('-48')
-48.0
>>> float('+45')
45.0
```

help() *This function is useful to access the built-in help system.* The following example has omitted most of the result for the sake of space. Try it yourself and have a look at the complete results.

```
>>> help('string')
Help on module string:

NAME
    string - A collection of string constants.

DESCRIPTION
    Public module variables:

    whitespace -- a string containing all ASCII whitespace
    ascii_lowercase -- a string containing all ASCII lowercase letters
    ascii_uppercase -- a string containing all ASCII uppercase letters
```

```
ascii_letters -- a string containing all ASCII letters

digits -- a string containing all ASCII decimal digits
hexdigits -- a string containing all ASCII hexadecimal digits
octdigits -- a string containing all ASCII octal digits
punctuation -- a string containing all ASCII punctuation characters
printable -- a string containing all ASCII characters considered printable

CLASSES
    builtins.object
        Formatter
        Template...
```

(I did not include the results from this point, but you get the idea.)

int() *This function converts a number or string into an integer, (whole number).*

```
>>> int('347')
347
>>> int(314.159)
314
```

max() *The maximum function returns the largest item or value in a list, tuple, or string.* If there is more than one argument, it will return the largest argument.

```
>>> atuple=('77','32','876','1')
>>> print(max(atuple))
876
```

min() *The minimum function returns the smallest item or value in a list, tuple, or string.* If there is more than one argument, it will return the smallest argument.

```
>>> atuple=('77','32','876','1')
>>> print(max(atuple))
1
```

range (start, stop, step) *Normally used for loops when you want to control how many times the computer loops through your code.* It produces arithmetic progressions. The range function can use three arguments; start", "stop", and "step." All the arguments must be integers. You may omit the third argument, (step). In this case it will default to 0.

**If you type all of these in IDLE and play with them you will learn much more than if you just read them.*

```
>>> list(range(7))    # using one argument
[0, 1, 2, 3, 4, 5, 6]
>>> list(range(1, 7)) # using two arguments
```

```
[1, 2, 3, 4, 5, 6]  # Continued
>>> list(range(0, 7, 2)) # using three arguments
[0, 2, 4, 6]
>>> list(range(0, 7, 3))
[0, 3, 6]
```

Let's look at the results of using a range function in a for loop.

```
>>> for x in range(7):  #using one argument
      print( "anything" )

anything
anything
anything
anything
anything
anything
anything
```

```
>>> for x in range(7):  #using one argument and a formula
      print(x+1)
1
2
3
4
5
6
7
```

```
>>> for x in range(1,7):   # using two arguments
      print (x)
1
2
3
4
5
6
```

```
>>> for x in range(1,7,2):   # using three arguments
      print (x)
1
3
5
```

Don't get confused by the results of using the third "step" argument. We are not telling Python we want every "even" number; but *every second number after the number "1."* If you use "0" as your first argument you would get "0" plus the even numbers lower than "7."

To do a countdown you would use:

```
>>> for x in range(7,0,-1):    # using three arguments
        print (x)
7
6
5
4
3
2
1
```

Notice that you have to think in Python; the first number in the sequence is included but the last number, (in this case "0"), is not printed.

So what happens if we use a "nested" range function?

```
>>> for x in range(2):
      print ("this")
      for y in range(2):
          print("that")

this
that
that

this
that
that
```

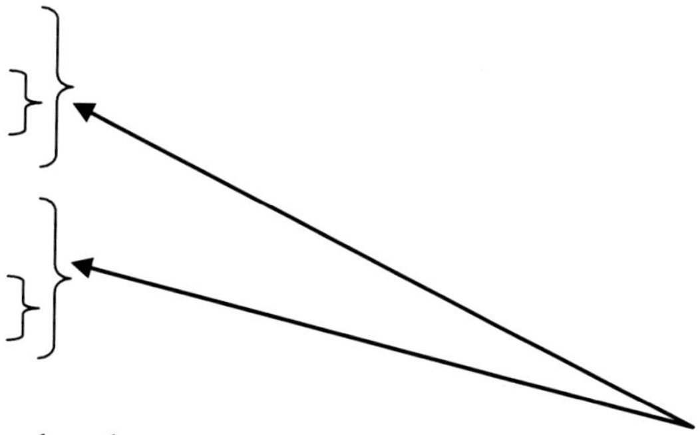

Notice that there are two groups created by the first for statement, and two instances of "*that*" created by the nested **"for"** statement in each of the two groups.

Still don't quite get it? Let's go line by line:

```
>>> for x in range(2):
```

Look at the "x" in "for x" as a blank line, space, or box. The first line is saying; "for this_blank_space we will make a range of "(2)" blank spaces.

Then “:”...

```
>>> for ?  in range(2):
```
makes:

?
?

} our range of two of these “?” things.

**Where “?” = a line, blank space, box, or variable to put something in.*

```
>>> for x in range(2):
  print ("this")
```

Here the print function is indented to make it a slave of the first line and will print:

```
this
this
```

But wait!!! We put a *__function__* in a *__function__*, ***(nested** a function)!*

```
>>> for x in range(2):

    for y in range(2):
            print("that")
```

So, the “for y in range (2)” is saying that each time the first function makes a “this” to fill the two, (range), blank spaces in the first part of our function; the function inside of it must make a “that” for each of its blank spaces before going on to the next “this” group.

In other words your output is two groups created in the first function each having two things in them made by the second function:

Parent function’s first output.

Parent function’s second output.

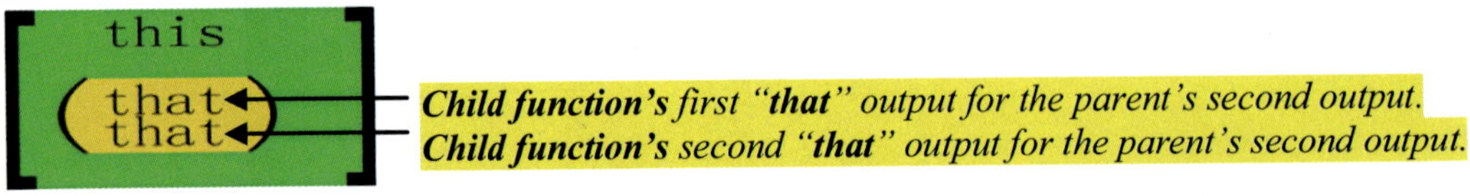

More on Keywords and Expressions

We will have another brief look at more common keywords and expressions in case you find a need for them. You can get more detailed information at *Python. org*. Let's have another look at the chart we saw before:

and	continue	except	global	lambda	pass	while
as	def	False	if	None	raise	with
assert	del	finally	import	nonlocal	return	yield

You will now recognize some of these keywords from using them in the previous lessons. The following is a review of some of the key words we did use and a brief description of those we didn't use:

assert *allows you to insert debugging code into your program.*

break *breaks out of a block of code even if the while statement remains true.*

continue *tells Python to skip the remaining statements in the current loop block and jump to the next loop block.*

else *statement offers a choice in a while loop...do this or else.....do...*

for...in *looping statement to find if something is in a list*

if *if a statement is true...*

is *similar to the == operator*

not *works like the English "not" and makes something the opposite meaning*

pass *acts as a neutral place holder in some statements*

return *returns a value from a function that can be assigned to another function*

while *while true repeatedly run this block of code*

with *statement has to do with writing new classes.*

yield *has to do with execution flow control and "freezing."*

REVIEW

Quiz 7:

7.1 Define the following terms and check your answers on the next page:

1. class
2. namespace
3. mapping
4. binding
5. attributes
6. descriptor
7. weak reference
8. constructor
9. instance
10. methods

7.2 Answer the following questions:

1. When reading a program description, a noun could indicate you should create a ______.
2. A verb could mean you should make a _______.
3. An Adjective could mean you should create a ________.
4. What is the syntax for making a class?
5. What is an advantage and disadvantage of importing an entire module rather than specific functions from within it?

VOCABULARY

class *a template that will contain your methods, functions, and other data for that object.*
namespace *are spaces reserved for names assigned to objects or code blocks.*
mapping *another way to refer to namespace assignment.*
binding *the assignment of a name to an object.*
attributes *are extra characteristics or pieces of information.*
descriptor *an object attribute that can over-ride default attribute behaviors.*
weak reference *a way to clean up the cache and free memory by not keeping objects "alive" beyond their current use.*
constructor *makes a new instance of an object*
instance *this particular appearance of a class or object in your code.*
methods *are functions that are made to be used exclusively within a particular class or object. Methods belong to a particular object or class.*
ordinary functions *are the common type of functions that follow a mathematical model and return a value using the return statement.*
procedural functions *have no parameters.* This kind of function *doesn't use the return* statement *and doesn't return a value.*
Built-in functions *are functions that come within Python.*
User-defined functions *are functions you make yourself.*

7.2 Answers:

1. Classes.
2. Methods for the class.
3. Attributes.

4.

```
>>>class NameofMyClass:
    pass
```

5. The disadvantage is importing the entire module takes more memory. The advantage is that namespace problems or name conflicts are less likely to occur.

Lesson 8: Most Common Data Structures

<u>WHAT YOU WILL LEARN:</u>

- **MORE ON LISTS**
- **STACKS AND QUEUES**
- **INTRO TO COMPREHENSIONS (HUH?)**
- **SEQUENCES**
- **WHAT'S A SET (INTRO TO COMMON SETS)**
- **FROZEN SETS**

MORE ABOUT LISTS

We introduced objects as being like mini-programs or pieces of code used to put together like blocks. Now that you understand what a tuple, string, list, function, etc. is; you can understand that these are the "objects" or building blocks of programs. *Lists, strings, and tuples are also called* ***data structures***.

Remember that a list or a tuple acts like a container in which you can put different kinds of data. You can move containers around or put containers into containers, (one of the wonderful things about Python). *A list with many types of data:*

```
a_variable_name=[7.7, 8,  'some words' , (1, 2, 3, 4),
( '3' ,' 4' )]
```

Here you can see a "*container*" or list that includes a float, an integer, a string, a sequence, and a tuple all in one big happy family! However, if you will need to add variables together, you may need to convert the data to common data types before Python can combine them.

Here are some tips on combining data:

```
>>>a=(1, 2,)
>>>b=(3,4)
>>>a+b
(1, 2, 3, 4)

>>>c=[5,6]
>>>d=[7,8]
>>>c+d
[5, 6, 7, 8]
```

The same data types can be combined, (lists can be added to lists, tuples to tuples, etc)

To combine a list and a tuple you must convert the tuple into a list by using

`list(tupleVariableName):`

```
>>>b=(3,4)
>>>d=[7,8]
>>>list(b)+d
[3,4,7,8]
```

Both lists and tuples can be multiplied by an integer; but cannot use other mathematical operators in this way:

```
>>> a = (1,2)
>>>a*2          #This is ok.
(1, 2, 1, 2)
>>> a+2         #This is not.
Traceback (most recent call last):
  File "<pyshell#10>", line 1, in <module>
    a+2
TypeError: can only concatenate tuple (not "int") to tuple
```

What is "concatenate?" ***Concatenate*** *means to "**glue together**" **or to combine in a sequence*** rather than as two numbers in addition. The error here is just telling you that you can't glue an integer to a tuple together. But, you can glue two tuples together.

The most commonly used data structures in Python are lists, stings, tuples, and dictionaries. Remember that lists are mutable, (editable), while strings and tuples are immutable, (not directly editable). Also remember that lists can be inside of other lists. If you forgot and need practice do the following exercise.

If you have no doubts and this stuff is too easy; then skip it and go on.

Practice 8.1:

Make a list of at least five items you had to eat today. Make another list of at least five drinks you had today, (or on an imaginary day).

1. Combine your two lists into one new list.
2. Replace one item in the list with a new item.
3. Add or "append" a new item into the list.
4. Remove an item from the list.
5. Print a slice of your list from index position 2 to 5.

Review lesson four to if you forgot how to do this.

Try each of these for practice and to increase your understanding. When would you use these in real games and software? Think of an example for each one if you can.

Appending a list (adding to it):

```
listname.append(x)
```

Where "listname" is the name of our list and "x" is the list item to add. For example in lesson 4 we used:

```
Family.append(Catouse)
```

Removing an item:

```
del listname[index position]
```

Remember that the number of the index position is the slice before the actual item in the list (Lesson4).

Combining lists:

```
print(listname1+listname2)
```

Inserting to a specific location:

listname. insert *(index position, " item")*

This is useful for inserting an item into a list at any position you choose. The first argument is the index position before the place you want to put the item. If you want to insert item as the first in the list you could use listname.insert(0,"item"). If you want to specify your item should be in index position 4, you must input the position before it,(index position 3). Remember to add the item at the end of the list you can use append. *Look at the following examples and play with these until you understand them.*

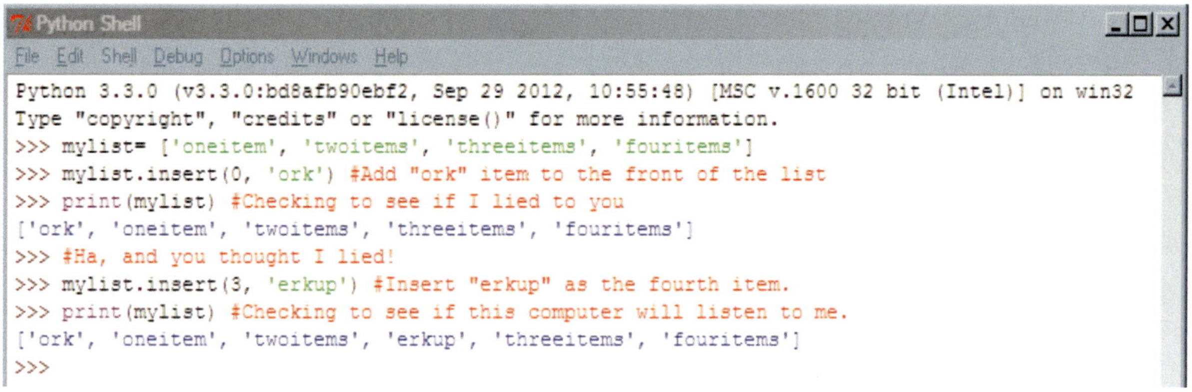

```
Python Shell
File Edit Shell Debug Options Windows Help
Python 3.3.0 (v3.3.0:bd8afb90ebf2, Sep 29 2012, 10:55:48) [MSC v.1600 32 bit (Intel)] on win32
Type "copyright", "credits" or "license()" for more information.
>>> mylist= ['oneitem', 'twoitems', 'threeitems', 'fouritems']
>>> mylist.insert(0, 'ork') #Add "ork" item to the front of the list
>>> print(mylist) #Checking to see if I lied to you
['ork', 'oneitem', 'twoitems', 'threeitems', 'fouritems']
>>> #Ha, and you thought I lied!
>>> mylist.insert(3, 'erkup') #Insert "erkup" as the fourth item.
>>> print(mylist) #Checking to see if this computer will listen to me.
['ork', 'oneitem', 'twoitems', 'erkup', 'threeitems', 'fouritems']
>>>
```

****REMINDER:** *ALWAYS REMEMBER AND NEVER FORGET TOO! YOU DON'T BEGIN COUNTING ITEMS IN YOUR LIST; BUT COUNT THE SLICES BEFORE EACH ITEM! Index position 0 is actually before the first item; index position 1 is before the second item; and so on.*

Finding the index value of an item:

listname. index(item)

This will output the index number of the item in your list.

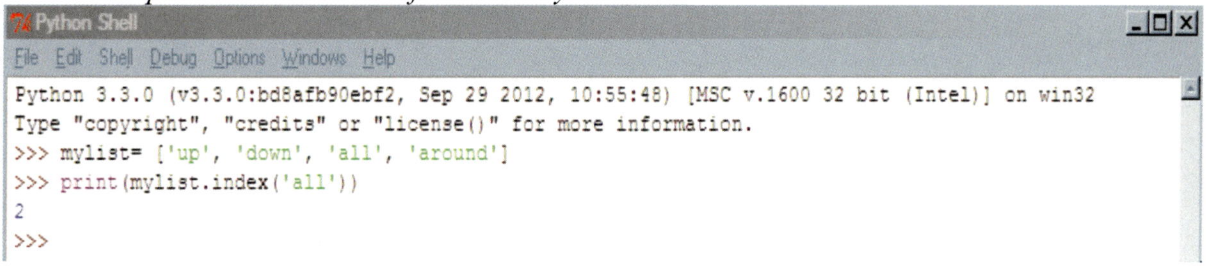

```
Python Shell
File Edit Shell Debug Options Windows Help
Python 3.3.0 (v3.3.0:bd8afb90ebf2, Sep 29 2012, 10:55:48) [MSC v.1600 32 bit (Intel)] on win32
Type "copyright", "credits" or "license()" for more information.
>>> mylist= ['up', 'down', 'all', 'around']
>>> print(mylist.index('all'))
2
>>>
```

How many in my list?:

listname. count(item)

This will count how many entries of an item are in your list.

```
>>> mylist= ['ooo', 'wow', 'eek', 'oof', 'wow', 'uhg', 'wow']
>>> mylist.count('wow')
3
>>>
```

Reversing the order of items:

`listname.reverse()` The first will be last; and the last will be first.

```
Python 3.3.0 (v3.3.0:bd8afb90ebf2, Sep 29 2012, 10:55:48) [MSC v.1600 32 bit (Intel)] on
win32
Type "copyright", "credits" or "license()" for more information.
>>> mylist= ['aaa', 'eee', 'iii', 'ooo', 'uuu']
>>> mylist.reverse()
>>> print(mylist)
['uuu', 'ooo', 'iii', 'eee', 'aaa']
>>>
```

Sorting the order of items:

`listname.sort()`

This puts the numbers in order from lowest to highest and alphabetizes your word items.

**Numbers take priority over words in Python.*

```
Python 3.3.0 (v3.3.0:bd8afb90ebf2, Sep 29 2012, 10:55:48) [MSC v.1600 32 bit (In
tel)] on win32
Type "copyright", "credits" or "license()" for more information.
>>> mylist= [ 'apple', 'dog', '1', 'elephant', 'bird', 'cat', '4', '2', '3']
>>> mylist.sort()
>>> print(mylist)
['1', '2', '3', '4', 'apple', 'bird', 'cat', 'dog', 'elephant']
>>>
```

Extending (copy and add to) your list:

`listname.extend(listname)`

This puts the power of a photocopier in your list! It makes a copy of your list, (or items in your list), and adds it/them to the end of your first list. This can save a lot of time typing.

```
>>> mylist= ['almonds', 'chocolate', 'stuff', 'morestuff']
>>> mylist.extend(mylist)
>>> print(mylist)
['almonds', 'chocolate', 'stuff', 'morestuff', 'almonds', 'chocolate', 'stuff',
'morestuff']
>>>
```

Popping your list:

```
listname.pop()
listname.pop(index position)
```

Pop can be used to remove items, but some programmers complain that it is much slower and less reliable than using append. The details of listname.pop will be easier to understand as we use it in the next section.

The official definition in the Python manual says; *"Removes an item at a given position in the list and returns it. If no index is specified* **listname.pop** *removes the last item in the list."*

```
Python Shell
File Edit Shell Debug Options Windows Help
Python 3.3.0 (v3.3.0:bd8afb90ebf2, Sep 29 2012, 10:55:48) [MSC v.1600 32 bit (In
tel)] on win32
Type "copyright", "credits" or "license()" for more information.
>>> mylist= ['clouds', 'ocean', 'sea', 'see', 'c']
>>> mylist.pop(3)
'see'
>>>
```

Cloning your list:

```
newlistname=oldlistname[:]
```

Cloning the list allows you to make a new copy to change or edit without changing the old copy.

```
>>> oldlist= [1,2,3]
>>> newlist= oldlist[:]
>>> print(oldlist)
[1, 2, 3]
>>>
```

An aliased list:

```
name_one=[list_items]
name_two=name_one
```

What's your alias? *A list is* ***aliased*** *when it has two or more names.* Two or more names referring to the same list can be useful, but remember changes made in either name will affect the original list.

Making a list from a large series of words:

some_animals= "dog cat horse pigeon pig cow frog duck chicken panda python vulture anteater bear tasmanian devil wombat wolverine racoon" . split()

In this example, the ".split()" method will cause each of the words within this sequence to be seen by Python as individual elements of a list. Python uses the spaces to detect each element. As you can see, there would be one problem in this sequence during conversion. "Tasmanian devil" is one animal with two words in its name. Each of these words would be detected as separate elements in the list when using the .split() method. Using this method can save on typing, *but only if each element is a single word.*

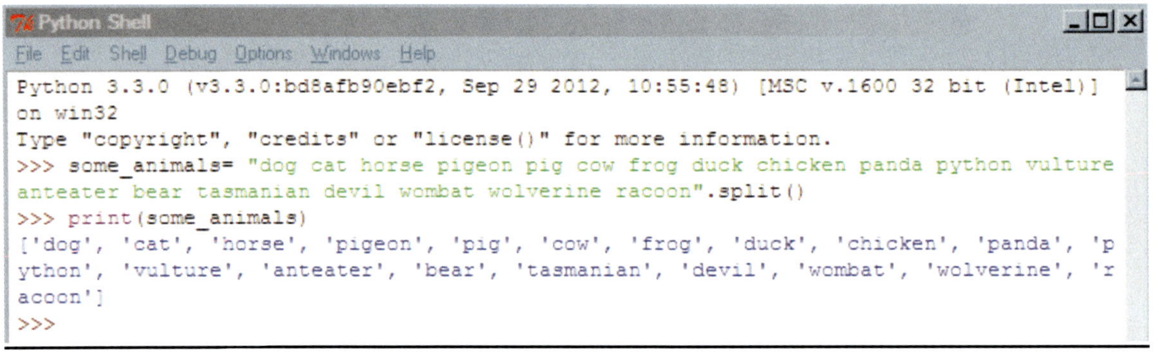

Practice 8.2:

Its time to try it; (if you haven't done it already).

1. *Make a list and insert a new item at index position 3.*
2. *Choose any item in your list and find out it's index value using IDLE.*
3. *Let IDLE tell you how many items are in your list.*
4. *Reverse the order of the items in your list.*
5. *Sort your list according to the proper order.*
6. *Extend or copy your list into itself.*

Review this lesson to confirm your answers.

STACKS AND QUEUES

Yeah I know, it sounds like a new kind of game. Stacks and queues are just two ways of storing and retrieving data in a particular order in and out of your lists.

What is a LIFO structure? No, not a new form of LIPO suction. *LIFO structure refers to last-in first-out data retrieval in a* ***stack***. That's just a fancy way to say that we call it a stack when we remove the last item on our list first.

*If we remove the first item in our list first we call it a **queue**. A queue has a FIFO structure, (first-in; first-out).*

When we append or add an item, it goes at the end of our list in both the stack and the queue. To add an item we use listname.append('itemname').

*To pop an item off with the **stack method** you would **use listname.pop().***

*To pop an item off with the **queue method** you would use **listname.pop(0).***

Think of it this way:

1. With LIFO you have a stack of cookies and you add a cookie to the top (or end) of the stack. When you eat the cookies you eat the ***last arrival on top of the stack***.
2. With FIFO you have a queue of cookies you just told to line up. When a new cookie walks in it goes to the end of the line; but when you eat one you eat the one at the front of the line.

The best way to understand this is to just do it. *Let's make a list and try it:*

```
Python Shell
File Edit Shell Debug Options Windows Help
Python 3.3.0 (v3.3.0:bd8afb90ebf2, Sep 29 2012, 10:55:48) [MSC v.1600 32 bit (Intel)] on win32
Type "copyright", "credits" or "license()" for more information.
>>> eatum= ['cookie1', 'cookie2'] #Make a list
>>> eatum.append('cookie3') #Add a cookie to the list
>>> print(eatum) #Just checking
['cookie1', 'cookie2', 'cookie3']
>>> eatum.pop(0)#Eat a cookie that is queued up/first in line.
'cookie1'
>>> print(eatum)#Checking
['cookie2', 'cookie3']
>>> eatum.pop() #Eat a cookie from the stack/list.
'cookie3'
>>> print(eatum)#Checking
['cookie2']
>>> #We removed/ate the first cookie in our queue and last cookie on our stack.
>>>
```

INTRO TO COMPREHENSIONS (HUH?)

Now let's talk about your list comprehensions; no I did not say your listening comprehension. However, if you read this out loud you can listen to see if you comprehend list comprehensions.

Anyway, list comprehensions are where you apply some change to each item in your list all at once to save some time. *A **list comprehension** applies an expression to every item on your list and out-puts a new list of the results.* A ***list*** comprehension uses ***brackets***; while a ***tuple*** comprehension uses ***parenthesis***. An expression followed by a "***for***" clause is placed within the brackets or parenthesis.

Examples:

```
Python Shell
File Edit Shell Debug Options Windows Help
Python 3.3.0 (v3.3.0:bd8afb90ebf2, Sep 29 2012, 10:55:48) [MSC v.1600 32 bit (Intel)]
on win32
Type "copyright", "credits" or "license()" for more information.
>>> mylist= [2, 4, 6, 8] #Make a list
>>> [elem *3 for elem in mylist] #Applying an operation to each list element
[6, 12, 18, 24]
>>> print(mylist)#Checking original list for changes
[2, 4, 6, 8]
>>> #Nope, it is all still there.
```

Ok, this out-puts the results of applying an operation to each list element, but what if you want to save it as a new list? *Here is one way:*

```
Python Shell
File Edit Shell Debug Options Windows Help
Python 3.3.0 (v3.3.0:bd8afb90ebf2, Sep 29 2012, 10:55:48) [MSC v.1600 32 bit (Intel)
] on win32
Type "copyright", "credits" or "license()" for more information.
>>> mylist= [2, 4, 6, 8]
>>> newlist= [elem *3 for elem in mylist]#Defining the name and new list contents
>>> print(mylist)
[2, 4, 6, 8]
>>> print(newlist)
[6, 12, 18, 24]
>>> #Mylist is the same and I have made a new list from it.
```

What if you only want to apply the changes to part of your list? Maybe you only want a new list applying changes only to members of mylist that are less than six:

```
>>> mylist= [3, 6, 9, 12]
>>> newlist= [elem *5 for elem in mylist if elem < 9]
>>> print(newlist)
[15, 30]
>>>
```

Comprehensions are powerful tools that can also include loops, if statements and all kinds of fun stuff.

SEQUENCES

There are many data types in Python that are used as variables; sequences, string literals (words), numbers, Boolean values, and dictionaries (mappings). You have already been introduced to most of these and will meet some of the other creatures soon.

*A **sequence** is a data type that contains items in a specific order.* In a sequence you have a first, second....and last item in your collection. Strings, lists, and tuples are examples of sequences. In fact, strings, lists, tuples, byte array, and bytes are the five sequence data types that are built-in to Python.

Let's take a look at the Python definition of bytes. Traditionally the term "*bytes*" referred to the smallest chunk of data a computer could comprehend. We won't go into extreme detail about why and how, but in Python, (since version 3), the term "*bytes*" has been redefined. The standard byte size has changed with technology and time. *A **byte in Python** is **a sequence data type** that can represent **raw text strings and binary data**.*

A sequence supports the size function (`len()`), the membership operator (`in`), slices (`[]`), and is *iterable, (supports looping one item at a time)*

- An **iterable** object is object code that allows you to loop through items one at a time, repeating until the desired result is achieved.
- An **iterator** is a construct that allows looping.

What's a "len?" *The* **len** *function returns the length of an object such as a string, tuple, or list. So what!?!* Well, this is very useful believe it or not. Let's try it first to make sure I am not lying to you before we talk about its uses.

For example:

```
Python Shell
File Edit Shell Debug Options Windows Help
Python 3.3.0 (v3.3.0:bd8afb90ebf2, Sep 29 2012, 10:55:48) [MSC v.1600 32 bit (Intel)] on win32
Type "copyright", "credits" or "license()" for more information.
>>> alist= ['this', 'that', 'and', 'the', 'other']
>>> print(len(alist))
5
>>> #Cool! It works!
>>>
>>> atuple= (2,4,6,8)
>>> print(len(atuple))
4
>>> #Yep, it works on tuples too!
```

Yep! Our friend, Lenny, does count things! *(Actually, "len" is for "length," not "Lenny").*

Ok, back to: *"So what?"* There are many times when you will want to know the length of your sequence or the position of items. *What if we want to have the computer tell us the index position of each item rather than figure it out for ourselves?*

```
Python Shell
File Edit Shell Debug Options Windows Help
Python 3.3.0 (v3.3.0:bd8afb90ebf2, Sep 29 2012, 10:55:48) [MSC v.1600 32 bit (In
tel)] on win32
Type "copyright", "credits" or "license()" for more information.
>>> listofweapons= ['gun', 'knife', 'wetnoodles', 'raygun'] #Make a list
>>> length= len(listofweapons) #Define the length
>>> for x in range(0, length): #Specify range to search
	print('The item at index %s is %s' % (x, listofweapons[x]))#Print length


The item at index 0 is gun
The item at index 1 is knife
The item at index 2 is wetnoodles
The item at index 3 is raygun
>>> #Yeah, let Python do the thinking!
```

We will look more at the len and range functions more as we use them. For now, just be happy with what you have and quit complaining.

WHAT'S A SET? (INTRO TO COMMON SETS)

*A **set** is an unordered collection of data of zero or more object references that are iterable and hashable.* As you recall, an iterable object is object code that allows you to loop through items one by on; while an iterator is a construct that allows looping.

***Hashable** objects have a _hash_( ) special method whose return value remains the same through the objects life.* They can be tested for equality using __eq__( ) special method. In other words; hashable is referring to a type of reference system something like a serial number that represents a book. It means that some data, referred to as a hash value, is given to represent a larger set of data. This value does not change during the objects life. You could also think of hashing as referring to a book by giving its index a special name or a value. You then arrange all of your indexes by their names or values. If you need more details form the book, the index name will refer you to the full details within that book or the full data set. This method allows the computer to sort data faster by using a smaller set representing the data rather than the entire set. Often hashing converts a large about of data into a single integer for reference.

What can you do with set objects? You can compare sets; check membership; and can apply many mathematical operations to them just as you would in mathematical "*sets*." They support operations like union, intersection, difference, etc.

Sets have the following qualities:

Sets...

- *are a collection of data in no particular order*
- *are iterable (allow looping items one by one)*
- *are hashable*
- *remove duplicate items automatically*
- *are mutable (you can add or remove items)*
- *cannot be referenced with index positions (since they are not in any special order)*
- *cannot be sliced (since you can't use index positions)*

You can create a set with one or more values by using curly brackets:

```
set_name = { 'item1' , 'item2' , item3' }
```

Dictionaries also use brackets, but *with **sets** you **don't use a colon** to create key-value pairs.*

Reminders:

- *You create an empty set with the* set( ) *function.*
- *Using* set{ } *creates an empty dictionary.*
- *For multiple arguments or items use* set([]).

- *Use* `new_set_name = (list_name)` *to convert a list into a set*

```
>>> mylist= ['one','two','three']
>>> my_set= set(mylist)
>>> print(my_set)
{'two', 'one', 'three'}
>>>
```

Practical example: Let's say you are making a war game and you have acquired a new army. Army1 is your old army and has certain resources. Army2 has some different resources and some that are the same as Army1. Since you just got Army2 to join you; you have to find out what these two groups have in common and what they don't have in common.

**Remember; for multiple arguments or items use* `set([])`.

Try this:

```
Python Shell
File Edit Shell Debug Options Windows Help
Python 3.3.0 (v3.3.0:bd8afb90ebf2, Sep 29 2012, 10:55:48) [MSC v.1600 32 bit (Intel
)] on win32
Type "copyright", "credits" or "license()" for more information.
>>> Army1= set(['tank', 'stealth bomber', 'ship', 'rotten tomatoes'])#Define Army1
>>> Army2= set (['boat', 'rotten eggs', 'tank', 'ship', 'carrier']) #Define Army2
>>> Army1 #Checking to see what is in this set
{'stealth bomber', 'ship', 'tank', 'rotten tomatoes'}
>>> Army1-Army2 #Checking what is in Army1 that is not in Army2
{'stealth bomber', 'rotten tomatoes'}
>>> Army1&Army2 #What do they have in common?
{'ship', 'tank'}
>>> Army1|Army2 #What do they have altogether or in either army?
{'carrier', 'rotten eggs', 'boat', 'tank', 'stealth bomber', 'ship', 'rotten tomato
es'}
>>> #Note that if the item is in both sets, it is only listed once
>>> Army1^Army2 #What is in either Army1 or Army2, but not in both?
{'carrier', 'rotten eggs', 'boat', 'stealth bomber', 'rotten tomatoes'}
>>> #Cool!
```

The built-in, non-hashable, mutable data types, such as dictionaries and lists can't be added to sets. They are not hashable because their hash values can change.

Review/reminder: Sets can use comparison operators and the size function (len()). The size function is to determine the length of a sequence.

```
Python Shell
File Edit Shell Debug Options Windows Help
Python 3.3.0 (v3.3.0:bd8afb90ebf2, Sep 29 2012, 10:55:48) [MSC v.1600 32 bit (Intel)] on win3
2
Type "copyright", "credits" or "license()" for more information.
>>> asequence= (['thing', 'monster', 'coffee'])#Define a set sequence
>>> len(asequence)#Checking the length of the sequence.
3
>>> #Sequence length is 3!!!
```

All hashable, built-in, immutable data types, such as; strings, integers, floats, tuples, and frozensets can be added to sets. *Frozensets? What's are frozen sets? You will be enlightened in the next section.* You may have to re-read or repeat sections of these lessons until you can remember and understand the important information. The same idea applies to this course. If you finish the course and still don't "get" everything; repeat it until you do.

FROZEN SETS

As you know, the normal set type is mutable. The ***frozen set*** is just as it sounds; it *is immutable or a frozen set of data.* Once you make it you can't change it.

`frozenset()` returns an empty frozen set if you have no arguments. Frozensets only accept one argument at a time.

Syntax for a few examples of what you can do with frozensets:

- `frozenset.copy` *(setname)*
- `frozenset.difference` *(setname1)- (setname2)*
- `frozenset.intersection` *(setname1)& (setname2)*
- `frozenset.union` *(setname1)| (setname2)*

Exercise:

1. *Create at least 2 sets and name them.*
2. *Within your sets have some common items.*
3. *Replace "setname1" and "setname2" with the set names you have chosen.*
4. *Try the examples of "what you can do with frozensets" from above.*

You should get something like this:

```
Python 3.3.0 (v3.3.0:bd8afb90ebf2, Sep 29 2012, 10:55:48) [MSC v.1600 32 bit (Intel)] on win32
Type "copyright", "credits" or "license()" for more information.
>>> mylunch= frozenset(['apple','meatball','scorpions','pepto bismol'])#Defining
>>> mysupper= frozenset(['meatball','apple','rocks','garbage'])#Defining 2nd set
>>> frozenset.copy(mylunch)#Trying this
frozenset({'apple', 'scorpions', 'meatball', 'pepto bismol'})
>>> frozenset.difference(mylunch)-(mysupper)
frozenset({'scorpions', 'pepto bismol'})
>>> frozenset.difference(mysupper)-(mylunch)#How about this way?
frozenset({'rocks', 'garbage'})
>>> frozenset.intersection(mylunch)&(mysupper)
frozenset({'apple', 'meatball'})
>>> frozenset.union(mylunch)|(mysupper)
frozenset({'rocks', 'garbage', 'scorpions', 'meatball', 'apple', 'pepto bismol'})
>>>
```

Play with these until you are comfortable and can make them without errors or typos.

REVIEW

Quiz 8:

8.1 Define the following terms and check your answers on the next page:

1. Data Structures
2. Concatenate
3. List comprehension
4. Sequence
5. Iterable object
6. Iterator
7. Set
8. Hashable
9. Frozen Set

8.2 Answer the following questions:

1. What is the syntax to pop an item from a list using the stack method?
2. What is the syntax to pop an item from a list using the queue method?
3. What is FIFO?
4. What is LIFO?
5. List five things you can do with lists.

Vocabulary

Data structures *Lists, strings, and tuples.*	
Concatenate *means to "glue together" or to combine in a sequence.*	
List comprehensions *applies an expression to every item on your list and out-puts a new list of the results.*	
Sequence *is a data type that contains items in a specific order.*	
Iterable *object is object code that allows you to loop through items one at a time, repeating until the desired result is achieved.*	
Iterator *is a construct that allows looping.*	
Set *an unordered collection of data of zero or more object references that are iterable and hashable.*	
Hashable *objects have a* _hash_( ) *special method whose return value remains the same through the objects life.*	
Frozen set *is an immutable or a frozen set of data.*	

8.2 Answers:

1. **listname.pop()**
2. **listname.pop(0)**
3. First In First Out
4. Last In First Out
5. Answers will vary, see text.

Lesson 9: Text Editors and Code Styles

What You Will Learn:

- **Other Text Editors**
- **Introducing PyScripter**
- **Coding with Style**

Other Text Editors

For convenience we have been using Python's default editor, IDLE, to this point in the course. Any text editor, even notepad, can work for programming. But, there are advantages to choosing a text editor with more bells and whistles. There are also times when using a different text editor would be better.

When using Tkinter in your program design, some programmers recommend that you choose an editor other than IDLE. *Why?* IDLE is written in Tkinter. To avoid code "mainloop" conflicts it is probably better to use a different text editor if you are writing some serious code using the Tkinter module.

I often use PyScripter when I am not using IDLE. PyScripter has many great features and is easy to install. However, it is limited to Windows operating systems. A fairly new comer that has great potential and is cross-platform is the "Ninja-IDE." These are just my opinions at this time and are based on trying a number of the most popular free IDE's and by reading many reviews about the best IDE's to use with Python 3 or later. Things are always changing and you may have a different opinion on what makes a "better" editor. New editors and some I am not yet aware of will probably alter my first choice in the future. Unless you have specific needs, there are plenty of free editors to choose from that work well with Python. Research and play with them to find which one(s) are best for you.

For the purposes of convenience and consistency, I have predominantly used IDLE in this course. I will not introduce you to all the editors out there, just one more so you get the idea.

INTRODUCING PYSCRIPTER

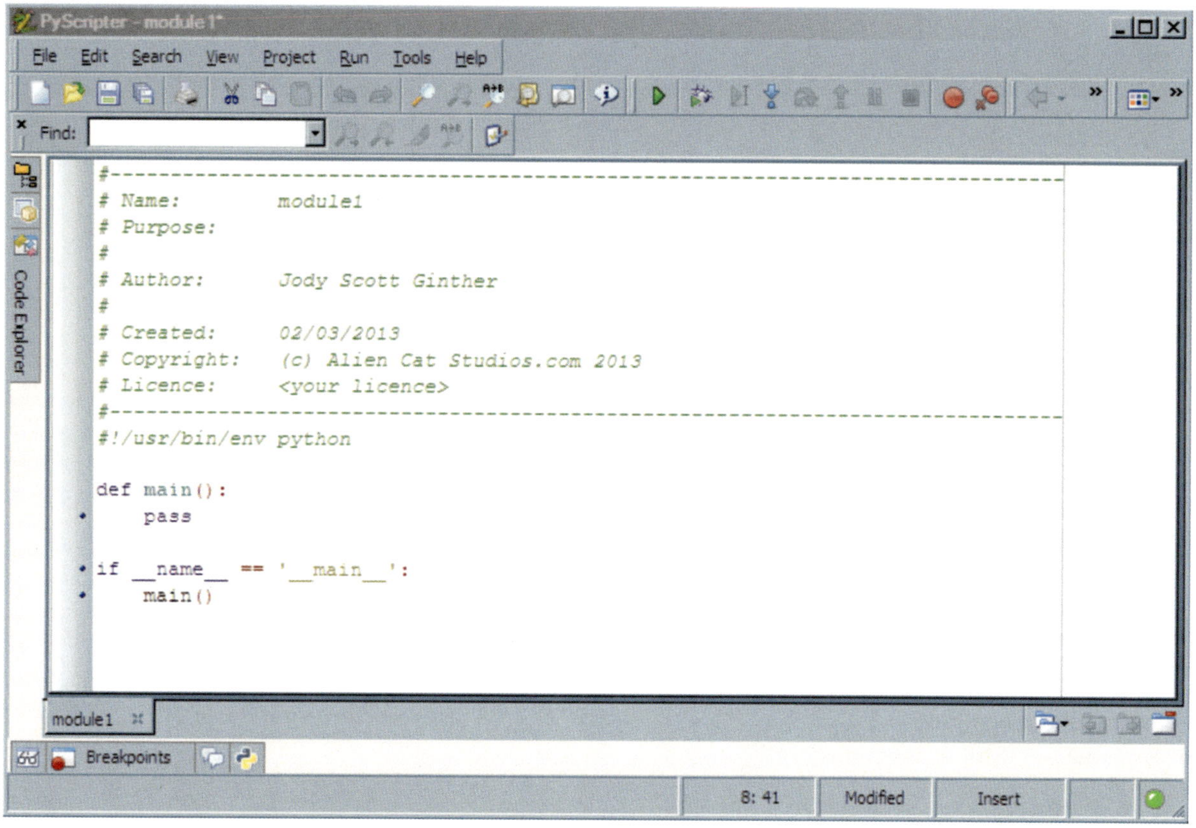

PyScripter is a lot prettier than IDLE. As you can see, it has a number of useful and time saving bells and whistles. It is a full-featured, stand-alone, IDE for Windows that was built in Delphi and is very Python friendly. If you are not running Windows, you could do a search for other open source IDE's that will not conflict with Tkinter or Easy GUI. Pyscripter is free and the latest version is available for download from: http://code.google.com/p/pyscripter/

When you start PyScripter it will automatically load a standard template. You can change default template or the look and feel of the PyScripter window according to your preferences.

PyScripter comes with some good help files and a Python manual. After you install it; play with the buttons and have a look at the help files and comments to get an overview of how to drive this thing. Some people learn faster by trial and error, pushing buttons until something explodes; while others; learn best by reading the documentation. It's your call, you know you better than I do.

You can customize PyScripter to choose a "theme" you are familiar with or just looks good to you. You have some power to organize the user interface to customize your work place to the way you work. Just some of the features offered include; *syntax highlighting editor, integrated Python interpreter, integrated debugging, disassembly and HTML editor views, code explorer, file explorer, project explorer, integrated unit testing, to do test, find and replace, regular expression testing, and find definition/find references.*

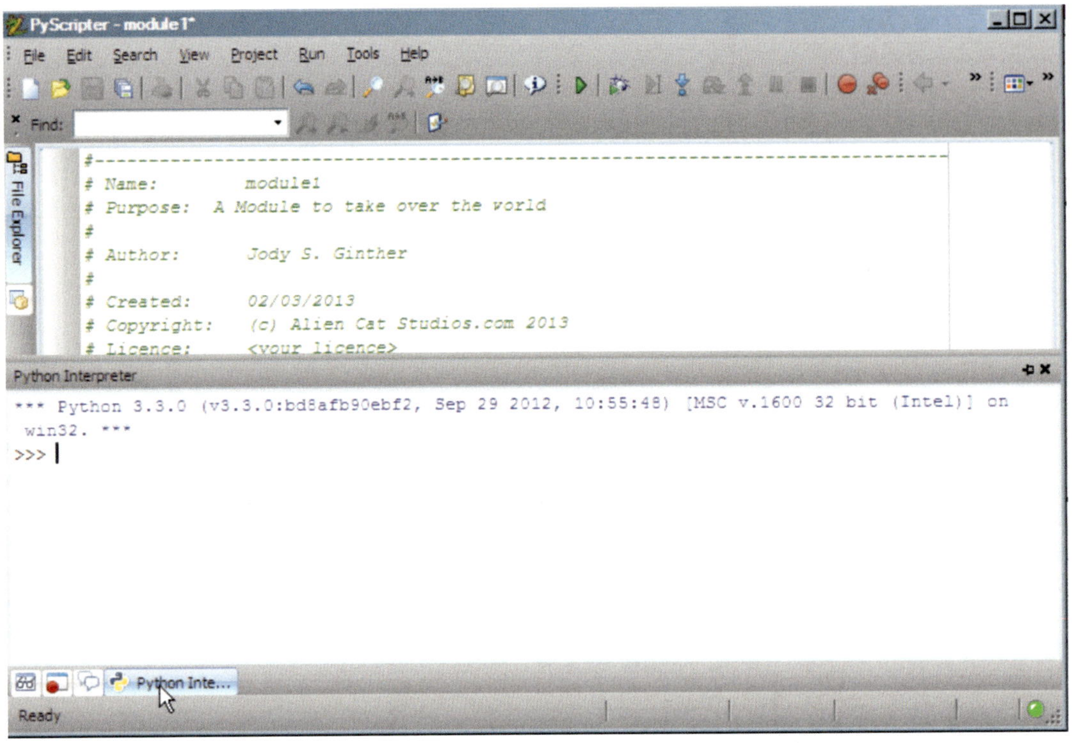

By arranging and pointing at view tabs you will have pop-up windows of your choice to make your coding experience more pleasant. *(No, I am not doing a paid commercial here, I am just giving my opinion).*

There are many other free text editors online. You can try a few and choose the one that you prefer. You can even buy an editor if you have money laying around that serves no useful purpose. Many of the most widely used editors in the Python community are not yet compatible with Python 3x at the time of this writing. Remember that the more complex your mix of external software tools and modules, the more chances you have for conflicts. Make sure all your add-on programs and modules match the version of Python and the operating system you are using with a minimum of conflicts. Experiment and find the write programming environment that works best for you. Your preferences will most likely change over time. For this course we will generally stick to Python's editor to prevent confusion and to allow you to make your own decision on when and which editor to use in the future.

Coding With Style

Up to this point I did not violently adhere to a particular style of typing code to point out that the code, even sloppy code, can work. There are also different approaches and philosophies on which style conventions are best for Python programming. If you need other people to work on your code or need to be able to read it more easily yourself; it is best to follow a particular style of writing. This will also make it easier for you and others to debug. Since the source code we write is about to get much longer, it is important to start thinking about a consistent style to follow.

The style you choose may be influenced by the kind of text editor you prefer or you could even create your own style. But, it is recommended to follow some traditions and conventions to make your life easier.

Generally, the standard style at the time of this writing for Python is the PEP 8 guide. What's a PEP? You can take a look at this ongoing work at http://www.python.org/dev/peps/pep-008. **PEP** stands for *Python Enhancement Protocol*. The purpose of PEP is to collect community input on particular issues and documenting them. For our purposes, we are looking at the style guide.

The objectives of this style of formatting code are to create easy to read and nice looking code. According to PEP guidelines, you should break the accepted style rules if it makes your code more readable or to be consistent with nearby code. With that in mind here are the main guidelines:

- Use **4-space indentation** for every level. Don't use tabs. If you insist on using tabs, be consistent and only use tabs. Mixing tabs and spaces will cause errors.

- **Wrap lines** longer than **79 characters**. Break the line after operators. *Why 79 characters?* To be readable on smaller displays or in multiple windows. Indent properly:

```
>>> erg._init_(self, width, height,
               color, blah, blah)
```

- Use two **blank lines** to separate top level functions and classes and larger blocks of code. Single blank lines are used around method definitions within a class.

- **Spaces** should be used after commas, colons, or semi colons. They should be used before and after operators. Use them after the close parenthesis in a function call, index, for slicing, etc.

```
oop(1)     good!       >>> dict['key']
oop (1) not good!      >>> dict ['key']
```

- **Don't use spaces** to surround the equal sign when it indicates a **default parameter value** or a **keyword argument**:

```
def this(blahblah, image=7.7):
```

- **Comments** should be complete sentences with capitalization, periods, and with spaces after each sentence. Don't use unnecessary comments unless it is a beginners tutorial. The "#" sign is generally used to indicate comments. It will only indicate a comment to the end of the line, so you may choose to use triple quotes for multiple line comments.

- Use **docstrings** for public modules, functions, methods, and classes. *What's a docstring?* A *docstring* is a *document string* used within source code similar to a comment. The difference is that a docstring is retained throughout the runtime of the program making it available for the program to see these lines to use as *metadata, (data about data),* or for an interactive help

system. Docstrings should be the **first statements** in modules, functions, classes, and in method definitions.

The **syntax for a docstring** just involves placing your note within **triple quotation** marks.

- Don't use blank lines before or after a docstring
- If the docstring is too long to fit on one line put the closing triple quotes on a separate line:

```
"""This is a short one."""

"""This is what to do if your document
string is going to be on multiple lines
"""
```

- Use "r," (raw), if you use backslashes in your docstrings:

```
r"""This is what to do if your \
document string is going to be \ on
multiple lines
"""
```

- Use Python's default encoding, UTF-8. If you must, you can use ASCII use plain ASCII, but only if you are certain your code is not going international. *Huh?*

What's ASCII or UTF-8? In the past, Python strings of code used to represent text in computers used the ASCII standard, (American Standard Code for Information Interchange). The problem with this type of coding was that it only worked well with languages based on Latin script/letters. Problems came up when code had to deal with languages with non-Latin characters such as Chinese. To overcome this problem the Unicode standard was developed to cover all known written languages.

UTF-8, (Transformation Format - 8bit), can represent all characters in Unicode's character set. Unicode is the industry standard encoding to represent text in computers for most of world's languages. The Unicode standard currently consists of more than 110,000 characters. UTF-8 is variable width encoding and has become dominant on the World Wide Web. It is backwards compatible with ASCII.

Python 3x was updated to use UTF-8 as its default encoding. Since Python version 3 was created, a string in Python can represent characters for international languages.

➢ Naming Conventions:

- **Be consistent.** The common convention is to use `CamelCase` for classes and `lower_case_with_underscores` for functions and methods. Remember that spaces have meaning in Python so it is best to use underscores to separate words in a name. All **caps** are generally used for abbreviations like HTTP.

- **Don't use** the lower case letter "L", (l), or the uppercase letter "o" (O) as single characters variable names. These can be confused with the numerals one, (1), and zero, (0).

- **Module and Package** names should be short. Modules may use underscores if necessary for readability but avoid them with Packages. Packages should use lower case names.

- **Class** names should use `CamelCase.` **Internal classes** use a leading underscore.

- **Function and Method** names should use lower case letters and underscores.

- **Constants** generally use all capital letters with underscores.

For more details refer to http://www.python.org/dev/peps/pep-008.

All these conventions were not followed strictly in this course. This was intentional to show you the code will still work written different ways. I also chose to deviate from this standard to emphasize certain aspects of the code for better understanding. Some deviations were made because some symbols and characters are not as easily seen when placed in a text document like within these lessons. Anyway, those are my excuses.

However, now you have some experience and know that programming will generally require enough social skills to communicate and work with other programmers. You should develop some consistent habits in your coding style. The PEP standard is probably the best to go with to make your code easy to read and understand for other Python programmers. Chances are you will rarely develop entire software alone if you are going to get a job with a software company. If you are not someone who can follow the crowd; at least loop around it once in a while so you can see what they are doing and communicate in a conventional way with them. That is where the PEP standard can come it.

REVIEW

Quiz 9:

9.1 Answer the following questions:

1. *What are notepad, Ninja-IDE, IDLE, and PyScripter to programmers?*
2. *What is PEP?*
3. *When don't you use spaces around an equal sign?*
4. *What is a docstring and what kind of quotation marks are used with it?*
5. *Spaces should be used _____(before/after) commas, colons, and semi-colons.*

9.1 Answers:

1. *Text editors.*
2. *Python Enhancement Protocol; a standard style of writing code*
3. *Don't use spaces to surround the equal sign when it indicates a default parameter value or a keyword argument.*
4. *A docstring is a document string used within source code similar to a comment.*
5. *Spaces should be used **after** commas, colons, and semi-colons.*

Lesson 10: More Modules and GUI's

WHAT YOU WILL LEARN:

- STANDARD LIBRARY INTRO
- WHAT'S A GUI?
- WHAT'S "EASY GUI"
- THE EASY GUI TOUR

STANDARD LIBRARY INTRO:

The standard library is the library of modules, functions, and exceptions that Python includes with the standard version of Python. Most of the standard library consists of modules. If you have Python installed, you should have the standard library. There are additional add-ons depending upon the distribution you downloaded. Python's standard library includes many things you might need. The standard library includes modules for; tkinter and other graphics, HTML, web browsers, data bases, email, GUI, wave files, multi-threading, template stuff, math modules, data compression, cryptographic services, generic operating system services, internet tools, networking, debugging, internationalization (language services), documentation generator, etc. The huge list of modules and functions in the Standard Library is intimidating. Occasionally make time to browse through available modules in the Python documentation. Finding modules to do your work for you will save you time in the future.

Some modules are written in C and others are written in Python. Modules are provided to allow interfaces that are operating system specific to access particular hardware. These are also useful for specific application domains like the World Wide Web.

Python's standard library includes a number of built-in functions that don't require the use of the import statement. You have already been using many of these in previous lessons, (like the print function). Some functions are part of modules that have to be imported.

Here is a very mini sample of some modules within the standard library and some of their uses:

calendar	*Calendar related functions*
cmath	*For complex numbers.*
codecs	*Code registry and base classes.*
collections	*Container types*
datetime	*Basic time and date functions.*
decimal	*Fixed point and floating point arithmetic.*
fractions	*Rational numbers.*
gzip	*Support functions for gzip.*
itertools	*Functions for efficient looping.*
math	*Math functions including Trigonometric, powers, number theoretic, logarithmic, etc.*
numbers	*Numeric base classes including basic math operations.*
operator	*Standard operators as functions.*
pdb	*Debugging.*
re	*Regular expressions operations including matching objects, searching, checking for pairs, simulating scan, and finding adverbs.*
stringprep	*Internet string preparation.*
struct	*Interprets bytes as packed binary data including byte order, alignment, and size.*
textwrap	*Just as it sounds; it is for textwrapping.*
tarfile	*Read and write tar archives.*
zlib	*Gzip compatible compression.*

You will need to consult Python.org's documentation for details on these and other modules in the Python Standard Library. Don't get overwhelmed, use them as you need them and be aware of what is available.

WHAT'S A GUI?

***GUI** stands for graphical user interface.* In Chinese *mu gui* means ghost, demon, or monster, (that was just some useless information for your amusement). GUI is just a fancy way of saying that instead of staring at a prompt and some letters to communicate with your computer; you get to use windows, boxes, frames, entry fields, widgets, and other
visually pleasant ways to interact with your computer. A GUI produces those colorful little boxes that say things like; "install now," "yes, no, cancel," or "enter your password."

In earlier lessons you were introduced to Tkinter and how to import it as a module. To call it a module is a bit simplistic since it actually includes many modules. Tkinter is often referred to as a GUI toolkit that comes with Python. We will take a quick tour of Tkinter in shortly. For now, let's have a look at a simpler GUI.

WHAT'S EASY GUI

If you want to take a shortcut, there is an easier GUI interface than Tkinter. What GUI you choose will depend upon your experience, preferences, and goals. You can search the internet to find out what other easier GUI's are out there, but at the time of this writing there are very few for Python 3x. Check the licensing requirements and compatibility with Python 3x. To get you started, we will use Easy GUI in this lesson.

First you will have to download and install the appropriate version for your computer configuration. http://www.easygui.sorceforge.net/download/version_0.96/index.html Check for new version and make sure it is compatible with your version of Python. You should also consider changing to another editor. Many programmers suggest getting away from IDLE when using Easy GUI or Tkinter because there are potential conflicts. Since IDLE is a Tkinter application; Easy GUI is a collection of Tkinter routines; and Tkinter is Tkinter; there are potential problems with running these within IDLE. My preference is to use PyScripter for safety.

THE EASY GUI TOUR

Once you have downloaded it you need to put it where Python can find it. Make sure you also download the file that includes help files and tutorials. Installation notes for your operating system are on the site. For Windows (type all of the following stuff in quotes ***without*** the quotation marks):

1. Download the .zip files

2. Copy the zip file to **directly** to your Python 3x**site-packages directory** and unzip it in there, (where "x" is your version of Python). The unzipped files **cannot** be too deep into a subdirectory. If you put it in the wrong place your import statement will fail. If you unzipped them elsewhere, move them to your Python\Lib\site-packages directory. On my computer I unzipped the file to:

C:\Python33\Lib\site-packages

3. Open a console window or "Dos box", (click on "start"; "run"; then type in "cmd" in the entry field on XP).

4. Navigate to the temporary directory you made and to a clean "C:\>_" blinking prompt. (If you see a number of directories in front of the C prompt; type "cd.." and the enter key to go back one directory. Repeat this until you see "C:\>_"

5. Type "cd C:\Python33\Lib\site-packages" (or the location and name you used for your temporary directory).

6. At the command prompt type:
   setup.py install

7. A "build" file will appear in the directory if you were successful.

8. Go to your "build" file in windows, double click; then double click the "lib" folder; finally double click the "easygui.py" file. If you have more than one version of Python installed, you will have to open Python's IDLE and navigate to the "easygui.py" file from the open file menu or open it with the matching version of PyScripter.

You should see something like this:

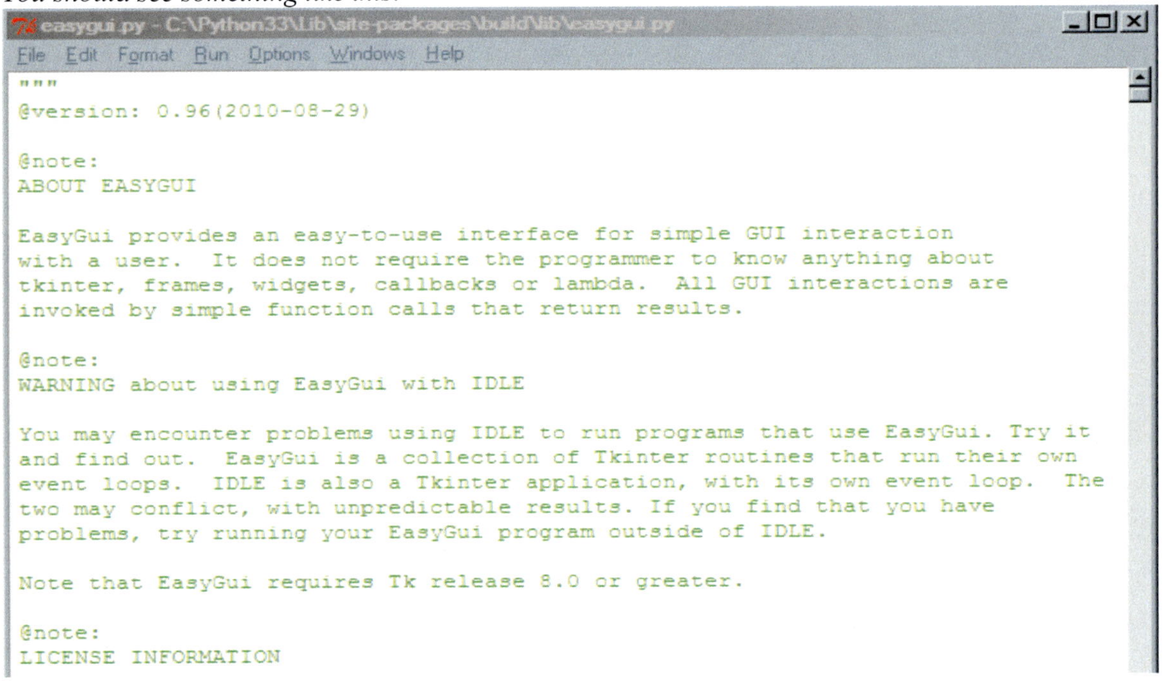

9. Now run the module.

You should be looking at this:

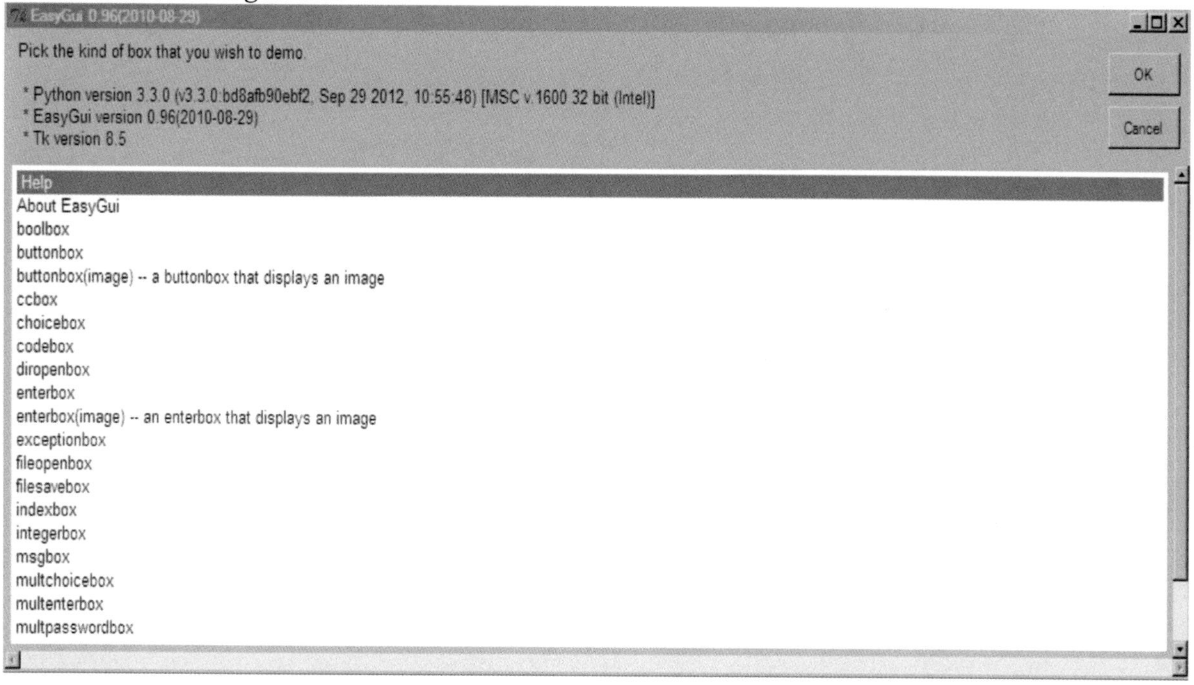

In fact, the box you are looking at to select a demo box, is itself an example of what Easy GUI can do. You can also have a look at the gallery.html. There are a number of ways to access Easy GUI's functions. We won't go into all of them here since this is a brief introduction. If you like, you can click on one of the items in this menu to see more detailed information or you can just click on "cancel" to close the box.

In the first screen you can find a warning about possible conflicts if you are using IDLE. For the remainder of this lesson you should probably be using another text editor. I will use PyScripter to walk you through a few examples. Feel free to chose another text editor, if it is compatible with Python 3x you should get the same results.

If you are using PyScripter open it and delete everything in a new window.

Let's make our first box:

```
from easygui import *

msgbox( "and some kind of message here" )
```

Click on the green "run" button if you are using PyScripter:

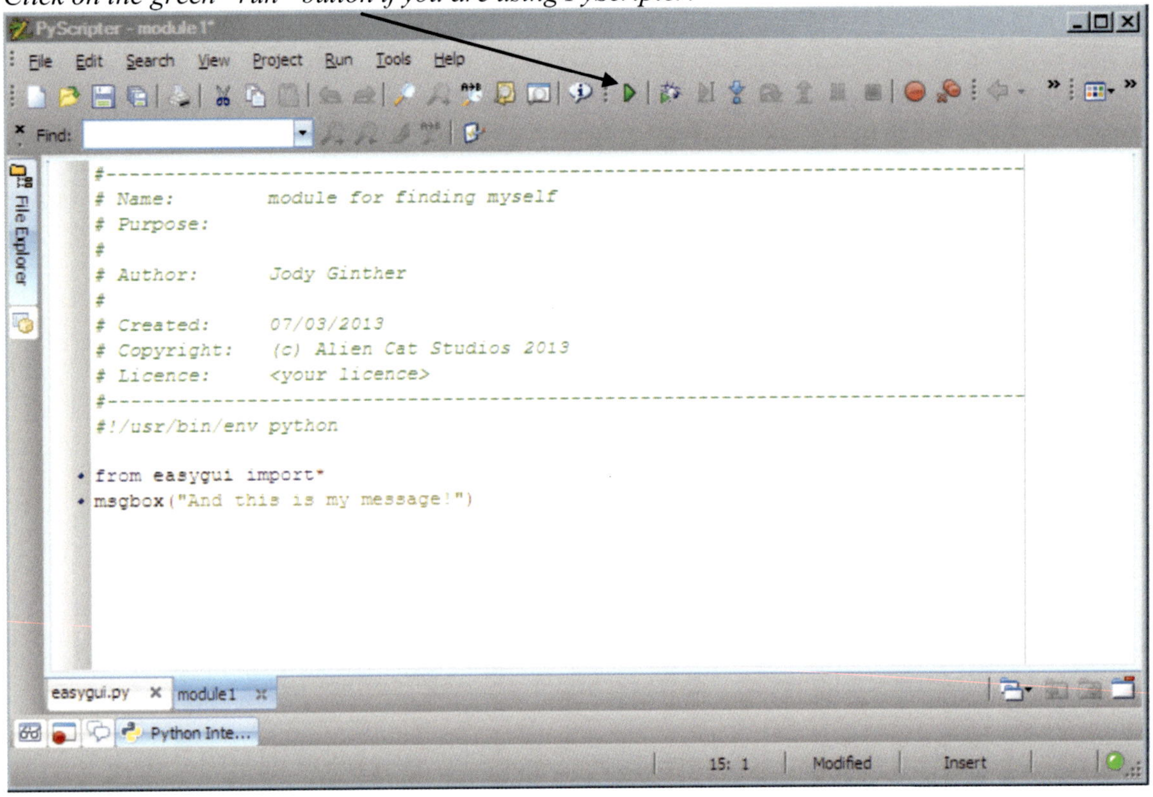

You should see something like this:

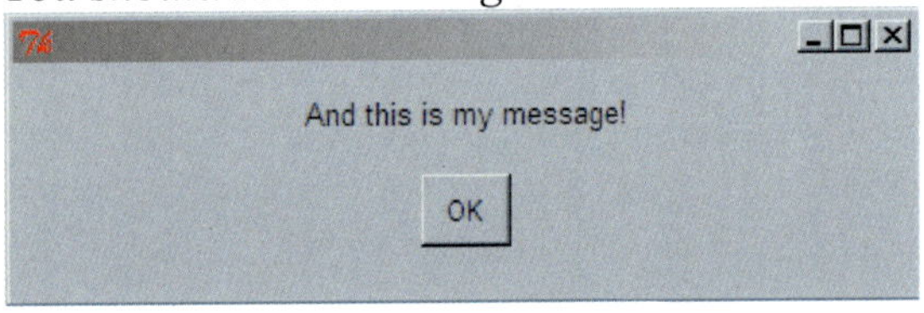

Ok, that was really easy. Just click on "ok" to close the box. Since Easy GUI is so easy and their help files cover the syntax, commands and examples so well; I will only show you a few examples in this lesson. You will learn it best by knowing what it can to and then just playing with it.

The following example includes the Eyes.gif image I created in *Gimp, (a free image editor)*. You can use an image of your own or this same image in the "FilesAndAssets" folder provided with this course. If you got the pirated version of this course you can still download these files free at our website www.tooncat.com . While you are there; please feel free to feel guilty enough to donate something for the time I put into this and to encourage me to not stop writing this stuff.

This box offers you some choices. You must indicate in your code where EasyGUI can find the image you are referring to. I placed the image in my Python 33 directory.

The code could look like this in PyScripter:

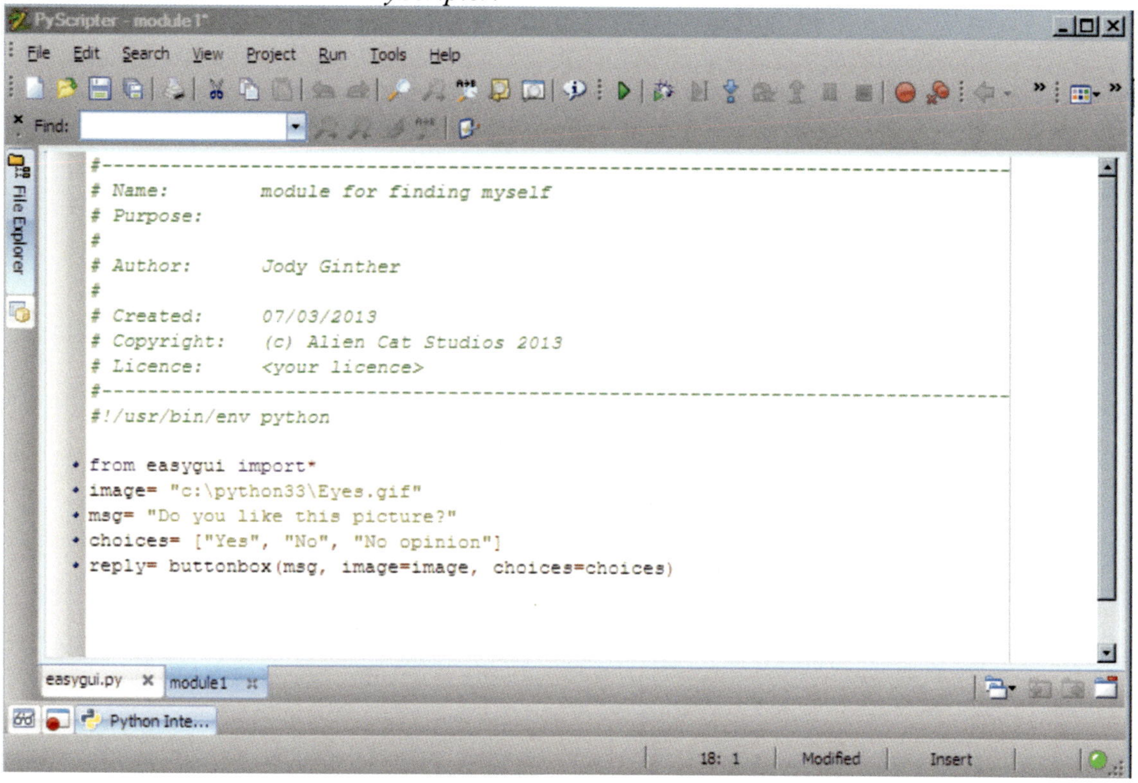

The result of running the code looks like this:

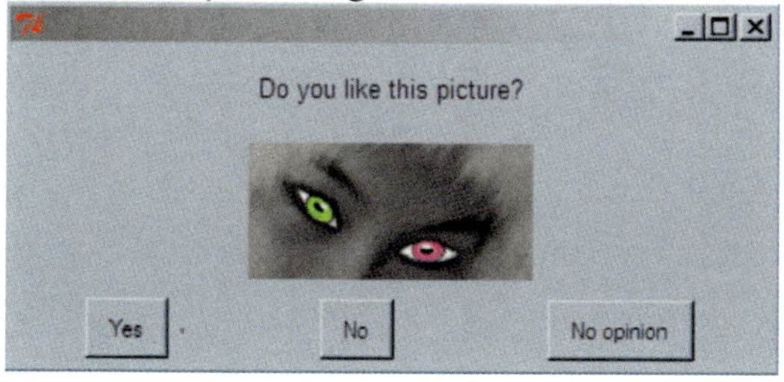

Easy GUI only supports images in a gif format. An animated gif will not work in this example. It will remain a still image of the first frame. In the above example, we first defined image, msg, and choices. Then we defined the reply to be a buttonbox that included these definitions. Remember to use the argument; image = and to include a reference path whenever you want to place an image in a box.

The following is a partial reference list of what you can create with Easy GUI with some examples of the code syntax. Choose some or all of them to practice and make your own examples. Remember that programming is best learned by doing it. You may have to change the indentations if you are using some versions of PyScripter and get error messages.

All boxes have a default set up to save you time if you choose to use them. You can over-ride these defaults if you choose to do so. The first argument for all boxes is for the message; the second argument is for the title.

In our previous example of a simple message box, the default button was the "ok" button. To add a title to the box and change "Ok" to your own words, you would add the following arguments:

```
msgbox("Hey! What's up?", title=" My Box Title" , ok_button="Nothing!")
```

My box now has a title!

Next, let's have a look at how to create a Boolean box:

```
boolbox(msg='Shall I continue?', title=' ', choices=('Yes', 'No'), image=None)
```

> **Note that an integer value is returned rather than "true" or "false." The default is for the first choice to return 1. Otherwise, 0 is returned. A cancelled dialog will also return 1.*

A Quick Look at some of Easy GUI's other main functions:

This section will briefly introduce you to some of the other common boxes you can create easily in Easy GUI. The defaults, syntax, and other details can be found in the tutorials and help files that come with Easy GUI, so we won't repeat them here.

buttonbox *A box of multiple buttons.*
ccbox *Offers the choice to continue or cancel an action.*
choicebox *Offers a list of choices.*
diropenbox *A dialogue box to return the name of a directory.*
egdemo *Runs Easy GUI's demo.*
enterbox *Allows the user to enter some text.*
exceptionbox *A display box to show information about an exception.*
fileopenbox *A dialogue box to open a file.*
filesavebox *Yep! You guessed it! Saves a file.*
integerbox *The user can enter integers.*
multchoicebox *Multiple choice options.*
multenterbox *Multiple data entry fields as you define them.*
passwordbox *Password entry box where text is masked with asterisks.*

ynbox *A message box with "yes" and "no" choices.*

REVIEW

Quiz 10:

10.1 Answer the following questions:

1. What is the Standard Library?
2. What is a "Boolean box?
3. What is PyScripter
4. What are packages?
5. What is a GUI?

10.1 Exercise

With what you know so far; design a Boolean box with a "yes" and "no" button where each button will return a different message in another box when chosen. When you finish you can look at one possible solution on the next page..

10.1 Exercise:

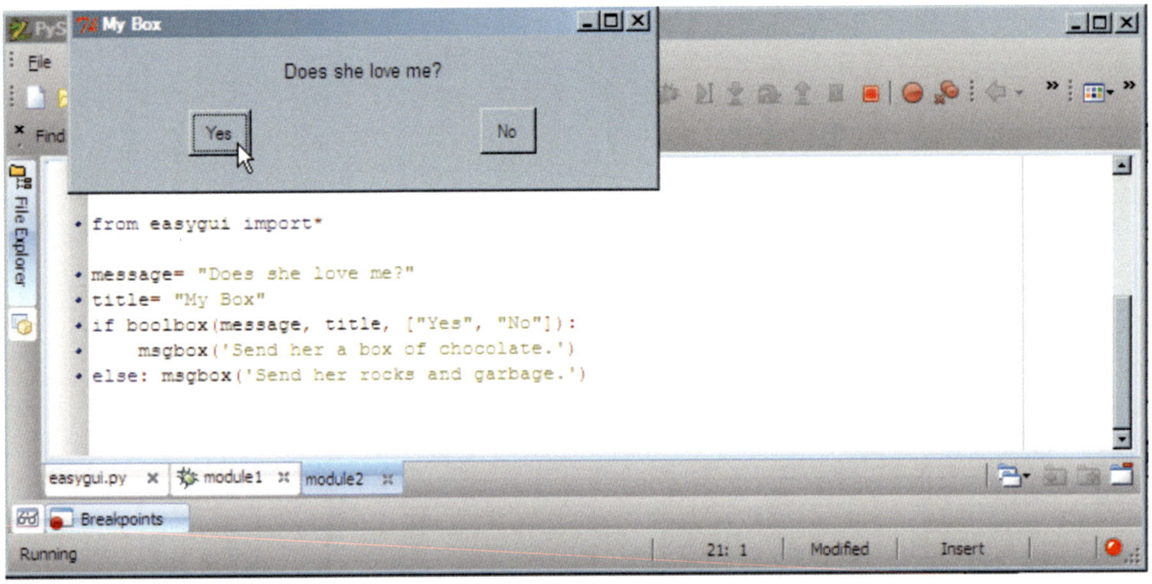

If the answer is "yes":

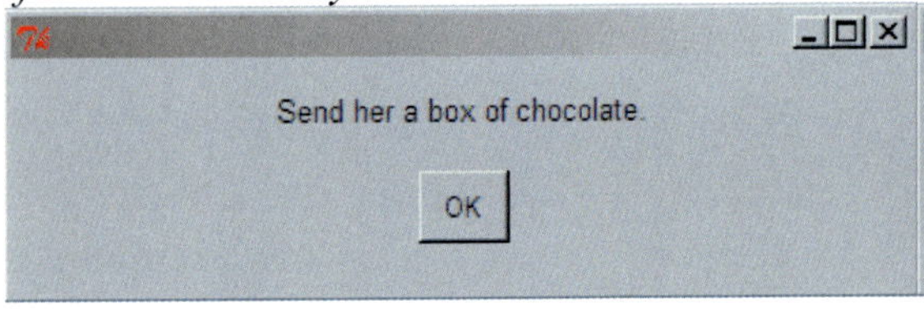

If the answer is" no":

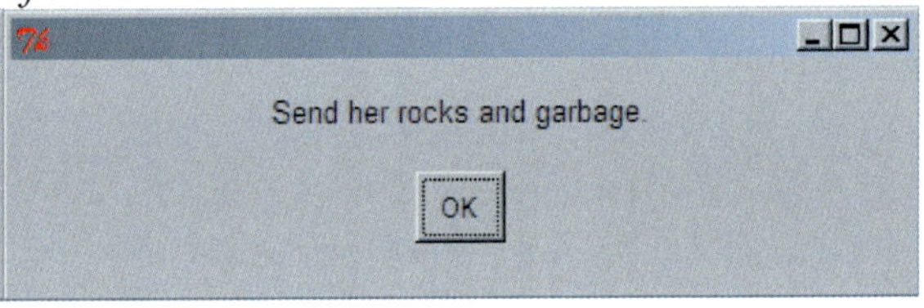

10.1 Answers:

1. The Standard Library in Python is a huge collection of modules and functions.
2. A graphical interface of a decision making box.
3. PyScripter a great text editor for Python.
4. Collections of related modules.
5. Graphical User Interface; a way to interact with a program using graphics like windows, input boxes, etc.

Lesson 11: Tkinter Tour

- WHY USE TKINTER?
- UNDERSTANDING TKINTER
- SPEAKING TKINTER
- TKINTER'S MAIN WIDGET CLASSES
- WIDGET TOUR
- CUSTOMIZING WIDGETS

WHY USE TKINTER?

Why do I need Tkinter if I have EasyGUI? Tkinter gives you more advanced control over many GUI functions. You may want to use EasyGUI for simple applications and switch to Tkinter when you have something complex in mind. There are other GUI's out there to explore if you wish; but Tkinter comes with Python and is open source. So, it is a good idea to know a little about it.

UNDERSTANDING TKINTER

One of the first questions I often hear about Tkinter is, "Can you make games with it?"
Technically, yes, I have seen a few simple games made with it. But, your life would be much easier if you stuck to using Pygame for game making, (we will talk about this one later). Tkinter is good for your graphical interface needs and to combine with your other Python code.

I will not attempt to cover every aspect of Tkinter in this course. That would require a separate course. We will take a tour and get a general overview of Tkinter so you know some of the things you can do with it and for you to understand when you may need it.

When learning about GUI's, understanding all the new vocabulary can get confusing. Some words can mean almost anything. The term "***widget***" often can just be interpreted as *"thing." It could refer to icons; drop down menus; buttons; and many other graphical interface "things."* A **frame** *is a rectangular box that can contain many widgets.* You will be working with frames and adding text or widgets to them.

The Tkinter module is actually a collection of modules that includes the Tk interface.
First of course, you must tell Python to import the module. You could use the import Tkinter statement; but in most cases you would use:

```
from tkinter import *
```

This will import all the related functions and classes that you may need. In Lesson 6 I introduced you to a Tkinter widget but did not explain things in detail. In this lesson we will look a little closer at how things are done in Tkinter.

SPEAKING TKINTER

To understand some basic Tkinter terms and how they are used will save you hours of headaches in dealing with Tkinter. Let's begin with some commonly used terms:

- *A **widget class** in Tkinter is a fancy way of referring to what kind of widget thing it is. Is it a canvas, a button, a label, a menu, etc?* These are referred to as widget classes. Common widget classes will be listed and defined one-by-one in the next lesson. You will also learn to use some of them.
- *A **style** in Tkinter is the over-all appearance of the widget class.*
- *A **theme** is a set of widget styles grouped together.*
- ***Elements** are the parts of a widget. A style of widget is composed of different parts. A button widget will have a label element, spacing element, border element, etc.*
- *A **layout** is how the elements are arranged or "laid out."*
- ***Padding** is the extra space around some element or widget.*

TKINTER'S MAIN WIDGET CLASSES

Before we take a brief tour of some of Tkinter's widgets and how to make them, you should be aware of some common Tkinter widget classes, (kinds of widgets):

- **Button** *A button for executing a command.*
- **Canvas** *can be used to draw, create graphics, complex widgets, and could even be used to make paint and graphics programs, (graphic editors).*
- **Entry** *For entering text into a specific field.*
- **Frame** *We already mentioned that this one is like a frame or container for other widgets and elements.*
- **Label** *Can display an image or text.*
- **Listbox** *Just as in EasyGUI, it displays a list.*
- **Menu** *Used to make pulldown and popup menus.*
- **Menubutton** *Creates menu buttons.*
- **Message** *Can display text with auto-text wrapping.*

- **Radiobutton** *Represents one value of a variable that can have one of multiple values.*
- *It is most commonly used to give a list of mutually exclusive answers for questions like: "What country are you from?" or "What planet are you on?"*
- **Scale** *A slider for changing numerical values.*
- **Scrollbar** *makes scrollbars.*
- **Text** *To edit and format text or imbed images or windows.*
- **Toplevel** *Can display a window on top of other windows.*

Widget Tour

This is an interactive tour. If you don't plan to use Tkinter as your GUI but want to know what it can do, you can just read it. However, if you plan to use Tkinter it would be best to actually make the widget examples to practice and understand them. In the following examples we are not importing Tkinter with a wildcard, (*). We are also not creating a frame for our widget. Although this is much less code to type, this method also limits our options to edit colors and text as easily as we did in our QUITBUTTON example. We will use this method just for our quick tour. This will also allow you to focus on how the code changes according to the widget class. For all the widgets in this tour we will use the following syntax pattern:

```
import tkinter as tk

root = tk.Tk()

# Here we will add the code for a specific type of widget.

root.mainloop()
```

Practice time: *Write the following widget type code to produce these examples. The first one is done for you.*

1. Widget type code: `tk.Label(root, text="Hello Aliens").pack()`

The examples:

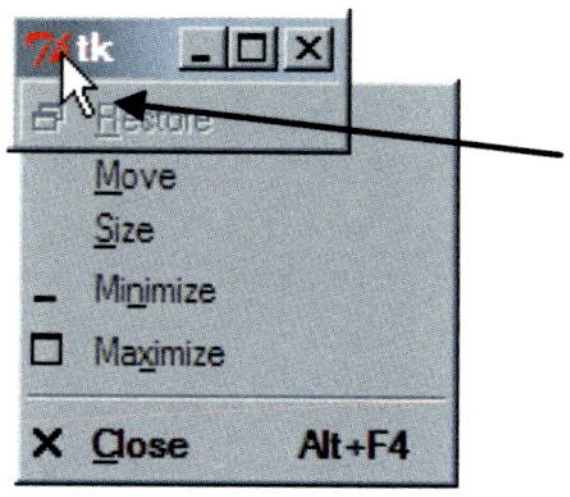

You can see if you click on the left corner of the window, a drop down menu appears in this default setup.

Try writing the code for this yourself first, then look at the next page for the answer.

The complete code syntax (the answer):

```
import tkinter as tk
root = tk.Tk()
tk.Label(root, text="Hello Aliens").pack()
root.mainloop()
```

Ok, now you do it. I will supply the widget type code and the results/examples you should see. You type them in the complete code to practice getting the correct syntax patterns.

2. Widget type code:

```
def pressed():
    print ('I lied!')
tk.Button(root, text='Push to explode.', command=pressed).pack()
```

The example:

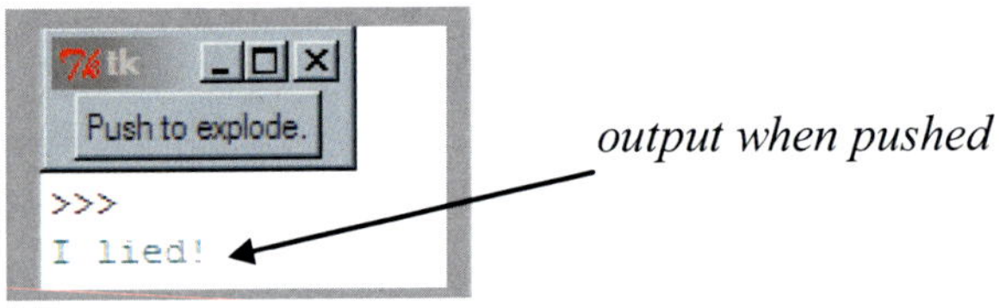

3. Widget type code:

```
entry = tk.Entry(root)
entry.pack()
entry.insert(0, 'Enter text here')
value = entry.get()
```

The example:

4. Widget type code:

```
value = tk.StringVar(value='Your Choices')
tk.OptionMenu(root, value, 'Play', 'Sleep','Work').pack()
```

The examples:

5. Widget type code:

```
variable = tk.IntVar()
tk.Checkbutton(root, text='Check this out!',
variable=variable).pack()
value = variable.get()
```

The example:

6. Widget type code:

```
text = tk.Text(root)
text.pack()
text.insert(tk.END, '''YOU CAN TYPE STUFF HERE.''')
```

The example:

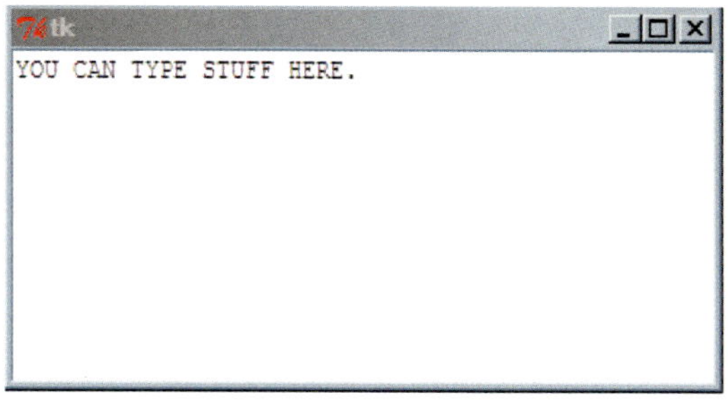

7. Widget type code:

```
scale = tk.Scale(root, from_=0, to=50)
scale.pack()
```

The example:

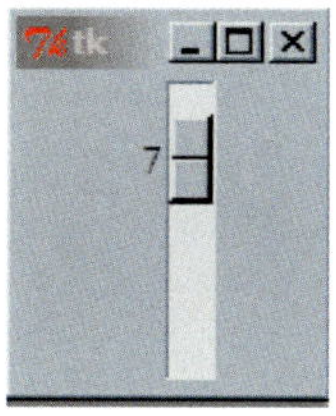

Customizing Widgets

You can customize your widgets *color, fonts, borders, size, relief settings and even the type of cursor* it will use. Although we won't go into how to do all of these, if you are aware of them, you will know what can be done in Tkinter. Once you know what Tkinter can do you can look at the documentation to see how to do it. It is just a matter of looking up the syntax for the code you need and practice applying it.

In the examples given above, the code was kept as simple as possible for easier understanding. Generally, you will create a widget class for your widget. Let's take a look at how to do that. Don't worry if you don't understand all the code at this point. You will when you get to later lessons. For now, we are just taking a brief tour to see what can be done with Tkinter.

Try this example to make a widget within a class object:

```
from tkinter import *
class Application(Frame):
    def say_Yeh(self):
        print("Yeh! Your button just did something!")
    def createWidgets(self):
        self.QUITBUTTON = Button(self)
        self.QUITBUTTON["text"] = "QUIT BUTTON"
        self.QUITBUTTON["background"] = "purple"
        self.QUITBUTTON["fg"]    = "white"
        self.QUITBUTTON["command"] =  self.quit
        self.QUITBUTTON.pack({"side": "left"})
        self.do_something = Button(self)
        self.do_something["text"] = "CLICK TO DO SOMETHING BUTTON"

        self.do_something["command"] = self.say_Yeh
        self.do_something.pack({"side": "left"})
    def __init__(self, master=None):
        Frame.__init__(self, master)
        self.pack()
        self.createWidgets()
root = Tk()
app = Application(master=root)
app.mainloop()
root.destroy()
```

You should end up with something like this.

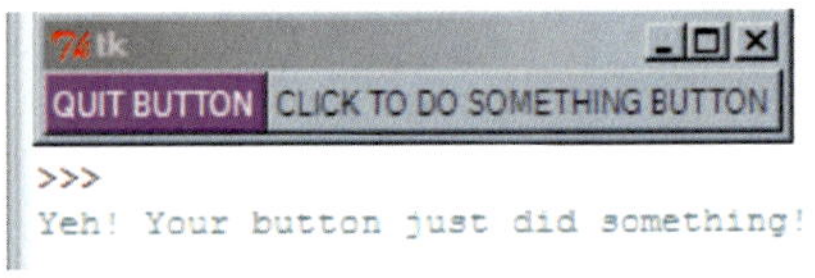

When you hit the "quit" button the widget will exit; when you hit the "Click..." button it will output the words you entered.

You can designate some colors by their common names or choose very specific colors by their RGB values. **RGB values** *are number values used to indicate how much Red, Green, or Blue will be mixed together to create a specific color.* You can also change the foreground and background colors of the text or widget. Play with some color names like; tan, cyan, red, blue, green, etc. and get familiar with changing the code. You can also change the color of the letters on your buttons.

Exercises:

1. Change the background of the click to do something button to tan with:

```
self.do_something ["background"]="tan"
```

Result:

2. Change the font of one or both of your buttons using the following syntax:

```
self.BUTTON_NAME_HERE["font"]="Times, 7"
```

> **Remember to use only the most commonly found fonts for most operating systems. To choose a font that doesn't exist on another computer can crash your widget and the programs you make.*

You can also change foregrounds, other text elements, borders, and even thc type of cursor.

3. Play around freely to change things until you understand the purpose of most of these lines of code.

REVIEW

Quiz 11:

11.1 Define the following terms and check your answers on the next page:

1. Widget class
2. Style
3. Theme
4. Elements
5. Layout
6. Padding

11.2 Answer the following questions:

1. What is a widget in Tkinter?
2. What is a "canvas" in Tkinter?
3. What is a frame for in Tkinter?

4. What is the syntax for importing part of Tkinter?

VOCABULARY

widget class *is the type of widget such as; a canvas, a button, a menu, etc.*
style *is the over-all appearance of the widget class.*
theme *a set of widget styles grouped together.*
elements *parts of a widget like; label elements, spacing elements, border elements, etc.*
layout *the arrangement of elements*
Padding *the extra space around some elements or widgets.*

11.2 Answers:

1. *It could refer to icons; drop down menus; buttons; and many other graphical interface "things."*
2. *Canvas is used to draw, create graphics, complex widgets, and could even be used to make paint and graphics programs, (graphic editors).*
3. *A rectangular box that can contain many widgets.*
4. from tkinter import *

Lesson 12: Debugging Basics

WHAT YOU WILL LEARN:

- **INTRODUCING THE "UNKNOWN BUG"**
- **SYNTAX ERRORS**
- **LOGIC OR SEMANTIC ERRORS**
- **EXECUTION OR RUNTIME ERRORS**
- **HUNTING BUGS**
- **PYTHON'S DEBUGGER**

INTRODUCING THE "UNKNOWN BUG"

I am sure by now; you have already experienced a rise in blood pressure when you see the cryptic error messages and exceptions Python hisses out and spits at you. I know, it's hard to believe, but these can be helpful and in more advanced programming you will cause some exceptions to happen on purpose! Let's talk about bugs.

What is debugging? No, it is not buying a flea collar or using special shampoo. ***Debugging** is finding and solving problems in a program*. The term "bug" became the traditional way of referring to computer problems thanks to a very famous moth. No one seems to remember the moth's name, but the memory of the "unknown moth" will remain throughout history. According to the legend, one of the first major computer systems in computer history experienced an unexplainable crash. After many days, (who knows maybe it was many months or even many minutes), a moth was found inside the computer. It seems this historical moth short circuited the mother board with its wings in an evil plot to take over the world. A moment of silence for the unknown moth please.............................. So, the unknown moth courageously, (or perhaps sniveling and whining in total terror), gave up its life to become the world famous "computer bug." So, like a ghost, (with friends), it returns for revenge. Bugs continue to infect programs and computers. Since computer guys have to speak their own cultural language, the term "exception" pops up whenever the computer code of honor and legal code are violated. ***Exceptions** are important and exceptional, (exceptionally bad), events that generally interrupt the running of the program.* So an "exception" is just another way of saying "***Hey look! This is bad!***"

An ***un-handled*** exception is what Python generally spits out to tell you *something happened but nothing was done about it.* When running the program, un-handled exceptions will generally stop the program from continuing to run. *A **handled** exception is when you expected it and wrote some code to tell Python what to do if or when it happens.*

There are also many tools and modules available to help you. Python comes packaged with some very useful modules and in interactive mode will display exceptions. Various text editors also come with code de-bugging options. PyScripter has it's own approach to helping you prevent and eliminate bugs in your code.

To be a great programmer you will have to learn to enjoy, or at least be good at, debugging. You can think of yourself as a detective, looking at the clues, and hunting killer bugs. As long as people make mistakes, debugging will be a necessary talent for programmers to develop. In this lesson we will keep things simple. However, debugging can get really complex depending upon the complexity of your strategies and the complexity of the code you are debugging.

One of the advantages of using an interpreted language like Python is that you will discover many errors while you are writing code; rather than trying to find them all after your entire code is compiled and executed.

The Big Three:

1. Syntax Errors
2. Logic or Semantic Errors
3. Runtime or Execution Errors

SYNTAX ERRORS

*What's a syntax? No it is not a "sin" tax or we would all be in trouble. **Syntax** refers to the proper structure of the words, indentation, spelling, capitalization, sentences, spaces, punctuation, etc.* I'm sure you noticed by now that syntax errors are some of the most common causes of exceptions. Syntax errors occur when the interpreter finds something ***"illegal,"*** *(that it does not understand).* It's Python language for; "Huh?" As with most snakes, Python's have poor eyesight, so the error will often not be where it is seen by Python.

*Python inserts the error **when** it detects one; not always **where** the error is located.*

All you know for sure is that the error is in the code that ran before the error message appeared. If you are lucky, it is in the first line of code before the error message.

An arrow " ^" may indicate where the error was detected.

The best way to deal with these errors is to not make them. Of course, back in the real world we know that we will often make mistakes. Finding errors takes experience, detective work or trial and terror, (or is that "error"?) Let's practice finding some of these errors.

Exercise 12.1:
Find as many of these types of errors in the following code as you can, (hint = 7):

```
coins = 2
diamonds = 4
run = 2
while run:

    guess = int(input(the 2 or the 4    '))
    if guess = coins
        print ('Yeah! You can buy a hamburger with your coins!!" )
        run = False
     if guess == diamonds:
        print ("YOU CAN'T EAT DIAMONDS!!!")
        IntroTwo()
Print ( Game Over! Your Full!!)
```

Logic or Semantic Errors:

There's a demon in my computer! ***Semantic errors, (logic errors),** are when your code runs fine but does not do what you expected or wanted it to do.* To find semantic errors you may have to work in reverse and do some detective work by looking at:

1. *The output you are getting, (if any).*
2. *The output you want to get.*

Python is like a blind policeman to these errors because it does not see anything illegal.

Errors in logic can be very difficult to find. Sometimes adding print functions and using the "divide and conquer" approach becomes necessary. Divide and test each suspected block of code and look closely at the results you are getting compared to what you should be getting. If you can't find the error, you can sometimes benefit by making a visual representation or diagram of what each block of code should be doing. You can also use print statements to see what is really happening in a particular block of code.

EXECUTION OR RUNTIME ERRORS: FAILED EXECUTION

*A **runtime error** is when a problem shows up as you run the code. It will generally cause an exception or crash your program.* An illegal action is detected but it could be caused by a logic error in the previous code or an illegal action in or near the line where execution fails. *How do we hunt down bugs?*

HUNTING BUGS

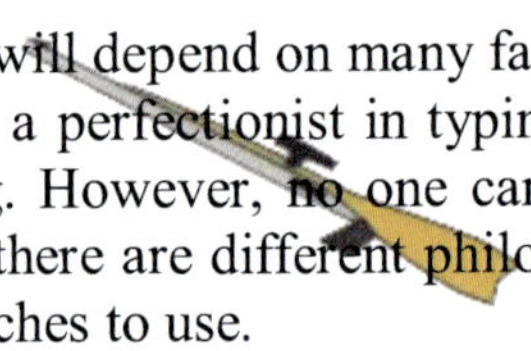

The way you choose to debug a program will depend on many factors. *Of course, the first level of defense against bugs is not to make them.* Being a perfectionist in typing, understanding logic, and practice are your first priorities to good code writing. However, no one can claim they can continually write good programs without debugging skills. But, there are different philosophies and different circumstances that will help you to understand which approaches to use.

The "Fight or Rewrite" Approach

If your source code is very brief and you have no idea where the problems are, you may consider just re-writing it. Choosing this approach is appropriate *when debugging will take longer than re-writing.*

The "No Debugger" Approach

Some programmers feel that using a debugger can just make things more confusing. The debugger may output so much vague, cryptic, or even wrong information that it may cause you to waste valuable time chasing butterflies in the wrong directions. The simplest approach to debugging is to use the print function and a *step-wise or step by step* strategy. *The* ***step-wise*** *approach just means line by line testing and analysis.* With this approach it is recommended:

1. *Use the print function in blocks of code to find the problems.*
2. *Test and fix as you go. Test small blocks of code as you write them.*

Utilizing Python's interactive interpreter is useful for this strategy.

The TDD Approach

Test-Driven Development, (TDD), *uses continual testing during the development cycle* to prevent or reduce debugging with the final product. Although it slows down the development of the software, it can eliminate or radically reduce debugging time at the end of the development cycle. In TDD:

1. *Make a detailed plan with examples for the features you want the code to have.*
2. *Write code examples with the expected output.*
3. *Test the code examples.*
4. *Rewrite them as needed. (For every change the code is retested).*
5. *Test them again and repeat the cycle until the code passes all test(s).*

What tests? The two main types of tests are *functional tests or acceptance tests,* and *unit* tests. ***Functional or acceptance tests*** *are user acceptance tests*. These are checklists or tests often created by users or customers about the features that are expected. There are acceptance test writing tools available on the internet for specific applications such as web design, data base, etc.

Unit testing *involves isolating individual modules for testing.* If external data or dependencies are necessary for testing; *fakes objects* or *mocks* will play as substitutes.

There are various third party testing tools available on the web. Python's standard library also provides modules for these kinds of tests; **unittest** and **doctest**.

The DDD Approach

*The **Document-Driven Development, (DDD),** approach is detailed documentation on the code.* Text documentation will include:

1. ***What it does.***
2. ***How it works.***
3. ***How it should be used.***
4. ***Clear code examples.***

PYTHON'S DEBUGGER

Python's debugging module, pdb, *provides interactive debugging.* For details, check Python's documentation under "*Debugging and Profiling.*" This module provides single-step, (line by line), debugging control statements and other useful tools for debugging. If you are in a hurry an "instant user's manual" is provided in the Python documentation. Documentation of Python's debugger is extensive so expect to spend some time going through it. Mastering logging techniques can also be valuable in debugging complex programs.

One simple approach to debugging is to use the try...except...else block. The syntax for this strategy is:

```
try:
    the code to test here
except  exceptions to the rule
    print( 'Oops, there is a problem. ' )
else:
    print( 'No problem' )
```

An easy way to understand this is to examine the error of trying to divide by zero. To Python that would be a "ZeroDivisionError."

Try this (save and run in the shell window; not the interactive window):

```
*Untitled*
File  Edit  Format  Run  Options  Windows  Help
def being_bad(num1, num2):
    print(num1/num2)
being_bad(7, 0)
```

Running it causes an exception:

```
>>>
Traceback (most recent call last):
  File "C:/Python33/tmp.py", line 3, in <module>
    being_bad(7, 0)
  File "C:/Python33/tmp.py", line 2, in being_bad
    print(num1/num2)
ZeroDivisionError: division by zero
>>>
```

Let us imagine that we are a little slow upstairs. We need to test division by zero and compare it to division by another number to understand the ZerroDivisionError. We can use the try...except statement or add an additional else statement to test the code if no exception occurs.

Try this:

```
*tmp.py - C:/Python33/tmp.py*
File Edit Format Run Options Windows Help
def being_bad(num1, num2):
    print(num1/num2)
try:
    being_bad(7, 0)
    print(num1/num2)
except ZeroDivisionError:
    print('No division by zero')
```

Outputs:

```
No division by zero
```

Now try:

```
tmp.py - C:/Python33/tmp.py
File Edit Format Run Options Windows Help
def being_bad(num1, num2):
    print(num1/num2)
try:
    being_bad(10, 5)

except ZeroDivisionError:
    print('No division by zero')
else:
    print('It works.')
```

Outputs:

```
>>>
2.0
It works.
>>>
```

This last module will print the answer and "It works" or "No division by zero" depending on the pair of numbers you use. You could also use the pass statement rather than print('It works') to allow the code to continue running if no exception occurs.

*You will have times when you want an exception to occur for some reason, this is called **raising** and exception. **User-defined exceptions** are ones that you create.*

Alien Cat Studios.com, 2013

Most of Python's exception messages are self-explanatory. We will only list a few that are not so obvious:

- **OverflowError** happens when calculations are beyond the maximum limit.
- **EOFError** happens when input was expected or not acceptable.
- **KeyboardInterrupt** is when the user uses the keyboard to interrupt the running of the program. (Ok, this one may be obvious to some people).
- **IndexError** happens when an index is not found in a sequence.
- **UnboundLocalError** happens when an attempt to access a local variable in a function or method but there is no value assigned to it.
- **IOError** happens when an input output operation fails.
- **RuntimeError** is the generic message for errors that don't fall into specific categories.

TIPS

- Be consistent in your coding style and syntax.
- Be a perfectionist.
- Watch: spaces, indentation, and case sensitivity at all times.
- Avoid using names that already exist or are similar to other names and keywords.
- Provide clear documentation in comments and docstrings.
- Update any and all changes within the comments and docstrings.
- Divide and Conquer.
- Join Python forums to interact with experts.

Study your code, compare it to similar code that works. If you must; test your code block by block, or even line by line, to narrow down the problem. A good IDE can often help you isolate the problems in your code. Inserting the "print" function to determine actual output of certain blocks of code is very useful.

REVIEW

Quiz 12:

12.1 Define the following terms and check your answers on the next page:

1. Debugging
2. Exceptions
3. Syntax errors
4. Runtime error
5. Semantic error
6. Un-handled exception
7. Handled exception
8. Functional testing
9. Unit testing

12.2 Answer the following questions:

1. *When is it best just to rewrite the code from the beginning?*
2. *What do you do with the "no bugger" approach?*
3. *Describe TDD.*
4. *What is pdb?*

VOCABULARY

Debugging *finding and solving problems in a program*	
Exceptions *are important or exceptional events*	
Syntax *refers to the proper structure of the words, indentation, spelling, capitalization, sentences, spaces, punctuation, etc.*	
A ***runtime error*** *is when a problem shows up when you run the code. It will generally cause an exception or crash your program.*	
An ***un-handled*** exception is what Python generally spits out to tell you *something happened but nothing was done about it.*	
A ***handled*** *exception is when you expected it and wrote some code to tell Python what to do if or when it happens.*	
Functional or acceptance tests *are user acceptance tests often designed by users*	
Unit testing *involves isolating individual modules for testing.*	
Semantic errors *refer to when your code runs fine but does not do what you expected or wanted it to do.*	

12.2 Answers:

1. *When it would take more time to debug it than re-write it.*
2. *Use the print function and test as you go.*
3. *TDD is Test-Driven-Development, meaning continual testing during development using functional and unit tests.*
4. *Python's debugger module.*

Exercise 12.1 Answers:

```
coins = 2
diamonds = 4
run = 2
while run:

    guess = int(input(' the 2 or the 4    '))
    if guess == coins:
        print ('Yeah! You can buy a hamburger with your coins!!")
        run = False
    if guess == diamonds:
        print ("YOU CAN'T EAT DIAMONDS!!!")
        IntroTwo()
Print (' Game Over! Your Full!')
```

① 2 equal signs; not 1
② missing colon
③ Mismatched quotation marks
④ indentation
⑤ missing quotation mark
⑥ wrong capitalization
⑦ missing quotation marks

Lesson 13: Designing Your Software

<u>WHAT YOU WILL LEARN</u>:

- **SOFTWARE DEVELOPMENT**
- **SOFTWARE VERSIONING**
- **PLANNING STAGE**
- **DEVELOPMENT CYCLE**
- **MAINTENANCE AND SUPPORT CYCLE**
- **UPDATE AND NEW RELEASE CYCLE**
- **THINKING ALGORITHMS TO MAKE A GAME**

SOFTWARE DEVELOPMENT

In this lesson you will be introduced to the world of software design. Remember that one of the primary purposes of this course is to give you some confidence in doing some actual programming while giving you an overview of Python. Python is a language, and as a language it is best learned by using it and diving into deeper levels as you understand it. For most of this lesson, we will take a break from new vocabulary and have a brief look at software design theory and architecture.

Now that you have played a little and know that you truly are clever enough to become a programmer; you can understand the world of software design theory. You can dive deep into the world of software design. How deep would depend upon your goals and how well you can swim. You may need to study psychological aspects, artificial intelligence, or look at demographics, distribution, and marketing. Programming and software design covers a wide, wide world. You have to make some choices about which languages to use and what kind of software you want to design. ***Everything in a programmer's mind should begin with:***

1. **What result do I want?**
2. **How to get there?**
3. **Make it happen.**

1. **"What?"**
2. **"How?**
3. **"Do it and refine it"**

Do you want to program games, mobile apps, business software, web pages, everything? *What programming languages should you use?* In advanced programming you may want to use more than one language to make your software. You must choose the tools that you have available and will do the best job.

Most programming languages can make nearly any kind of software. However, the reality is that different languages are better for different jobs. You should learn more than one, but you shouldn't bother learning thirty or forty either, (unless your job requires it). Being a master of a few languages is better than being a beginner in ten languages.

Mastering a programming language is like and artist mastering the use of his paint brushes; the resulting programs are your works of art. Some languages, like Python, are versatile enough to use for nearly anything. However, some languages are better than others at certain jobs. Often C is used in combination with Python to increase speed and help deal with heavy 3D graphics engines. Choose those languages that will fit your goals as a programmer. Python is a wonderful place to start because it is easier to learn than many languages and is powerful enough to get the job done. Be cautious on getting advice or sucked into the "newest" languages. Some are like fads that pass away quickly. Some programmers follow a language like following a religion and have very emotional opinions about the languages they use. Also understand that "new" does not always mean better. LISP is one of the oldest popular programming languages, yet it is still relied on by NASA and other high tech organizations because it can be used to solve some problems in ways that are unique and more powerful than some newer languages.

An advantage of some of the latest languages is that they are often more user friendly and faster for development. A big disadvantage is their dependencies on other code. For example, the .NET Framework is very useful for making software design easier. On the flip side, if Microsoft© techs wake up in the night and decide to radically change it; any software designed to rely on it could become useless overnight. I like the idea of my software being as independent as possible. This way it is not at the mercy of; nor is its use totally controlled by people I don't know. I am using my own translation but De Vinci once said something like: **"Don't learn knowledge that will be useless and forgotten tomorrow."** If I learn all the "easy" or point and click development tools that are totally dependent on underlying algorithms I don't know or control; I am going to have problems. Someone will change the interface at will and the underlying algorithms. I will wake up one day to find all my current knowledge is useless and my programs no longer work. My hours of work and time spent learning this stuff was for nothing.

To plan your programs design you define exactly what you want to do and how you will do it. Spending extra time here can save you endless frustration later. Consider the life cycle of the program. The life stages of a program could be dived into three phases from the programmer's point of view. The life cycle would be quite different from a businessman's or marketing point of view. Since this is not a business book; you can skip reading that last sentence.....and this one too. For now, just put your mind on a programmer's overview of software development. It is probably most accurate to collectively call these the four stages of the development "cycle" since this process is generally repeated.

Four Stages of the Software Development Cycle:

1) Planning
2) Development
3) Maintenance and support

4) Update and New Release

Software Versioning

*A **versioning system** refers to the method that various software developers use to keep track of changes during the lifecycle of their software.* There are now laws that demand a particular system be followed so many have developed. It is generally best to follow some standard system to avoid confusion. One of the most popular systems is as follows:

Pre-Alpha

The pre-alpha stage refers to all the stages of software development prior to complete functionality and major testing. This would include requirement analysis, software design, and software development.

Alpha

In this phase the software will undergo testing. The final features are added to the software. The software may be unstable at this point, causing crashes and possible data loss. Testing for stability and revising the code are part of the process. A "feature freeze" is usually placed on the software at the end of this stage.

Beta

The software is theoretically feature complete and will be tested for the first time outside of the organization that developed it. Users are referred to as "beta testers." Beta testing can be used to promote the software while testing it among a larger group of users. Hopefully, small problems will be discovered and corrected before releasing the software to the general public.

Some software developers use an open beta and closed beta phase. The closed beta version is released to a selected group of users for testing. The open beta version may be available to a larger group, sometimes anyone who is interested in testing the software. Bugs are reported by users and the software is revised and refined for release to the public.

The software version is referred to as code complete when the development team feels there will not be any entirely new source code added to the software.

RTM

"*Release to manufacturing*" or "*release to marketing*" is the phase where the software is released to a manufacturer for mass production. It can also be referred to as "*going gold*" since engineers often release a "*gold master CD*" for duplication.

GA

"*General acceptance*" or "*general availability*" is the phase where the software is released to the general public. The product is said to have "*gone live*" and should be a stable release.

Version Numbers

Software numbering conventions can get confusing since various developers use different systems. Generally, they should indicate minor or significant changes. One scheme uses 0.9 for beta software and three or four place values to indicate changes. For example; *version 1.1.1* going to *1.1.2* may reflect minor bug fixes, going from *1.1.1* to *1.2.0* may reflect significant changes; and going to *version 2.0.0* may indicate major rewriting of the code. Of course, every developer uses their own system so there are no strict rules about numbering schemes. Some developers will jump numbers to indicate a significant change in software versions. They may want to let the customers know that major changes have taken place by changing a version from 1.0.0 to 1.5.0.

Some developers use the following scheme:

major.minor.revision

Some companies will add a "b" to indicate a beta version, (1.2.1b). 1.2.1**b2** would indicate a beta version with bug fixes; 1.2.1**rc** may indicate release candidate; 1.2.1**r** may indicate the version ready for commercial release with bug fixes indicated by adding a number after the "r," (1.2.1**r3**). The use of letters is often restricted to internal use within the company and is often dropped when the product is actually released to the public to avoid confusing potential customers.

The version scheme you use will depend on your personal choices or the conventions used by the company you work for. Regardless of the scheme you use, be consistent to avoid confusion.

Planning Stage

We begin with planning and brain storming sessions to answer a few questions:

1. *What will it do?* Entertain you, solve a problem, or transport you to another dimension?
2. *Who will use it?* Child, teen, adult, tech, scientist, alien?
3. *What kind of operating systems should it run on?* Linux, XP, Win7, Vista, Mac, palm computer, cell-phones, gaming counsels, or super-computers?
4. *Who will work on this project?* Programs can be simple and take a matter of hours or so complex they take armies of programmer's years to complete. You have to consider your resources, time, skills, and goals to evaluate who will be needed to do it. If it is just you; then understand the time, mental, and physical, limitations of your own biological machine.
5. *Will it be used on the internet?*
6. *How fast does it need to be?*
7. *Will it be networked to many computers, be portable, etc.*
8. *How long will it take to develop the program?*
9. *Who will buy the program?*
10. *What programming languages will we use to make it?*

Development Cycle

- Write it and make a prototype. ***alpha stage***
- Test it. ***beta version/ beta stage***
- Fix It and Refine It
- ***Release version*** 1 *(dropping the Greek and speaking English phase)*

Maintenance and Support Cycle

- Verify bug rumors, (their existence and power). Label them; super bug lame bug, or ghost/no bug here.
- Test to see if you really killed it; or it is in hiding?
- Make bug guards to prevent future anticipated problems.
- Test and repeat cycle until it looks good.
- Release a patch software, new version, or upgrade.

Update and New Release Cycle

- Consider all problems and possible new bugs learned from the maintenance and support cycle.
- Decide what new stuff you want to add to your program to make it cooler.

Plan how to:

- Change the program
- Test the new stuff
- Fix it
- Beta test (give it to some other people to try and report problems)
- Fix it again.
- Repeat all the stuff mentioned above until you are happy.
- Release a new version and wait for replies, suggestions and death threats.
- Sort through the reports and filter them accordingly:
    - *not true*
    - *useless blabbing*
    - *true*
    - *maybe true*

- Apply the new stuff you know to a patch or new version and release it.
- Repeat until it is not practical to continue supporting, upgrading, or changing the software, *(you've reached the end of the products life cycle).*

THINKING ALGORITHMS TO MAKE A GAME

To design algorithms you must learn to think in good algorithms, (vs. evil ones). You must practice translating words and sentences into algorithms. This brings us to some new questions. What does a good algorithm look like? Will an algorithm get along with my cat?

To illustrate how to think in algorithms, I will give you some examples followed by a practical exercise mostly with code you already know from earlier lessons. However, we will give you the power to add random elements to your code in this lesson.

Let's say you want to make a word game. (Yeah I know; word games are boring, but for your current level of programming they are best for you to practice and understand). *Remember that your writing teacher said;*

"All good writing begins with a good outline."

First, you *outline the instructions or main events you want to happen.* This is called a ***level one solution***.

This sequence of statements will be the instructions that we will change into our source code later. In a level one solution, keep things simple.

Exercise 1: Simple Shell Game

1. Player is told a diamond is placed under one of three shells.
2. Shells are shuffled.
3. Player chooses a shell.
4. Player is told if he found the diamond, he has won; if he didn't he must try again.
5. Game is over when he finds the diamond

<u>Now we begin a *level two solution where we add more details that start sounding like the code* we will write.</u>

1.1 Player is told a diamond is placed under one of three shells.
1.2 He is told to press "enter" to continue. He hits "enter."
2.1 Player is told that shells are three colors; blue, red, and green and that the shells will be randomly shuffled around when he hits the "enter" key.
2.2 Player hits "enter."
3.1 Player is told that the shells have been shuffled and he should choose one.
3.2 Player chooses shell by INPUTTING a shell color..
4.1 IF player chose correctly he is told; "You won a diamond." and the game is over.
4.2 ELSE if the player is wrong he is told: "You are wrong! Try Again if you dare!" UNTIL he guesses correctly.
5.1 Game ends when IF; ELSE is true (player chooses correctly).

Your level two solution should give you the details you need to begin writing your code. It may also help to make a control flow chart to visualize what should happen.

Make it Visual: Going with the Flow (chart)

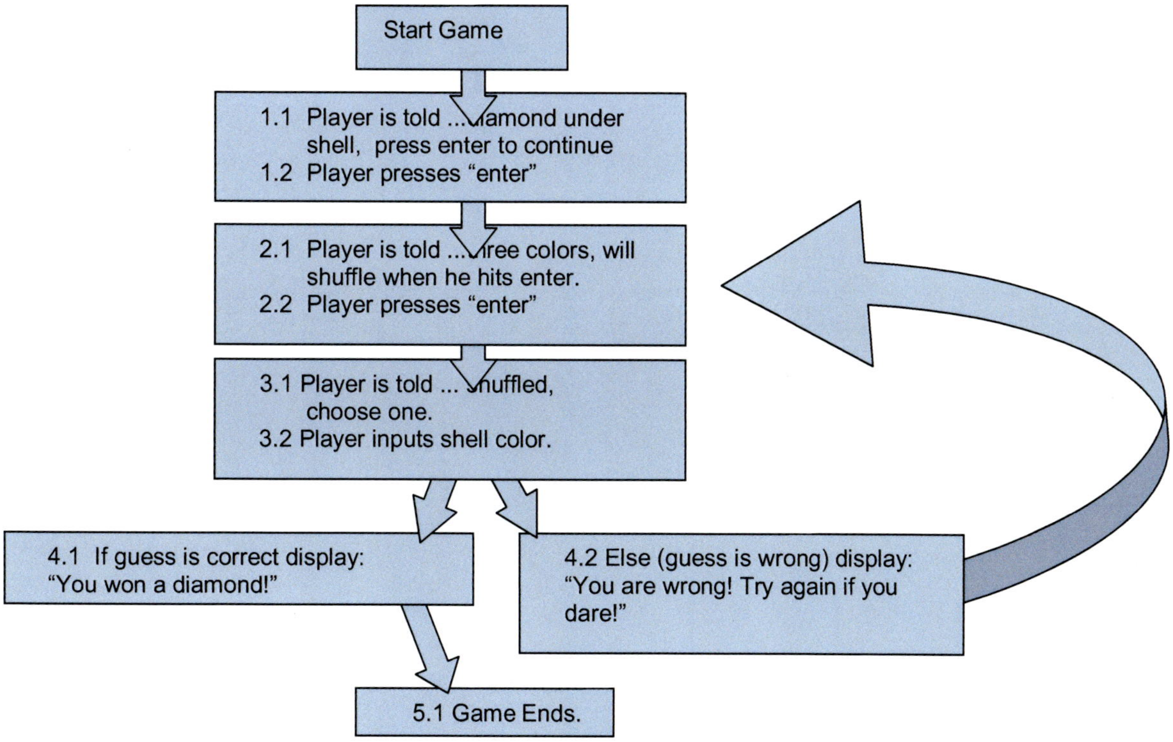

Making your game visual can help you design your program. Sometimes visualizing your code will help you debug your program if things are not working the way they should. Your flow chart don't need to be fancy, if you can sketch boxes and arrows on a piece of paper, you can make a data flow diagram.

Study your level two solution and look at the numbers. What blocks will need to go together and what details or "code" words need to be added? *If your program is complex and you need more details, you can also write a level three or level four solution.*

On the first time through, keep it simple. Once your game is working you can modify and play with it a bit until you understand it. You could even add more interesting elements to the game like; if player selects the wrong shell he reads; "Pow!! You just set off a bomb shell! Game over!" To pull this off you will need to remember how to make a loop and will need some new information coming up next. Review previous lessons if you get stuck. The new info you need is to understand how to generate random numbers to use for seemingly random events in your games.

Making Things Random

Many games will need to generate random events or numbers. A roll of a dice, choosing a card, or any random event requires some code to give you control over random events.

In a computer things are not truly random, but are based on something to fake or simulate random results. Python has many ways to create formulas to emulate random results and can even give you some control on creating you own formulas. As long as the player doesn't know the formula he will see an apparently random result. For the purposes of this course we will only introduce you to random number generation. "Random" is another example of a built-in function in Python.

To look at an overwhelming definition of built-in functions you can try Python's help module:

```
>>> help("builtins")
```

The information is probably more than you can handle at this point, but look through the first part at least for future reference.

Python has a built-in module just for allowing you to get creative with randomizing stuff.

There are many ways to code the information for the game we are working on. We will code this game primarily by using code you already know. When you are more confident you will think of better ways to get the same results with less, more efficient source code.

Type the following code into Python's Shell to get familiar with it. Play for awhile and then look at the explanations that follow.

```
Python Shell
File Edit Shell Debug Options Windows Help
Python 3.3.0 (v3.3.0:bd8afb90ebf2, Sep 29 2012, 10:55:48) [MSC v.1600 32 bit (In
tel)] on win32
Type "copyright", "credits" or "license()" for more information.
>>> import random
>>> shells= ['blue','red','green']
>>> random.choice(shells)
'red'
>>> answer= shells[1]
>>> print(answer)
red
>>> random.shuffle(shells)
>>> print(shells)
['blue', 'red', 'green']
>>> print(answer)
red
>>> random.shuffle(shells)
>>> answer= shells[1]
>>> print(answer)
green
>>> print(shells)
['red', 'green', 'blue']
>>> random.shuffle(shells)
>>> print(shells)
['red', 'green', 'blue']
>>> random.shuffle(shells)
>>> print(shells)
['blue', 'red', 'green']
>>>
```

**Note that with only three items to shuffle, there is reasonable probability that they could be shuffled back into their original position.*

<u>Explanations that followed:</u>

```
import random
```

Remember that to access a module in Python you must import it.

```
shells=[ 'blue' ,' red' ,' green' ]
# Here we are just defining the variable "shells" as a list, (see lesson four if you forgot).
random.choice(shells)
```

Here we are asking the computer to make a random choice from our "shells" list. My computer chose 'red.'

```
answer= shells[1]
```

We are telling the computer to place whatever is in the 1st position of our list will be a variable called "answer." We will need to do this so the game can keep track of the correct answer for the player's future guesses.

```
print(answer) # We typed this to test our code.
red  # Yeah! It worked.
```

If you forgot that we count slices from 0, review lesson four.

```
random.shuffle(shells)
```

Here we are shuffling the list called "shells" to re-arrange it.

```
print(shells) #Just checking to see if it worked.
[ ‘blue’ ,’ red’ ,’ green’ ] #Yep! It worked.
print(answer) #Just checking.
red
```

What happened? Position [1] is now 'blue' not 'red'!!! Sorry, the computer remembers that we already filled that variable with the color red. So, if we want it to change with the shuffle; we have to define the "answer" variable again.

```
random.shuffle(shells) # Again with the shuffling.
answer=shells[1]  # Re-defining  “answer.”
print(answer) # Just checking.
green  # Seems to work.
print(shells) # Checking to see it really chose position [1] in the list.
[ ‘red’ ,’ green’ ,’ blue’ ]  Yes it did.
```

```
random.shuffle(shells) # Trying again.
print(shells) # Checking again.
[ ‘red’ ,’ green’ ,’ blue’ ]  # Is it shuffling? What happened?
```

```
random.shuffle(shells) #Let’ s try that again.
print(shells) # Checking yet again.
[ ‘blue’ ,’ red’ ,’ green’ ] # Yes, it is shuffling.
```

Just as in a real shell game, especially with only three shells, you could randomly shuffle them back into their original position. That's what happened in this example.

Ok, now you have almost everything you need to create our shell game. You do need one more thing. In earlier lessons we introduced the "while" loop. There are more kinds of loops we will talk about later. We learned how to break out of a while loop when one of our variables becomes untrue. But, what if we want to break out of the while loop when one of our variables is true? Huh? If the player in our shell game chooses the right answer, how with our current knowledge of code can we *break* *out of the while loop at that point*?

With none other than *the break command!* Just put the word "break" without the quotes after the code that has become true, (when the user chose the right shell). You now have all the tools you need from previous lessons to write the code for the shell game.

Try your best to write the source code for this game without looking at the answer. Start with your level two solutions; line by line. To do a run test on your code; you may have to save and restart the interpreter occasionally to get things to work right.

Hint: If you need to retype your code because you typed something wrong in Shell mode; you can go to the shell drop down menu and click on "restart shell" or hit Control-F6.

In this section, I don't want to take you by the hand. I want you to stumble, fall, get up, and learn to walk into coding by yourself. Check the answer when you are too bruised up to continue or when you have found a solution.

I will use only code I have already taught you for my answer. My code choices were made to get the proper results while reinforcing old ideas and new concepts. The main idea at this point is; does your game work properly? If not; what needs to change? Try to figure it out and review previous lessons before jumping ahead to check the solution. If you do, feel guilty and try harder next time. Building the programming muscles in your brain is like body building.

Reminder: open up the IDLE Shell window to use like scratch paper to test your lines of code. When you are happy with the result of each line, open a new window to type or copy the code you are happy with into the Editor window. Save the code you are happy with in your Editor window. (Leave both windows open while you are working).

Do your best before going to the next page to see one possible solution.

Blank Thinking Space

One solution (from IDLE's edit window):

tmp.py - C:/Python33/tmp.py

File Edit Format Run Options Windows Help

```
import random
print('Welcome to the Shell Game!')
print('A diamond has been hidden under one of three shells.')
print('The shells will be shuffled and you must choose one')
print('The three shells are blue, red, and green.')
print('Press the Enter key when you are ready to begin.')
input()
print('Choose blue, red, or green')
run= ['red','green','blue']
random.shuffle(run)
answer= run[1]
while run:
    guess= input('Enter your answer: ')
    if guess== answer:
        print('Yes! You won a diamond!')
        print('Game over.')
        break
    elif guess!= answer:
        print('You are wrong! Try again if you dare!')
```

Explanation: Remember that a List uses [ ] and can be edited/is mutable while the Tuple uses ( ) and can not be edited/is immutable. The input() was used just to cause the program to pause until the enter button is pushed. The while run statement at the beginning of the while loop was used to make looping continue until the computer reached the break in the code. The other code has been explained in previous lessons so we won't repeat the explanations here. I used the code already covered in previous lessons and tried to make it as simple as possible; while giving you and understanding of each concept.

Exercise: Go ahead and try the game a few times. If you haven't already, change all the printed lines that can be grouped together into a function and add some improvements to your game.

REVIEW

Quiz 13:

13.1 Answer the following questions:

1. *What are the four stages of the software development cycle?*
2. *What are the first three stages of versioning software?*
3. *List at least three of the questions you should ask during the planning stage.*
4. *What are some things you should do before releasing a new version?*
5. *What is a level one solution?*

VOCABULARY

level one solution is an *outline of the instructions or main events you want to happen.*
versioning system *refers to the method that various software developers use to keep track of changes during the lifecycle of their software.*

13.1 Answers:

1.

1) Planning
2) Development
3) Maintenance and support
4) Update and new release

2.

1) Pre-alpha
2) Alpha
3) Beta

3. At least three of the following:

1) What will it do?
2) Who will use it?
3) What kind of operating systems should it run on?
4) Who will work on this project?
5) Will it be used on the internet?
6) How fast does it need to be?
7) Will it be networked to many computers, be portable, etc.
8) How long will it take to develop the program?
9) Who will buy the program?
10) What programming languages will we/can we use?

4. Some of the following:

1) Consider all problems and possible new bugs learned from the maintenance and support cycle.
2) Decide what new stuff you want to add to your program to make it cooler.
3) Plan how to
4) Change the program
5) Test the new stuff
6) Fix it

5. *A* ***level one solution*** is an *outline of the instructions or main events you want to happen.*

Lesson 14: Intro to Game Making

- What's Pygame?
- Getting help Tips
- Looking at A PyGame
- Introducing Pygame Modules
- Graphics to the Screen
- Colors
- Animation

Introduction

Congratulations! If you made it this far, you will now learn how to make more interesting games and applications.

Keep in mind that some software took huge teams of programmer's years to create. With time restraints and the complexity of large programs, a single programmer must count the cost before attempting to write a huge program on his own. If you can't do it alone, you will need to develop social and management skills to launch and manage a software project team.

Programming a common 3D game generally takes a large team of programmers, graphic artists, musicians, etc. and a few years to produce. Simple 2D games and software are possible for a lone programmer with some effort. These would include games like Tetris, card games, chess, etc.

You can take short cuts to making games by using commercial game engines, but you will often be limited by license requirements in selling your games and by pre-requisite software dependencies to run the games you create. For example, if a game engine requires a certain version of .net framework to run, the game you created is at the mercy of Microsoft's .net framework policies. A radical change in their code and supported versions could render your game useless on future operating systems. Yes, you will save much time with a game engine rather than by programming it all with fewer dependencies; but consider the cost and thoroughly research that game engine before choosing this road.

Most commercial games use combinations approach; combining Python with other languages such as C to speed up 3D graphics and other aspects of the game. Don't panic, you can create a game entirely in Python with the skills you learn in this course. For simplicity we will use available modules and add-ons that allow commercial production of your games.

To create a game also requires that you either create or find assets that you can legally use in your game. Game development will not get far without music, sound files, and graphic arts. You can create them yourself, use free assets, meet license requirements to use assets created by others, or you can buy the rights to them. Check out our free resources page at http://www.toonzcat.com to get started.

WHAT'S PYGAME?

You could write games entirely with Python from scratch and forget about Pygame; but that would make your life much more complicated. Pygame was designed to make use of Python programming but provide the programmer with modules and integrated programs to help him/her make games faster and easier. You needn't design everything from scratch. Pygame has provided powerful tools to use when you make games and has done many of the common game programming tasks for you. Pygame is often described as a multi-media library for creating 2D games. Saving time is a life-saving need for the lone programmer. It is good for the beginning programmer to see real results of his work as soon as possible. Producing a game you would not be ashamed to show your friends can diminish the "forget programming" syndrome. Studying programming for months only to produce word games and pathetic looking shapes that move can be discouraging for new programmers. So, PyGame to the rescue! *(But, if you are a hardcore, diehard, never give up, psychotically motivated beginner; skip all this and code everything from scratch in pure Python. The less motivated salute you!)*

The technical description is that ***Pygame** is a Python extension library wrapped around the SDL library. The **SDL** library, (Simple Direct Media Layer), is a cross-platform multi-media library that allows access to hardware such as a mouse, keyboard, joystick, etc.*

Environmental Planning

Prepare your computer environment to make some games. Unless you can just copy my configuration, you may need to research and select a different mix of software versions and modules to match your operating system and machine. Keep in mind that you must make sure the version of Pygame you download is compatible with the version of Python and other software or modules you will put together. Help on installation and version selection is available on the relative websites. You needn't have the same configuration as I used for this course. Just make sure all your installations and versions of Pygame and Python are compatible with your operating system.

My configuration for the following lessons:

- *XP sp2*
- *Python 3.2 and 3.3 (I used 3.2 when using Pygame for stability since 3.3 came out as I was writing this)*
- *Pygame 1.9.2a0 win32 py3.2 msi* http://www.pygame.org

Install Pygame to the same directory path where you installed Python. For example:

C:/Program Files/Python 32

If the auto install wizard does not detect the correct location use the "Python from another location" option and type in the directory path to your Python folder.

To check if it is installed correctly, open up IDLE and type the following:

```
import pygame
print(pygame.ver)
```

This should produce:

```
>>> import pygame
>>> print(pygame.ver)
1.9.2pre
>>>
```

If you got nothing or an error message rather than the Pygame version; it did not install correctly where Python could find it.

GETTING HELP TIPS

Remember that module help can be accessed in Python by using:

```
help(module name here)
```

To see what functions or methods are available for a variable use:

```
dir(variable name here)
```

For example, let's define a variable as a number and another as a string to see what functions are available for each (using IDLE):

```
>>> myname= 7
>>> dir(7)
['__abs__', '__add__', '__and__', '__bool__', '__ceil__', '__class__', '__delatt
r__', '__divmod__', '__doc__', '__eq__', '__float__', '__floor__', '__floordiv__
', '__format__', '__ge__', '__getattribute__', '__getnewargs__', '__gt__', '__ha
sh__', '__index__', '__init__', '__int__', '__invert__', '__le__', '__lshift__',
 '__lt__', '__mod__', '__mul__', '__ne__', '__neg__', '__new__', '__or__', '__po
s__', '__pow__', '__radd__', '__rand__', '__rdivmod__', '__reduce__', '__reduce_
ex__', '__repr__', '__rfloordiv__', '__rlshift__', '__rmod__', '__rmul__', '__ro
r__', '__round__', '__rpow__', '__rrshift__', '__rshift__', '__rsub__', '__rtrue
div__', '__rxor__', '__setattr__', '__sizeof__', '__str__', '__sub__', '__subcla
sshook__', '__truediv__', '__trunc__', '__xor__', 'bit_length', 'conjugate', 'de
nominator', 'from_bytes', 'imag', 'numerator', 'real', 'to_bytes']
>>>
```

```
>>> myname= 'A string of useless words.'
>>> dir(myname)
['__add__', '__class__', '__contains__', '__delattr__', '__doc__', '__eq__', '__
format__', '__ge__', '__getattribute__', '__getitem__', '__getnewargs__', '__gt_
_', '__hash__', '__init__', '__iter__', '__le__', '__len__', '__lt__', '__mod__'
, '__mul__', '__ne__', '__new__', '__reduce__', '__reduce_ex__', '__repr__', '__
rmod__', '__rmul__', '__setattr__', '__sizeof__', '__str__', '__subclasshook__',
 'capitalize', 'center', 'count', 'encode', 'endswith', 'expandtabs', 'find', 'f
ormat', 'format_map', 'index', 'isalnum', 'isalpha', 'isdecimal', 'isdigit', 'is
identifier', 'islower', 'isnumeric', 'isprintable', 'isspace', 'istitle', 'isupp
er', 'join', 'ljust', 'lower', 'lstrip', 'maketrans', 'partition', 'replace', 'r
find', 'rindex', 'rjust', 'rpartition', 'rsplit', 'rstrip', 'split', 'splitlines
', 'startswith', 'strip', 'swapcase', 'title', 'translate', 'upper', 'zfill']
>>>
```

You can play with some of these functions to see what they do; but with some of them you will have to look them up. For the functions in quotes use the *dot syntax*:

```
myvariablename.thefunctionname
```

```
>>> myname= 'This is a string'
>>> myname.lower()
'this is a string'
>>> myname.upper()
'THIS IS A STRING'
```

Note: This will not always work in all IDE's. If you need help and your IDE does not work, use IDLE to have quick look.

If you have a question that you can't find the answer via help files; join one of the many forums on Python or Pygame to ask someone in the Python community....don't be shy! The only stupid question is the one you didn't ask. Always experiment a little before asking questions though, sweat and tears will help you remember new programming concepts better than if someone tells you how to do it. Ah....the joy of frustration! Programming is best learned by doing it; just as a basketball is not learned well from a book, (unless you can dunk a book from half court).

Check websites, especially python.org to get more information and answers to common questions. Remember that you can also do an online search for Python communities that you can join or blogs about your particular question. Other members are sometimes happy to help you with questions and problems.

Looking at A PyGame

I think the most fun way to introduce you to PyGame is to show you a simple game. But first, you should know where you can find the documentation for Pygame in your computer.

After you have installed PyGame, you will find some tutorials and documents in the following directory, (unless you installed it somewhere else):

C:\Python32\Lib\site-packages\pygame\docs

PyGame comes with a number of examples you can try. Let's look at game example. Find the examples folder, (C:\Python32\Lib\site-packages\pygame\examples), and open "aliens.py" by double clicking it. COOL! A game!

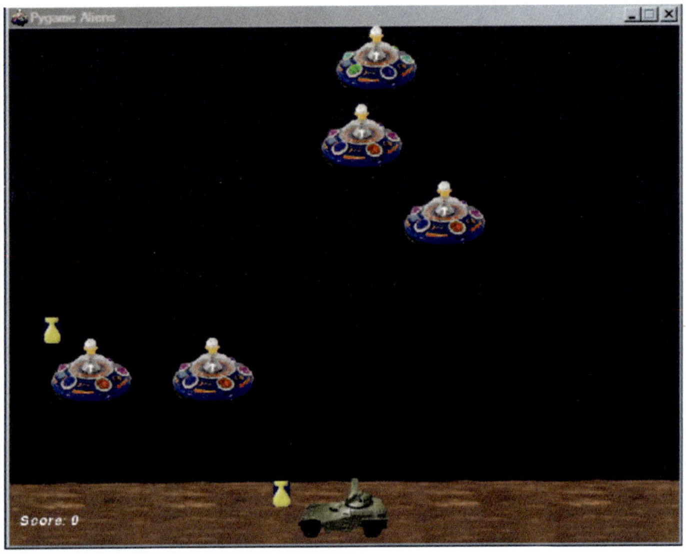

Now use your favorite IDE and open the alien.py file with it. Take a little time to look at the code. See how much of it you can understand. Aha! You are starting to reach the next level of programming! Ok....maybe you can't understand all of it yet...but you are on your way! We won't explain all the code at this point; we will play with it later. If you find the file and double click, in Windows it will generally launch the game. If you right click and choose "edit with IDLE" or you open it with IDLE, you can see the source code. You can play with the code and alter it to learn more about how things work.

Alien Cat Studios.com, 2013

INTRODUCING: PYGAME MODULES

cdrom	manages cdrom devices and audio playback
cursors	loads cursor images including standard cursors
display	controls the display window or screen
draw	draws simple shapes on a surface
event	manages events and the event queue
font	creates and renders True type fonts
image	loads and saves images
joystick	manages joystick devices
key	manages the keyboard
mouse	manages the mouse
movie	playback of mpeg files
sndarry	manipulates sounds with Numeric
surfarray	manipulates images with Numeric
time	controls time
transform	scale, rotate, and flips images.

We won't repeat everything in the PyGame tutorials and docs. You can read through the PyGame docs and play with the examples when you have time. Study the code and tweak it to gain some confidence.

GRAPHICS TO THE SCREEN

As you know, you can use inches, centimeters, pixels, or your foot to measure things. Each measurement has an appropriate usage. For example; your friend may prefer you use centimeters rather than your foot to measure his birthday cake. Pixels are a good way to measure things on a computer screen.

Think of your computer screen as a square with made of many little boxes called pixels. You find your way around by knowing what row and what column a particular pixel is in.

*The **coordinates**/location of a particular pixel is referred to by using a pair of numbers, separated by commas, within a set of parenthesis, (0,0). The **"x-axis"** is indicated by the first number in a number pair, (**0**,0), and can be used to represent width. The **"y-axis** is indicated by the second number in the pair, (0,**0**), and can be used to represent height.*

The number of pixels on a particular computer will depend on the resolution of the screen. The least it would be is 640 columns by 480 rows. So, to be safe and make sure our screen would look ok on any type of computer display; 640x480 could be used. If you want your app to work on mobile devices you will have to research the target devices display resolution. The pixel position of (0,0) would be the top left corner of our screen. *The pixel at (0, 0) is referred to as the **origin.***

Computer Screen Coordinates

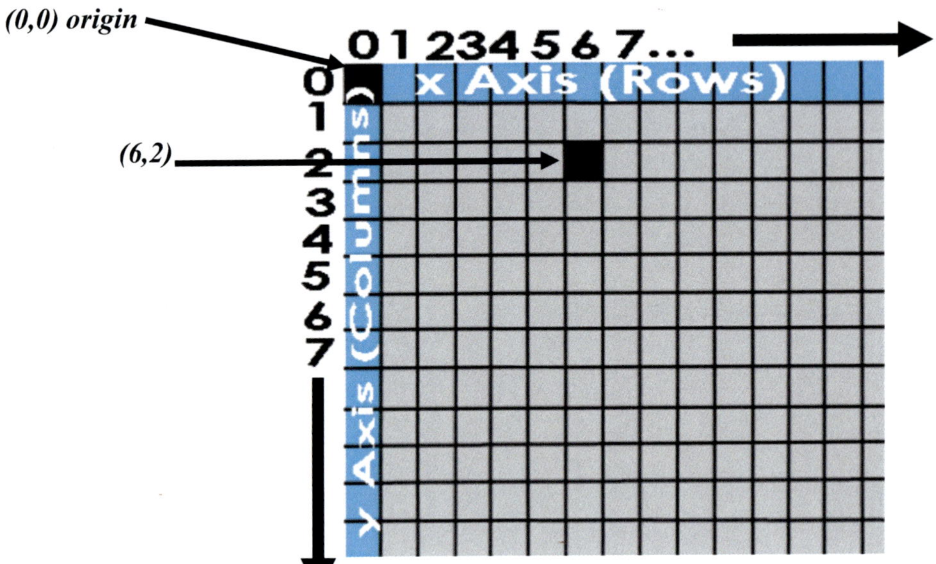

This image is not to scale, so just use your imagination.

Syntax for setting screen size in Pygame:

```
size = [640, 480]
screen = pygame.display.set_mode(size)
```

Or just enter the width and height as a tuple in double parenthesis:

```
screen=pygame.display.set_mode((640, 480))
```

Colors

Colors are defined in the computer world by numbers. Number values range from no color at zero to maximum for the computer screen at 255. *Red, Green, and Blue values, (**RGB**), define all the colors a computer screen can produce.* Huh? *They told me all colors were made from red, blue, and yellow in art class!?* This is true, but a screen is being painted with light, not paint. So, it works a little different. To a computer, when all three colors are off, (set to 0), we get black.

Basic color values:

```
black = (0, 0, 0)
```

```
white = (255, 255, 255)
```

```
red = (255, 0, 0)
```

```
blue = (0, 0, 255)
```

```
green = (0, 255, 0)
```

When all the colors are at maximum values, (255), we have white. When you want to control screen and other colors in your game, you will be setting the three values to define the colors you want. There are many free color picker tools on the internet if you want an easy way to pick a color and get its numerical value for your code.

You can add a fourth value for transparency. A t*ransparency value is referred to as the "**alpha value**."* Alpha values are also from 0 to 255. *Zero would be invisible* while *255 would no transparency, (the normal solid color).*

Animation

You can't make much of a game without the creating illusion of movement. You most likely already know that animation is creating the illusion of movement by using different pictures of the same thing in different positions or locations. Computer animation works the same way. The following is an example of a few of the frames for an animated Gif image. You can find this image at www.tooncat.com if you want to see it really move.

Jody Ginther ©2012

The point is that animated cartoons, gif images in web pages, and the illusion of movement within a game are all done by using a flashing sequence of images.

Movement in a game can be done by a sending a sequence of images to the computer screen, like frames in a movie or cartoon. The timing of the images appearing on the display will dictate the speed and smoothness of the movement.

The computer can also create animation by directly drawing images to the screen in a sequence. When the computer does the drawing, less memory is generally required than by using imported images.

For example, you could create a function that draws a simple rectangle in pixels and then redraws the rectangle in different pixels to create the illusion of movement.

You would define the coordinates for rows 1 and 2. Then the coordinates for rows 2 and 3; 3 and 4; 4and 5; and so on...to create a moving rectangle on the screen.

We will talk more about graphics and animation in the context of working on our source code for games in the next lessons. *Visit www.toonzcat.com for more about animation and graphic arts. You will also find free video tutorials and resources for Python and game making.*

To begin with a simple example we will start with another one that is provided with Pygame. But this time we are going to use our own modified code and the image provided by Pygame. Playing around will help you understand how things work, (and don't work).

Your first animation

Let's make an animation of our asteroid bouncing around in a window. Earlier versions of Python provided this code as an example for a bouncing ball. We don't have a ball, so we will use an asteroid. You can substitute your own image if you like. If your code does not work, make sure your files are in the proper directory and make sure every detail of the code has been typed exactly as in the example. Follow these steps:

1. *First, let's make a folder/directory under C:\Python32 (or your version of Python and the location you installed it), called "mycode."*

2. *Second make a copy of the asteroid.png image provided with this course, name it asteroid2.png and paste it into your folder, C:\Python32\mycode.*

3. *Open IDLE; carefully write the following code; and save it to your "mycode" folder:*

```
*Untitled*
File Edit Format Run Options Windows Help
black= (0,0,0)
import sys
import pygame
pygame.init()
size= width, height= 640, 480
speed= [1,1]
screen= pygame.display.set_mode(size)
pygame.display.set_caption("My First Game Window")
done= False
clock= pygame.time.Clock()
ball= pygame.image.load('asteroid2.png')
ballrect=ball.get_rect()
while done==False:
    for event in pygame.event.get():
        if event.type==pygame.QUIT:
            done=True

    screen.fill(black)
    clock.tick(270)
    ballrect= ballrect.move(speed)
    if ballrect.left < 0 or ballrect.right > width:
        speed[0]= -speed[0]
    if ballrect.top < 0 or ballrect.bottom > height:
        speed[1]= -speed[1]
    screen.blit(ball, ballrect)
    pygame.display.flip()

pygame.quit()
```

Run the code. If you did everything correctly, you will see a bouncing baby asteroid.
If you get an error, troubleshoot your code, and get it to work. First check all your syntax to make sure you did not make any errors in typing. Also make sure your image file name matches the name of your image exactly and that you placed it in the same folder as your .py file. Python will give you an exception message if it can't find the image. If you used a different image use the name of that image in your code rather than "asteroid2.png."

Important tip: If you ever need to know where Python is looking for modules and files just type:** "import sys; sys.path" **without the quotes and on the same line. This will present a list of directory paths that Python can see at the moment.

```
black= (0,0,0) # Define the color black for our background color
import sys  # Imports the sys module, containing special functions
import pygame # Imports the pygame module
pygame init() # Turns on or initializes pygame
```

```
size= width, height= 640, 480 # define size variable to set the size of
the display screen
speed= [1,1] # set a speed variable for movement
```

```
screen pygame.display.set_mode(size) # applying the size to the display
pygame.display.set_caption ( "My first game window" ) # creates a title
for our window
done = False # defining a done variable to break out of a loop
```

```
clock= pygame.time.Clock() # The clock statement is for controlling the
speed the screen will be updated.
```

```
ball= pygame.image.load( "asteroid2.png" ) # assign image loading to the
name "ball"
ballrect= ball.get_rect() # defining ballrect to provide a rectangle
surface for our image
```

The *Rect class* in Pygame provides the **rect** ***variable*** *to represent the rectangular dimensions of an image or sprite*, (we will talk about sprites later). Pygame places the image or sprite where the *x and y coordinates* are set.

```
while done == False: # beginning of our main game loop and establishing truth for breaking out of the loop. It means "while done is not true, continue reading this code..."
```

```
    for event in pygame.event.get(): # user causes keyboard event, (user does something).
        if event.type == pygame.QUIT: # quit pygame if user closes the window
            done = True # boolean trigger to exit this loop
```

```
    screen.fill(black) # fill the screen with the black we defined earlier as (0,0,0).
    clock.tick(270) # setting our refresh speed; like frame rates in an animation, (see notes below).
    ballrect= ballrect.move(speed) # setting movement speed of the rectangle under our image to [1,1] as defined earlier in "speed."
```

In making movies or animations this is the rate of frames per second that will be displayed to control the speed and appearance of the animation. A slow frame rate will cause choppy movement or snail-like movement. With computers it is more accurate to say *hertz per second,* but the convention is *fps*. Due to the variable speeds of monitors, graphic cards, and computer memory it is usually best to use the clock statement to control the speed of the animation. *You can play with this number to change the speed of the asteroid.*

```
    if ballrect.left < 0 or ballrect.right > width:
     speed [0]  = - speed [0]
```

The ballrect was defined earlier as our rectangle but the ".left" part is to indicate the integer value for the x coordinate of the left side of our rectangle on the screen. The ".right" part is to indicate the integer value for the x coordinate of the right side of our rectangle on the screen. So, this statement is saying; "if the left side of the rectangle becomes less than 0; or the right side greater than the width of the screen; then change the speed of the movement."

```
    if ballrect.top < 0 or ballrect.bottom > height:
     speed [1]  = - speed [1]
```

The ".top" part is to indicate the integer value for the y coordinate of the top of our rectangle on the screen. The ".bottom" part is to indicate the integer value for the y coordinate of the bottom of our rectangle on the screen. So, this statement is saying; "if the top of the rectangle becomes less than 0; or the bottom greater than the width of the screen; then change the speed of the movement."

```
screen.blit (ball, ballrect)
```

*To **blit** an image is to copy it to onto a **surface** object on the screen. A **surface** is a pre-defined 2D shape, like a rectangle, circle, ect.* The computer must be told to put the ball image onto the rectangle object and bring a copy to the screen. You could think of it like gluing a copy of a photo to a rectangular tile to display on screen.

```
pygame.display.flip() # see notes below
```

You **must** flip images to the screen when drawing objects. If you don't they won't appear on the screen. *"**Flip**" updates the entire screen and images to objects on the screen.*

REVIEW

Quiz 14:

14.1 Define the following terms and check your answers on the next page:

1. Pygame
2. SDL
3. Alpha value
4. rect variable
5. Flip

14.2 Answer the following questions:

1. *With a rectangle object the x axis would represent the _____ of the rectangle.*
2. *With a rectangle object the y axis would represent the _____ of the rectangle.*
3. *What are the coordinates of the two points below?*

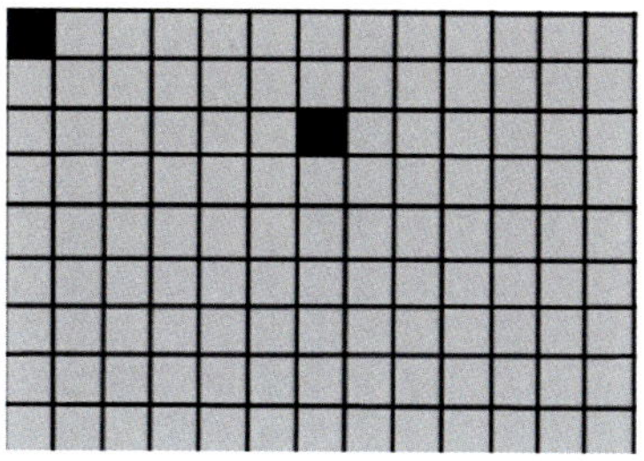

4. *Define the numeric value of the color black in a tuple.*
5. *Define the numeric value of the color white in a list.*

VOCABULARY

Pygame *is a Python extension library wrapped around the SDL library.*	
SDL *library, (Simple Direct Media Layer), is a cross-platform multi-media library that allows access to hardware such as a mouse, keyboard, joystick, etc.*	
coordinates*/location of a particular pixel is referred to by using a pair of numbers, separated by commas, within a set of parenthesis, (0,0).*	
alpha value *is the transparency value. Zero would be invisible* while *255 would no transparency, (solid color).*	
rect *variable* *represents the rectangular dimensions of an image or sprite*	
Flip *updates the entire screen and images to objects on the screen.*	

14.2 Answers:

1. *With a rectangle object the x axis would represent the* ***width*** *of the rectangle.*
2. *With a rectangle object the y axis would represent the* ***height*** *of the rectangle.*
3. *What are the coordinates of the two points below?* ***(0, 0) and (6, 2)***

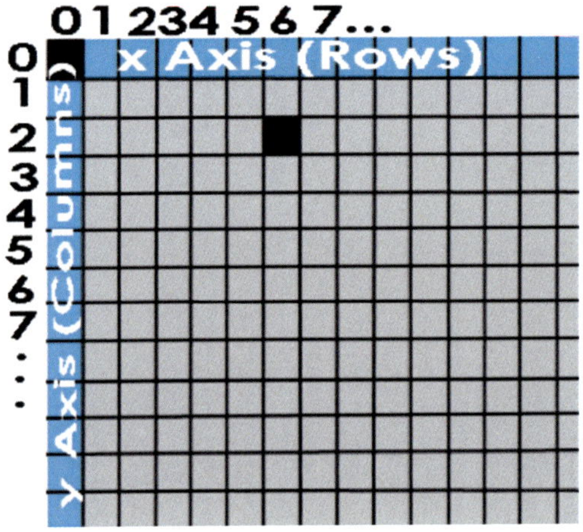

4. black = (0, 0, 0)
5. white = [255, 255, 255]

Lesson 15: Taking Control!

- CONTROLLERS
- KEYBOARD CONTROL
- MOUSE CONTROL
- CRUISING THROUGH SPACE

CONTROLLERS

***Controllers** are any of the devices we use to control things in a game, (keyboard, mouse, joystick, etc).* First, we will need an object to control. For simplicity we will have the computer draw a rectangle. We will begin by defining a function to draw our rectangle. Roll up your sleeves and get ready to type.

Syntax:

```
def draw_rectangle(screen, x, y):
```

Typing practice for perfect accuracy is one of the most important skills you must practice. The number one cause of errors in programming is in typing the syntax of the source code. Typing all the code in rather than copy and paste will also reinforce programming Python and Pygame into your memory. To help you avoid the copy and paste syndrome, most of the code in this course has been displayed within images rather than text. Our code is going to start getting longer and your typing accuracy is going to improve. If your programs don't work, go back and troubleshoot line by line.

KEYBOARD CONTROL

To set up keyboard functions in Pygame we often use the term "event" to describe something happening on the keyboard. We have to define what keyboard events the user will enter and what will happened when such event occurs. Whenever a keyboard event refers movement of some graphic(s) on the screen we will have to define the starting position of the graphic(s) and the speed of movement.

In this lesson we will place a rectangle on the screen and control it's movement with the arrow keys.
You have probably seen this type of thing in a number of arcade style games like ping pong or tennis.
If you are impatient to make a game of your own and want to challenge yourself; you can combine what you learn here and in Lesson 17 to make one of these games. For now let's look at the basics of keyboard events.

Carefully type in the following code and run it, (explanations are in the comments):

Untitled

File Edit Format Run Options Windows Help

```
import pygame
pygame.init() #initializing pygame

pygame.display.set_caption("My Keyboard Control") #Defining my screen title.
screen= pygame.display.set_mode((600, 500)) #Setting ths size of my screen.

#Defining colors:

black= (0, 0, 0)
green= (0, 255, 0)
red= (255, 0, 0)

def draw_background(screen): #Defining a function to create our background.
    screen.fill(green) #Set background color.

def draw_rectangle(screen, x, y): #Function to create our rectangle.
    pygame.draw.rect(screen, red, [0+x,0+y, 30, 25])

#We need a time reference to set speed of movement, (like miles per hour).
clock= pygame.time.Clock()

#Setting a beginning speed reference
x_speed= 0
y_speed= 0

#Setting beginning coordinates
x_coord= 30
y_coord= 30

done= False
while done== False: #Setting up our main/game loop.

    for event in pygame.event.get():
        if event.type== pygame.QUIT:
            done= True

        #When the user presses down on a key...
        if event.type== pygame.KEYDOWN:
            #Figure out that it is an arrow key and adjust the speed of movement
            if event.key== pygame.K_LEFT:
                x_speed= -7 # Setting speed on the x axis if the left arrow key
            if event.key== pygame.K_RIGHT:
                x_speed= 7 # Setting speed and direction of movement for the rig
            if event.key== pygame.K_UP:
                y_speed= -7 # Set speed and direction for the up arrow key.
            if event.key== pygame.K_DOWN:
                y_speed= 7 # Set speed and direction of the down arrow key.
```

(code continued on the following page)

```
        #Now we must define what happens when the user lets up on the key.
        if event.type== pygame.KEYUP:
            #If it is and arrow key reset the vectors back to zero.
            if event.key== pygame.K_LEFT:
                x_speed= 0
            if event.key== pygame.K_RIGHT:
                x_speed= 0
            if event.key== pygame.K_UP:
                y_speed= 0
            if event.key== pygame.K_DOWN:
                y_speed= 0

    #Move the rectangle object according to the defined speed.
    x_coord= x_coord + x_speed
    y_coord= y_coord + y_speed

    draw_background(screen)

    #Draw the rectangle to the screen at the defined coordinates.
    draw_rectangle(screen, x_coord, y_coord)

    #Flip the display.
    pygame.display.flip()
    clock.tick(60)

pygame.quit()
```

Ln: 78 Col: 0

If your code does not work go back and debug it. Check for typos and improper indentation. You should get the following results and be able to control the red rectangle with the arrow keys:

<u>Detective Questions:</u>

What happens if you delete this line and run the code? Can you predict what will happened before you try it? *Why does it do that?*

Play around with some of the numbers and re-run the code to see exactly what each line of code is doing. If you haven't already done it; indent some lines improperly and see what happens. have fun and see what kinds of cool errors you can produce. To be a good programmer, you must overcome the stress factor associated with errors, look at them like your occasionally irritating friends that you want to know anyway.

Mouse control

After you are successful, ***edit your source code*** *to make the rectangle work with mouse movement rather than the arrow keys by using the following code:*

```
import pygame
pygame.init()

pygame.display.set_caption("Mouse Power") #Defining my screen title.
screen= pygame.display.set_mode((300, 250)) #Setting ths size of my screen.

#Defining colors:

black= (0, 0, 0)
green= (0, 255, 0)
red= (255, 0, 0)

def draw_background(screen):
    screen.fill(black)
def draw_rectangle(screen, x, y):
    pygame.draw.rect(screen, red, [0+x,0+y, 30, 25])


clock= pygame.time.Clock()

done= False
while done== False:

    for event in pygame.event.get():
        if event.type== pygame.QUIT:
            done= True

    draw_background(screen)
    pos= pygame.mouse.get_pos()

    x= pos[0]
    y= pos[1]

    draw_rectangle(screen, x, y)

    #Flip the display.
    pygame.display.flip()
    clock.tick(60)

pygame.quit()
```

Move your mouse cursor around in the window that opens. The rectangle should now be attached to the movement of your mouse.

Questions for Detectives: What blocks of code were deleted compared to the "My Keyboard Control" algorithm? What code was added? Why?

**See PyGame's documentation to learn more about event handling code for using joysticks or other input devices in your games .*

CRUISING THROUGH SPACE

In this section we will learn how to control a moving image of a spaceship and cruise through the stars. First we will create the star field and then add our ship.

Write the following algorithm:

```
*Untitled*
File Edit Format Run Options Windows Help
import pygame
import random
pygame.init()

black= [0, 0, 0]
white= [255, 255, 255]
purple= [140, 45, 140]

screen= pygame.display.set_mode((640, 480))
pygame.display.set_caption('Star Field')

#Create some empty lists.
StarGroupOne= []
StarGroupTwo= []

# Loop 70 times and add a star at random x,y coordinates.
for i in range(70):
    x= random.randrange(0, 640)
    y= random.randrange(0, 640)
    StarGroupOne.append([x, y])
    StarGroupTwo.append([x, y])
clock= pygame.time.Clock()

#Loop until the user closes the window.
done= False
while done== False:
    for event in pygame.event.get():
        if event.type== pygame.QUIT:

            done= True

    screen.fill(black)
```

(continued)

This is part one of the code you need for a star field. Your algorithms are growing up. We are creating two groups of stars; one group of white stars and one group of purple stars to give it a more interesting appearance. Take a look at each line of code to make sure you understand it. Previous code explanations will not be repeated. If you missed something go back and review.

```
    #Process individual stars in our list.
    for i in range(len(StarGroupOne)):
        # Drawing some stars
        pygame.draw.circle(screen, purple, StarGroupOne[i], 2)
        pygame.draw.circle(screen, white, StarGroupTwo[i], 2)

        # Moving stars down by one pixel at a time.
        StarGroupOne[i][1] += 1
        StarGroupTwo[i][1] += 1

        #When our stars move off the bottom of the screen:
        if StarGroupOne[i][1] > 640:

            #Reset their location:
            y= random.randrange(-70, -10)
            StarGroupOne[i][1]= y

            x= random.randrange(0, 640)
            StarGroupOne[i][1]= x

        if StarGroupTwo[i][1] > 640:
            y= random.randrange(-70, -10)
            StarGroupTwo[i][1]= y

            x= random.randrange(0, 640)
            StarGroupTwo[i][1]= x

    pygame.display.flip()
    clock.tick(30)

pygame.quit()
```

Ln: 70 Col: 0

Play with the different values to see clearly which code does what. You can also delete, edit, and move lines of code around to see what happens. Of course, you should save your working code under a different name and play with copies in case you really mess it up.

You can also see that you could alter this code to simulate rain, snow, or other particles falling from the sky. Give it a try but save one version of this to edit and add our space ship to. Always experiment with copies of your source code rather than the original, *(I know, I often repeat myself; but most people need repetition to learn things well).*

If you really can't get yours to work, I did include a .py file of this code in the resources supplied with this course. You can run this "star_field" module if you need proof that this really works. Then go back to your code and find out what is wrong with it. If you got your code to run right on the first try; Congratulations! You are a rare breed and we mere mortals salute you.

Adding a Space Ship

We are ready to add a space ship to our star field. We will be using some of the same blocks of code that we used in our *keyboard control* code and the star field modules we wrote previously. We could just copy and paste these blocks into the appropriate locations and add the other necessary statements to add our image to the game. It would be better if you manually re-type the additional bocks of code for practice. Most of the new code statements are explained in the comments if they are not self-explanatory. Remember that you will have to move a copy of the "spaceship.png" image to the appropriate directory for Python to find it.

Create and run this"Space_cruise" module, ***(part 1 of 3):***

```
*Untitled*
File Edit Format Run Options Windows Help
import pygame
import random
pygame.init()

black= [0, 0, 0]
white= [255, 255, 255]
purple= [140, 45, 140]

screen= pygame.display.set_mode((640, 480))
pygame.display.set_caption('Space Cruise')
ship= pygame.image.load('spaceship.png') # Loading our space ship image.

#Function for placing our ship onto the screen.
def draw_ship(screen, x, y):
    screen.blit(ship, [0+x, 0+y, 30, 15])

# Speed (ppf), pixels per frame.
x_speed= 0
y_speed= 0

# Beginning ship coordinates placing it at the bottom middle of the screen.
x_coord= 225
y_coord= 350

#Create some empty lists.
StarGroupOne= []
StarGroupTwo= []

# Loop 70 times and add a star at random x,y coordinates.
for i in range(70):
    x= random.randrange(0, 640)
    y= random.randrange(0, 640)
    StarGroupOne.append([x, y])
    StarGroupTwo.append([x, y])
clock= pygame.time.Clock()
```

(continued)

Part 2 of 3:

```
#Loop until the user closes the window.
done= False
while done== False:
    for event in pygame.event.get():
        if event.type== pygame.QUIT:
            done= True

    screen.fill(black)

    #Process individual stars in our list.
    for i in range(len(StarGroupOne)):
        # Drawing some stars
        pygame.draw.circle(screen, purple, StarGroupOne[i], 2)
        pygame.draw.circle(screen, white, StarGroupTwo[i], 2)

        # Moving stars down by one pixel at a time.
        StarGroupOne[i][1] += 1
        StarGroupTwo[i][1] += 1

        #When our stars move off the bottom of the screen:
        if StarGroupOne[i][1] > 640:

            #Reset their location:
            y= random.randrange(-70, -10)
            StarGroupOne[i][1]= y

            x= random.randrange(0, 640)
            StarGroupOne[i][1]= x

        if StarGroupTwo[i][1] > 640:
            y= random.randrange(-70, -10)
            StarGroupTwo[i][1]= y

            x= random.randrange(0, 640)
            StarGroupTwo[i][0]= x

    # Indicate the event of a key arrow key press and speed.
    if event.type== pygame.KEYDOWN:
        if event.key== pygame.K_LEFT:
            x_speed= -7
        if event.key== pygame.K_RIGHT:
            x_speed= 7
```

(continued)

Pay close attention to the indentation of the "if" blocks. Why do you think they are not consistent? If you don't know re-read Lesson 1 on code blocks and indentation and ask yourself; "What does each group of code do as a unit?"

Part 3 of 3:

```
            if event.key== pygame.K_UP:
                y_speed= -7
            if event.key== pygame.K_DOWN:
                y_speed= 7

        # When the user lets the key come up.
        if event.type== pygame.KEYUP:
            if event.key== pygame.K_LEFT:
                x_speed= 0
            if event.key== pygame.K_RIGHT:
                x_speed= 0

            if event.key== pygame.K_UP:
                y_speed= 0
            if event.key== pygame.K_DOWN:
                y_speed= 0

        # Move ship according to set coordinates and speed.
        x_coord= x_coord+ x_speed
        y_coord= y_coord+ y_speed

        # Draw ship to defined coordinates.
        draw_ship(screen, x_coord, y_coord)

        pygame.display.flip()
        clock.tick(30)

pygame.quit()
```

Ln: 109 Col: 0

You made it!!! Does it work? Probably not the first time you typed it. Relax, go back and debug it. Do some comparisons with the code you made before that worked, check for typing errors, space, and indentation errors. Make sure your .py code is saved in the same folder as your image files.

Now, if you got it working; enjoy a cruise through space in your new space ship! Be careful, you can fly off the screen because we did not set limitations on the movement of our ship.

If you know how to make or alter png files in Photoshop, Corel, Gimp or some other image editor, feel free to make your own ship to fly around. Just replace the name the name of the png we used for your image and make sure your image is in the same folder as your module. We will look more at images, sprites, and image formats in the next lessons.

If you are dying of frustration and just can't get it to work load the Space_cruise.py file provided with this course to see how it should be working. Compare it to yours and fix your code.

REVIEW

Quiz 15:

15.1 Only one easy new term you probably already know for this lesson::

1. *Controllers*

15.2 Activity:

Activity: Before moving on to making an arcade style game out of this, study each line of code. Make a backup working copy; and a copy to play with.

1. *Change each value one by one and run the module to see what it does.*
2. *Move some code statements around to see what happens.*
3. *Rewrite or edit parts of the program to improve it according to your taste.*
4. *Write some notes on how the code statements and blocks work for yourself to refer to in the future.*

Vocabulary

Controllers *are any of the devices we use to control things in a game, (keyboard, mouse, joystick, etc).*

15.2 Activity:

Results will vary.

Lesson 16: The Game Plan

- TRANSLATING WORDS TO CODE
- PLANNING A GAME: PRE-ALPHA STAGE
- DEVELOPMENT STAGE 1
- ASSETS AND STUFF
- DIVIDE AND CONQUER
- SPRITE MAKING
- MAKING ASTEROIDS

TRANSLATING WORDS TO CODE

What will our program do? We should write a brief description of our game plan.
When designing a program, you will first write a program description. You will have to translate your program description into computer code. For example: "Player walks or runs to choose a car. He chooses the red car."

The ***nouns*** suggest classes we could create:
*"**Player** walks or runs to choose a **car**. He chooses the red **car**."*

The ***verbs*** could suggest methods for that class:
*"Player **walks** or **runs** to choose a car. He chooses the red car."*
We could create a class for the player and methods to define walking and running speeds.

The ***adjectives*** could suggest attributes for that class:
*"Player walks or runs to choose a car. He chooses the **red** car."*

Brief description of our game:

It will be an entertaining 2D space shooting game. The player will fly through space in his ***spaceship shooting asteroids*** with a ***plasma ball***. The object of the game is to shoot as many asteroids as possible without hitting one.

Notice the nouns, adjectives, and verbs for later development. Ha! And you thought all those English grammar classes were useless!

PLANNING A GAME: PRE-ALPHA STAGE

Before you can make a game, you need to collect the assets and other elements to make it. You will need background images, objects, other visual elements, and sound files. Let's make a shopping list of the things we will need for our program. You can find your own assets and image files, create your own, or use those provided with this course.

We need:

- A spaceship
- Small panel or display for displaying points.
- Asteroids *(We can actually get away with only one and clone it.)*
- A star field background. *(We can use the one we already created.)*
- Plasma ball
- Explosions
- Appropriate sound files *(Provided with the files in this course; if you don't have them you can find some on the internet.)*
- All source code for the game. *(Next lesson)*
- A way to package and create installation files if we want to distribute it. *(Later lesson.)*

Who will use it? Children to adults who like arcade style space games.

What kind of computer systems? For the purposes of this course, we will be writing on Windows XP but the game should work on other Windows operating systems. Our Python code is compatible on many platforms, but Pygame is for Windows so we limited ourselves to Pygame compatible operating systems by choosing it.

Who will work on this project? One lone programmer, so we will keep it simple. If you really wanted to make this game for a larger market and to be more interesting, you could arrange a team of developers. It would be best if you get some practice going it alone before working on a team project, *(unless required to do so by your teacher).*

What versioning system will we use? We are now in the *pre-Alpha stage* which involves everything we do until our first version is ready for testing. We will then do Alpha version testing and decide on the final features to *freeze*. The final Alpha version is the one we feel is complete. We can then think of how we want to create a package and installation file. If we have some friends who are willing, we can go to the Beta version by releasing it for outside testing. We will refer to this version released to the outside world for testing, as "Beta version 0.9.0." Revised versions of it will be called "0.9.1; 0.9.2," and so on. Finally, listening to feedback and doing some more revising; we can release what we will call our "release version 1.0.0" of this game. We will change the numbers later according to minor or major updates or bug fixes.

Development Stage 1

Detailed description:

We will need to develop a level one solution based on more details of the game. But first, we will think of more detailed descriptions of the game assets that will be needed.

Ok, let's choose a name and give more details of the game to clarify what game assets will be needed. We will keep it simple and just call it *"Space Cruise."*

First, let's be a little more detailed and clear about each asset in the game. *What view will the player be playing from?* Will it be a first-person view; a view from above; side-view; or a view from behind the space ship? *To use your current knowledge and code from previous lessons we will choose a 3rd person view from the top.*

More detailed description:

The player is *flying through* ***stars*** in a ***spaceship*** dodging and shooting ***asteroids***. ***Points*** are made when he *shoots asteroids with his* ***Plasma ball***. Asteroids ***explode*** when shot and on *impact with the ship*. The *game is over if the ship collides with an asteroid and explodes.*

The purpose of writing a more detailed description at this point is to focus on the *assets, (things),* you will need in the game. It also provides a place to start for planning what your blocks of code are going to do. For now, forget the coding until the next lesson. We will focus on the assets and game plan.

Assets And Stuff

For now, let's forget about the optional stuff for a higher level game. In the detailed description I underlined the assets we will need to collect or create before we get started. So, we will need the following assets:

- Spaceship
- Asteroids
- Points indicator
- Star field background
- Explosions
- Plasma ball

Optional considerations for a later and more advanced version:

- *We could load separate graphics of our spaceship window to visually display damage to our ship.*
- *We could create an entry box to enter a players name, and save his game.*
- *We could keep a high scores record.*
- *We could add asteroids of different sizes and speeds.*
- *We could add alien ships that shoot back.*
- *We could create different levels of difficulty or speed for the player to choose.*
- *We could add a fuel or life indicator and a way to get fuel or life during battle.*
- *We could add a mpeg movie clip at the beginning of the game.*
- *We could get really ambitious and make it all 3D.*
- *We could add joystick control for flying the ship in different directions through space...(and sell car-sick medicine at a discount).*

When you finish this course you can continually improve or change the "Space Cruise' game or write an entirely new one from scratch. You will have to further your practice and knowledge of Python and Pygame to continue your growth as a programmer.

Divide and Conquer

We already determined what assets we will need to make our game. Let's divide this list into types and think about how they will be created. We could go online and find assets to use in our games, but we would have to consider ownership and license limitations if we are going to use anything we did not create. Whether portions of code, graphics, or sound, you must consider the legal aspects of using them. Some assets are provided free online, but you can't guarantee they are really free unless you can trust the source. We will create some of our own assets in this course to avoid these problems and also to teach you how to make your own.

Review and break down the list one by one:

- ~~Spaceship~~ *(got one)*
- Asteroids
- Asteroid explosion or blackout
- Points indicator
- ~~Star field background~~ *(got one)*
- Plasma ball
- Ship explosion and/or blackout

Spaceship:
We already got our "spaceship.png" to use or alter. In reality we already have all the assets provided with this course already, but we will pretend we don't to walk you through the process of making or selecting them.

Asteroid:
The asteroid will be a combination of coding and some graphics. We will need to make an asteroid sprite. Don't worry, we will define sprites shortly.

For now, just trust me. We will need to do some coding and can add that part to our "code to write" list in the next lesson. We will make a list of "*sprites" to make* and add an asteroid to the list.

Score Indicator:
Add this to our "GUI Stuff" list. We can do it with a GUI or on screen. We have to decide if we want to use an onscreen indicator of points, like a digital watch type display or we want some nice graphical interface. If it will be using a GUI we will have to bring in Easy GUI, Tkinter or some other module to create it.

Star Field Background:
We can use or alter our code for the "Space_cruise" module.

Plasma ball:
We will create or find a sprite of a ball of plasma, code to make it move, and maybe sound files for it.

Explosions:
The asteroid explosion will be listed in our "*sprites"* list. We will code a "blackout" to indicate the ship has exploded. To simplify coding we will choose to make only one kind of explosion in this version of the game.

So, our list of lists of things to do or get is:

<u>General Code to Write (we will detail code tasks later</u>:

- ~~Spaceship movement with arrow keys,~~ *(got it)*
- Asteroid *(movement)*
- ~~Star field background,~~ *(got it)*
- Ship blackout *(or code and image for explosion)*
- *Point system and display*
- *Sounds and music*

<u>Gui Stuff:</u>
- Score indicator

<u>Sprites:</u>
- Asteroid
- Plasma ball

<u>Sound and video:</u>
- ~~Sound files~~ *(provided)*
- ~~Music files~~

- ~~Mpeg files~~ *(not needed unless we include movie clips for intros)*

Note: To simplify version one of this game we will skip adding mpeg intros and explosions to our game. I will introduce you to adding and looping sound. Explosions and video files can be added later if you choose to add them. (Reminder: Files and Assets for this course are at www.toonzcat.com).

Sprite Making

What's a sprite? No, to programmers it is not a soft drink. But, I'm glad you asked because you are about to learn how to make them. *A **sprite** is a picture, or an image that can be animated.* Remember that movement is an illusion. To create the illusion of movement, multiple frames of the object in different positions are created and flipped through to simulate a moving object. *Sprites are the objects, characters, explosions, and things that usually move around in your game.* You can make a single image to rotate and move around or you can make a *"sprite sheet"* which is a series of images on one sheet, (one page of images), that will be read in sequence. A 2D character walking would be an example. Each small movement is a separate image on the same page. If we made a sprite sheet of the frog dance image it would look something like this:

For this sprite sheet to work well, the black outlines on the frog would have to be more clear. This would help the computer distinguish it from the background color. To see this really move go to www.toonzcat.com.

Sprites have two main elements to consider. You must think about the space the sprite will occupy on the screen and the image that will occupy that space. *The space a sprite or image will occupy on the screen is referred to as the **surface.*** Remember that when we defined the ship variable in our Space Cruise module we used the syntax:

```
>>> ship = pygame.image.load("spaceship.png")
```

The pygame.image.load( ) function loads the spaceship.png image to a surface object. PyGame's default image type is uncompressed BMP, (bitmap), files. We later used screen.blit to *blit* the image to the screen. In other words ***blitting** is making a surface object with a copy of the image onto the screen. To "blit" just means to copy and move your image to the screen.*

PyGame can use other image file types; we will use .png files. PyGame uses an image class to load images as surface objects. The Surface class allows the manipulation of the images in screen space.

Before we get into programming and manipulating sprites, we must have the images we will be using. As mentioned, (and repeated so you get it), you could search the internet for images with an appropriate license, or you could create the images ourselves so you don't have any licensing restrictions.

So, how do you make sprites? You could use any graphics program that can create BMP or png images. Paint, Corel Draw, PhotoShop, or whatever graphics drawing program you prefer. Even if you don't use Gimp, read through the next section so you understand the process of creating sprites.

A free open source program called Gimp is very useful for most images. Gimp is not always as easy to use if you are not familiar with it, but it is a powerful program once you get used to it. http://www.gimp.org/downloads

Making Asteroids

We already decided that we will need the following sprites:

Sprites:

- ***Asteroid***
- Plasma ball

We will begin by making an asteroid image. If you are not interested in an overview of how to create assets or are not happy with the way your asteroid looks, you can just use the asteroid.png file provided.

When we create an image for a game, we need to consider the colors in our game. *Why?* Because when you make the image of the asteroid or other asset, your image is painted into a square, (surface object), like a piece of tile. We don't want a square picture of an asteroid flying around our space ship; so we must make the background of the asteroid picture seem invisible. We can do this by making the background of our asteroid image the same color as the background of our game; make an image with no background if the file type supports it; or in Pygame we can designate a color to be *"transparent."* For this option, we need to choose a solid color we can get the RGB code for and a color we will not be using for other game assets or background images. If we create or have an asset with no background, such as our .png file of the space ship, then we don't have to worry about it.

You wouldn't want this flying at you: *Ahh...this is much better:*

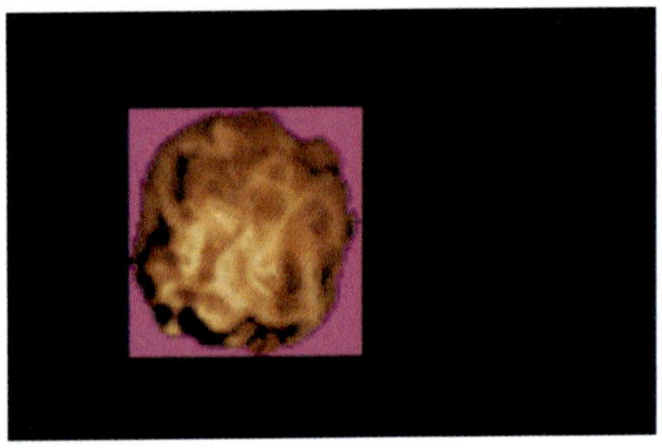

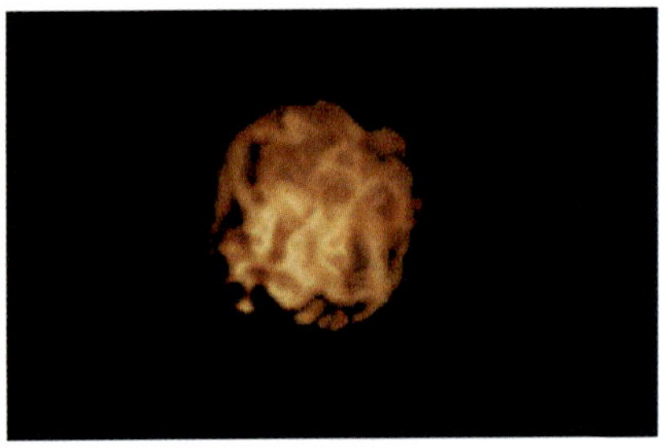

How you make an asteroid will vary depending upon your graphics program. However, I will list the basic steps:

1. Open Gimp or your favorite graphics program and create a new file 80x80 pixels. We must consider the influence of pixel size and memory usage when making assets.
2. Set the background color to transparent.
3. Select a circle with your circle select tool and use your bucket or fill tool to fill it with a brown-like color.
4. Use the paintbrush tool to paint some pits and bumps on your asteroid.
5. Erase some of the edges so you don't have a perfect circle.
6. Smear or soften the edges to get a more 3D like appearance.
7. Save your file as a .png or .bpm image.

You should try to end up with something that looks like an asteroid:

When creating graphics for a game; *choose a specific style*. *Do you want; arcade style; fantasy; cartoon looking; slightly realistic; very realistic?* Make your images consistent to the style you want to present in your game.

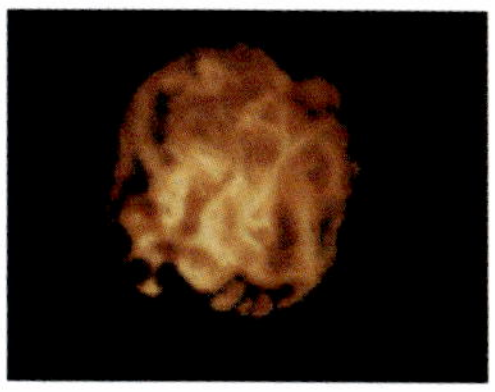

You just made your first game asset! Or not, (if you are using the files provided). Either way we can not cross this asset off of our list of assets to create.

Sprite images:

- ~~Asteroid~~
- **Plasma Ball**

Now you can create the other images on your own or use the ones provided with this course. There are no legal restrictions to using the assets provided with this course if they are used for non commercial or educational purposes. However, if you use these assets commercially, all I ask is that you link to the www.tooncat.com site and credit the graphics artist, *(that would be me)*. Once you have collected all your assets you are ready to start coding the rest of the game.

Being a graphic artist is yet another skill that programmers may need. This is a marriage of art and science. You don't need to be a great artist to create great games. Just look at the game assets in some of the most famous games in history and you will find some pretty lame 2D graphics and art. Some of the limitations on using quality graphics are limited memory and the desired game speed. These limitations have caused many games to be created with poor graphics. This can be an advantage to you as a programmer if you don't want to spend countless hours creating the many assets needed for your game. You must also consider the limitations of the devices your games are targeting. Mobile device graphics have far different requirements than hot gaming computers. Creating great graphic arts is beyond the scope of this course, refer often to www.toonzcat.com for more information.

REVIEW

Quiz 16:

16.1 Define the following terms and check your answers on the next page:

1. Sprite
2. Surface
3. Blitting

16.2 Answer the following questions:

1. What stage(s) of software design are we at this point?
2. What are the three ways we can make the background of our images invisible?

VOCABULARY

sprite *is a picture, or an image that can be animated. Sprites are the objects, characters, explosions, and things that usually move around in your game.*
surface *is the space a sprite or image will occupy on the screen*
blitting *is making a surface object with a copy of the image onto the screen.*

16.2 Answers:

1. Pre-Alpha
2. What are the three ways we can make the background of our images invisible?
    1) Create a .png or other file type that allows images with no background.
    2) Make the background of the image the same as the screen background.
    3) Choose a special background color, RGB value, to designate as transparent in the source code.

Lesson 17: Space Shooter Code

- **Final Assets**
- **GUI Stuff**
- **Code To Write**
- **Back to Class(es)**

Final Assets

Now we take a look again at any other assets we may need to make the game and make some decisions. We were also considering the following:

<u>*Gui Stuff:*</u>

- Score indicator

There are a number of ways we can make a score indicator. We can code a numerical display directly to the screen or we could use some type of GUI. We must first plan the score indicators details.

- How many digits do we want to display?
- Should it update in real time or in certain time intervals?
- Do we want the user to be able to save his game and score to continue playing the game later?
- Do we want to make a GUI to display and save high scores?
- What are the criteria for earning or losing points?

<u>*Sound and video:*</u>

- Sound files
- Music files
- Mpeg files (*if we include movie clips for intros)*

To collect or create our sound, music, and video files we must also make a number of decisions.

- Exactly what sound effects do we need?
- What music do we want and how do we want to "loop" it to save on memory?
- Do we record these files ourselves or buy the rights to them from others?
- What file formats should we use?

GUI Stuff

You were already introduced to Easy GUI and Tkinter. We could create some fancy GUI stuff to add to this game. We could add entry boxes for the player's name; make a fancy score indicator; or make some creative looking windows to add to our game. Since we are trying to keep the code as simple as possible in this game, we will not use a GUI for our score indicator. We will just create a score display directly to the screen by writing some code for it. If you want to add GUI elements to later versions of the game, you are encouraged to do so. So, we will just add this task to our "code to write" list.

Sound and Video

We will add some sound effects and music to our game. We will skip adding video files for now. The method used to add video is similar but can radically increase the size of your game. You can easily do this later if you like. I have supplied the required sound files with this course so you don't have to create or find them. If you don't have access to the sound files you may find some that are appropriate on the internet. So, you now have all the assets required for the game you will create.

Remember to get creative later and add a mpeg video to introduce the game or display credits at the end. Music loops would also add a nice dimension to the game. Just make sure you abide by license requirements for any assets used to avoid costly punishments, (keep your assets out of trouble).

Our assets list is now complete:

~~*Gui Stuff:*~~

- Score indicator (will code)

Sound and video:

- ~~Sound files~~ (provided)
- ~~Music files~~ (provided)
- ~~Mpeg files~~ (not used)

Let's get to designing and writing the code for the first version of our game!

Code To Write

General Code to Write (problems to solve):

- ~~Spaceship movement with arrow keys,~~ *(got it)*
- ~~Star field background,~~ *(got it)*
- Asteroids *(movement and explosions)*
- Asteroid explosion or blackout on collision with ship or plasma ball
- Plasma balls shooting at asteroids and exploding or blacking out on impact.
- Ship explosion or blackout on collision with asteroids
- Adding Sound
- Score Indicator
- Blackout, end of game, or restart.

We already have the code blocks we need for the first two problems in our "Space Cruise" module. We will begin adding each of the solutions to a copy of that module.

1st Level Solutions:

1. Asteroids appear in increasing numbers at the top of the screen and fly towards the player.
2. Asteroids blackout when they collide with the ship or a plasma ball hits them.
3. Plasma balls are shot from the ship.
4. You can hear the sound of the flying ship, laser shots, and explosions.
5. Points are scored every time the user shoots and asteroid.
6. Game ends when the ship is hit by an asteroid and final points are displayed.

Note: To keep things more simple we will use "blackouts" rather than "explosions." Good explosions require the use of a sequence of images.

2nd Level Solutions:

- *Asteroids* ***appear*** in *increasing numbers* at ***random*** *positions* at the top of the screen.
- *Asteroids* ***fly*** *towards the bottom of the screen.*
- ***If*** the asteroids ***collide*** with nothing they ***fly*** off the screen.
- *Asteroids* **blackout** when they **collide** with the ship ***or if*** they **collide** with *plasma balls.*
- *Ship* **shoots** plasma balls *towards* the asteroids when the player ***hits the spacebar***.
- The ***sound*** *of the space ship* continues in a ***loop*** *until* the ship *explodes*.
- You can ***hear*** the *zap of the laser* as the player shoots plasma balls from the ship.
- You can ***hear*** *explosions* ***if*** a plasma ball ***collides with*** an asteroid, ***or if*** an asteroid ***collides with*** the space ship.
- ***Points*** are ***scored*** and ***displayed*** on a *point indicator* ***if*** *plasma ball collides with an asteroid* or ***else*** *no points* are added to the *total score*.
- ***If*** the ship ***collides*** with an asteroid they *explode/blackout* together.
- *Final points* are ***displayed*** and the ***game ends***.

First we have to talk programming lingo and turn all actions in our solution to code statements we need to write. Pay attention to all relative verbs in your solution. We used the word "collide" rather than "hit" to point out that we have to code some "collisions" into our game.

Remember our general English guidelines

The *nouns* suggest classes we could create:
*"**Player** walks or runs to choose a **car**. He chooses the red **car**."*

In this case the *nouns* we need to consider creating classes for are:

1. asteroids
2. ship
3. plasma ball

We could also make a class for the star field background. *How do we decide what should be a class?* If functions, attributes, and methods are going to be unique for that object, then a class should be created. Another purpose of a class is to prevent unwanted behavior. If a statement or a function is to apply only to that object; we should place that statement or function within that object's class.

The <u>*verbs*</u> can suggest methods for that class:
*"Asteroid image **flies** towards the bottom of the screen and **disappear** off the screen.*

The <u>*adjectives*</u> can suggest attributes for that class:
*"Player chooses the **gold** spaceship."*

However, an attribute or method may indicate *what to do with a particular object.* You have been using the _init_ method to initialize objects within a class object. Remember that in Python everything is an object. You can think of a class as your classy car object, and the _init_ method as the key method for turning on the engine object.

We can think of the code to write as the problems we will be solving. It can help to make a list of specific problems you will be solving and then write all possible solutions for those problems.

Programmers must always think in terms of <u>problems and solutions.</u>

In this game we will use a star field as our background and use the code we already created for the "Space Cruise" module. So, in this case it is not really; "code to write" but is; "code to modify." It is time to get your hands dirty. This is a *"just do it"* lesson.

<u>*Just do it! Exercise 18.1:*</u>

So, open the <u>*Space cruise*</u> module in IDLE or your favorite editor, make a working copy, and then let's have a look at our first problems to solve:

*Asteroids **appear** in increasing numbers* at ***random*** *positions* at the top of the screen.
*Asteroids **fly** towards the bottom of the screen.*
If the asteroids ***collide*** with nothing they ***fly*** off the screen.

We already imported the random module, so no need to do that again. Before we start writing classes let's attach our asteroid image to a surface object, set coordinates, and blit it to the screen to see what it looks like. *Change the name of the module and the window label to; "Space Shoot."*

Before looking at the solution, see if you can place the following code into the right locations, run the module, and get the asteroid to appear:

```
asteroid = pygame.image.load("asteroid.png")
```

```
def draw_asteroid(screen, x, y):
```

```
x_coordtop=225
```

```
y_coordtop=10
```

```
draw_asteroid(screen, x_coord, y_coordtop)
```

Did you get good results? If not, check every detail of your code. Is your typing ok? How about the number of spaces? Did you miss any punctuation? Did you brush your teeth? Wash your hands? Wipe? Use paper? If you placed your code in the right locations and did everything correctly you should get something like this:

Beautiful! One more problem solved! ***Now we have to:***

1. Get copies of our asteroid to appear in random locations.
2. Get the number of asteroids to increase.
3. Get the asteroids to move to the bottom of the screen.
4. Get the asteroids to fly off the screen if they are not destroyed.

The following highlighted code should be added to your module. Always save more than one copy of your modules as you are working in case you really mess something up properly. Sometimes going back to a previously saved version is easier than debugging what you changed.

```
import pygame
import random
pygame.init()

black = [ 0, 0, 0]
white = [255,255,255]
purple = [215, 0, 215]

screen = pygame.display.set_mode((640, 480))
pygame.display.set_caption("Space Shoot")
ship = pygame.image.load("spaceship.png")
asteroid = pygame.image.load("asteroid2.png") #image to surface
object

def draw_item(screen,x,y):
    screen.blit(ship, [0+x , 0+y, 30, 15])

def draw_asteroid(screen, x, y):
    screen.blit(asteroid,[0+x , 0+y, 30, 15])

# Speed in pixels per frame,(ppf).
x_speed=0
y_speed=0

# Beginning coordinates placing ship at the bottom middle of the
screen
x_coord=225
y_coord=350
x_coordtop=225 # For placing the asteroid at the top middle of the
screen
y_coordtop=10
```

To just get the asteroid to appear, we don't have to mess with the middle of our main loop. Let's jump to the end of our source code to have a look at other necessary changes.

```
        # Draw the item (ship) to the screen at our coordinates.
    draw_item(screen, x_coord, y_coord)

        # Draw the asteroid to the screen at our coordinates.
    draw_asteroid(screen, x_coordtop, y_coordtop)

    pygame.display.flip()
    clock.tick(30)

pygame.quit ()
```

At this point we just copied and altered the code statements for the ship. We attached the asteroid.png to a surface object; defined a function that will blit the image to the screen; and set new starting coordinates for the asteroid. If you succeeded in getting your images to the screen you are ready for the next step.

Reminder: The `clock.tick()` function sets the number of *ticks* for an imaginary clock. ***Ticks*** represent increments of time, (named after the movement of the second hand on the old mechanical clocks). Ticks are units of seconds represented by floating point numbers. You guessed it! The `clock.tick()` function is used to influence timing of events.

Back to Class(es)

Sprite Class

To manage our assets better we are going to create some classes. Remember that the *nouns* in our solutions can often indicate the need for defining a class. In this case we will be looking at our asteroids, ship, and our plasma ball for consideration. PyGame comes with a sprite class that automates many tasks regarding sprites. By writing and using Pygame sprite classes we can skip a lot of algorithm design. Keep in mind, the code used is not the best way or the only way to solve our problems. Most of these solutions were chosen to help you understand the making of a game based on what you know so far. There are also intentional problems in the game for you to develop solutions for and solve on your own. Developing and solving your own games and solutions will give you the confidence to really believe you are a programmer reaching higher and higher levels in your quest.

Repeat after me;

"I am a programmer...
I am a programmer...
I am a programmer..."

When I count to ten you will wake up; quit being weird; and get back to work.

When do we use the sprite class in Pygame?

- *When you will use many instances of the same object on the screen.*
- *When you need to track objects for collision detection.*
- *When objects have similar functions or code that could cause unwanted behavior.*
- *When you plan to move, share, or reuse the class object in other modules.*
- *When you need a lot of control over individual object instances or groups.*
- *When you want to *increase speed, (of writing and running code for sprites).*

```
class Name(pygame.sprite.Sprite):

 def __init__(self):
     pygame.sprite.Sprite.__init__(self)
     self.image = pygame.image.load("my_image.png").convert()
     self.rect = self.image.get_rect()
     self.rect.center = (300, 200)
 Your own stuff.
```

When should we not use the sprite class?

- *When objects don't share much code.*
- *When you rarely or never need multiple instances of the object on the screen.*
- *When loops are event based.*
- *When the objects movement is always event or user controlled rather than automated.*
- *When we have read too many anti-class articles written by programmers who feel using classes is a bad way to do things. (We won't get into that debate but you should know the issue exists.)*

Before writing our sprite class we will have a closer look Pygame's sprite module, (pygame.sprite). Some of the code explanations and concepts have already been introduced. But, for the sake of review, reinforcement, and better understanding some will be repeated in the context of writing classes for our sprites.

The sprite class will make it easier to create solutions for problems like collision detection. The computer needs to know when two of our game assets hit each other and what to do about it. The easiest way to do this is to put these assets into classes and use the sprite module functions spritecollide and groupcollide.

Many of our objects will share behaviors and attributes. If we write a class for these shared behaviors we needn't repeat writing the same the code in every class object. So, let's create a "***sprite***" class to define common behaviors that will pop up in all of these objects.

Let's look at a generic sprite class design and break it down:

1. As usual, we define a class using the word "class" followed by the name we want to give it using CamelCase style syntax.
2. Within the parenthesis is the Pygame sprite class and all it's power.
3. We then use initialize _init_( ) to announce it's arrival; or turn on this instance of our class and to initialize Pygame's sprite class. *(Remember the ancient proverb; "It is difficult to drive one's car before you turn it on").*
4. Remember that "image" refers to a copy of your original image file; while rect refers to the place or rectangle it will be bound to. Here we are loading a copy of our image file into self.image. (This is the simplest, but not always the best way to load images.) The .convert( ) is optional, but speeds things up by making a pixel format of our image friendlier to the display. It is generally better to use it because it helps the image match the screen being used.
5. We are getting the image and rectangle to bind to one another until death do they part
6. We are setting up the starting location of our rectangle.
7. This is where we go back to the *verbs* in our solutions description. What behaviors and qualities do we need for this class object?

> *Asteroids* ***appear*** in *increasing numbers* at ***random*** *positions* at the top of the screen.
> *Asteroids* ***fly*** *towards the bottom of the screen.*
> ***If*** the asteroids ***collide*** with nothing they ***fly*** off the screen.

Now we need to think of how to reword these sentences into a workable level two solution. We need to add more details and think of ways to optimize our code. We could create many asteroids or we could make one asteroid with many copies of it to reduce the amount of memory that will be required. We need to think about which objects need collision detection and how to make our objects disappear from the screen. When objects collide or explode we need them to "blackout."

Before going on to the next page, write a possible level two solution for behaviors and qualities we just listed in number seven. There are different approaches to writing solutions. The important points are that the solutions contain all the qualities and behaviors required; and that the sentences clarify your approach to writing the code.

Asteroid Class

Our level two solution helps us with the details of our asteroid class:

1. *We need copies of the asteroid image to appear in increasing numbers at random positions at the top of the screen.*
2. *Asteroid images need to fly towards the bottom of the screen and disappear.*
3. *Asteroids need to blackout on impact with the ship or the plasma ball. We need collision detection and blackouts.*
4. *Asteroid collisions with the plasma ball should result in the accumulation of points.*

Write your own level two solutions for the other classes. What other "classes" should we create? *Remember that the special behaviors and attributes of game objects can indicate the need for a class:*

- The ***ship*** will require individual control input from the player.
- The *plasma balls* will shoot from the laser on the ship sprite and follow the position of the laser on the ship. The plasma balls will also require input from the player. Since the laser is part of the ship sprite image, a class should be created to represent the behavior of the plasma balls. We will refer to this class as the ***"Laser Class."***

All of our objects need to be tracked for collision detection and we need to keep track of rectangles for everything to be drawn to. There are many different approaches. For our game we will create the following classes:

Classes:

- ***Sprite Class***
- ***Rectangle Class***
- ***Asteroid Class***
- ***Spaceship Class***
- ***Laser Class***

The Sprite Class and the Rectangle Class will establish some of common behaviors and positions of our sprites. Remember that the size of the rectangles will influence where collisions will take place; not the image itself. Once you have written the code for the game, you can play around with changes in rectangle size coordinates and collision detection code to refine the game play.

Read through the following possible solutions. Don't worry if you can't understand all of it at this point. If you understand almost nothing, go back and review the previous lessons. If you understand most of it, congratulations! You are well on your way to being an independent programmer. The complete code will presented later for you to type into your module. Although I will provide code for a functional game; it will not be written in perfect form and will need further development by you to become a great game. Some problems will be left for you to solve. In this part of the lesson just read through each section of the following code. Think about the creation and purposes of these classes:

```
class Asteroids(Sprite):
        def __init__(self,x,y):

Sprite.__init__(self,asteroid_image[random.randrange(0,len(asteroid_image))])
                self.x = x
                self.y = y
                sprite_list.append(self)
                self.asteroid=True
```

Remember to distinguish "Sprite" with a capital from "sprite."

```
class Sprite:
        def __init__(self,image_path="data/asteroid.png"):
                self.direction = 1
                self.x = 0
                self.y = 0
                self.image = pygame.image.load(image_path)
                self.width = 30
                self.height = 30

        def update(self):
                        if self.x < 0:
                                self.direction = 1
                        elif self.x > screenW:
                                self.direction = -1
                        if self.y < screenH:
                            self.x += 1
                            self.y += 1
```

```
class Rectangle: # And a function to deal with intersecting rectangles
def __init__(self,x,y,width,height):
                self.left = x
                self.top = y
                self.bottom = y+height
                self.right = x+width

def rectangular_intersection(rect1,rect2):
        return not (rect1.right < rect2.left or rect1.left > rect2.right or
        rect1.bottom < rect2.top or rect1.top > rect2.bottom)
```

`rect.left` – refers to the integer value of the x coordinate on the left side of the rectangle.

`.right` – to the right side.

`.top` – to the y coordinate at the top

`.bottom` – to the y coordinate at the bottom of the rectangle.

The Spaceship class is written next, but the "keyboard" events that will allow you to fly your spaceship will be added to the game loop later in the code.

```
class Spaceship(Sprite):

        def __init__(self):
                Sprite.__init__(self,"data/spaceship.png")
                self.x = screenW/2
                self.y = screenH-130
                self.x_speed = 0
                self.y_speed = 0
        def update(self):
                self.x = self.x+self.x_speed
                self.y = self.y+self.y_speed
                if self.x < 0:
                        self.x -= self.x_speed
                if self.x > screenW-30:
                        self.x -= self.x_speed
                for sprite in sprite_list:
                        if sprite != self and not hasattr(sprite,"plasma"):
                                self_rectangle =
Rectangle(self.x,self.y,self.width,self.height)
                                other_rectangle =
Rectangle(sprite.x,sprite.y,sprite.width,sprite.height)
                                if
rectangular_intersection(self_rectangle,other_rectangle)and collision == False:
                                        global done
                                        done=True
```

In this class we made some functions to influence speed, updating, and collision detection.

Laser Class

Finally, our Laser Class:

```
class Laser(Sprite):
        def __init__(self):
                Sprite.__init__(self,"data/plasmaball.png")
                self.plasma = True
                laser.play()
        def update(self):
                global shots, score
                kill_list = []
                self_rectangle = Rectangle(self.x,self.y,self.width,self.height)
                for sprite in sprite_list:
                        if hasattr(sprite,"asteroid"):
                                other_rectangle =
Rectangle(sprite.x,sprite.y,sprite.width,sprite.height)
                                if
rectangular_intersection(self_rectangle,other_rectangle):
                                        kill_list.append(sprite)
                                        boom.play()
                                        if self not in kill_list:
                                                kill_list.append(self)
                                                shots -= 1
                                if
rectangular_intersection(self_rectangle,other_rectangle):
                                        kill_list.append(sprite)
                                        if self not in kill_list:
                                                kill_list.append(self)
                                                shots -= 1
                if self.y < 0:
                        kill_list.append(self)
                        shots -= 1
                for sprite in kill_list:
                        if sprite in sprite_list:
                                sprite_list.remove(sprite)
                                if hasattr(sprite,"asteroid"):
                                        score+=50
                self.y -= 1
```

In the next lesson we will add some sound effects and music. Finally, we will take care of all the other variables we need and add the game or "main" loop to complete this version of our program..

REVIEW

Quiz 17:

17.1 Review Grammar to code translation:

1. *Nouns can suggest _______ in our code.*
2. *Verbs can suggest _______.*
3. *Adjectives can suggest ______.*

17.2 Write "Yes" or "No" to indicate if a sprite class may be used for each of the following conditions:

1. _____ *When you will use many instances of the same object on the screen.*
2. _____ *When you need to track objects for collision detection.*
3. _____ *When objects don't share much code.*
4. _____ *When you rarely or never need multiple instances of the object on the screen.*
5. _____ *When objects have similar functions or code that could cause unwanted behavior.*
6. _____ *When you plan to move, share, or reuse the class object in other modules.*
7. _____ *When you need a lot of control over individual object instances or groups.*
8. _____ *When loops are event based.*
9. _____ *When the objects movement is always event or user controlled rather than automated.*
10. _____ *When you want to *increase speed, (of writing and running code for sprites).*

Quiz 17 Answer Key:

17.1 Grammar to code:

1. *Nouns can suggest* ***classes*** *in our code.*
2. *Verbs can suggest* ***methods****.*
3. *Adjectives can suggest* ***attributes.****.*

17.2 "Yes" or "No":

1. __Yes__ *When you will use many instances of the same object on the screen.*
2. __Yes__ *When you need to track objects for collision detection.*
3. __No__ *When objects don't share much code.*
4. __No__ *When you rarely or never need multiple instances of the object on the screen.*
5. __Yes__ *When objects have similar functions or code that could cause unwanted behavior.*
6. __Yes__ *When you plan to move, share, or reuse the class object in other modules.*
7. __Yes__ *When you need a lot of control over individual object instances or groups.*
8. __No__ *When loops are event based.*
9. __No__ *When the objects movement is always event or user controlled rather than automated.*
10. __Yes__ *When you want to *increase speed, (of writing and running code for sprites).*

Lesson 18: Complete With Sounds and Music

- **Adding Sounds and Music**
- **Coding the Main/Game Loop**
- **Putting It All Together**

Adding Sounds and Music

Adding sounds and music to our game is easy with Pygame. First, of course, you will need to record or find sound files that are compatible with your game. When using Pygame you can utilize MP3, WAV, or OGG files. You must consider the trade-off in choosing the type of sound files for your program. MP3 and WAV files are the most commonly available sound formats; while OGG is a loss-less compression format that is not universally supported. OGG is generally the smallest, yet good quality. MP3 is small and commonly supported but the quality is not as high as WAV files. WAV files can provide varying degrees of high quality sound, but can slow down your game and increate it's size dramatically.

Since our game is so small and has very little sound to deal with; I have provided WAV files for you to use. First we just initialize Pygame's mixer and define some appropriate variables for our WAV files:

```
pygame.mixer.init()
laser = pygame.mixer.Sound("data/laser.wav")
boom = pygame.mixer.Sound("data/boom.wav")
music = pygame.mixer.Sound("data/music.wav")
```

After setting up these things, we merely call the appropriate variables within the classes, events, and game code that require them. *Take a look at the complete code for our game at the end of this lesson.*

- *Notice where we put the above code to initialize the Pygame mixer and define the sound variables.*

- *Find and ponder the code where we called the boom and laser sounds:*

```
boom.play()
plasma = Laser()
                =
             Laser()
```

- *Find and ponder the code for the music file:*

```
music.play()
channel = music.play()
lastupdate = time.time()
        if not channel.get_busy():
                channel = music.play()
```

Now that you have been pondering what you have learned so far, *(if not get back there and ponder*!), you should have a basic understanding of how to find and apply sounds to a game. The ".play( )" is to call the sound or music and begin playing it. Python will not wait for the file to complete before continuing on to read the next line of code. Keep this in mind when calling sound files so they don't overlap unless you want them to. You could add more parameters to further limit or control your sounds.

In the parenthesis following ".play ( )" you could add (-1, 0.0) or other parameters. Adding -1 as an argument creates a loop that never ends. This is often used for creating irritation and repetitious background music. The 0.0 indicates the starting point within the sound file to begin playing. 0.0 starts playing the file from the beginning. By changing it to a larger integer you could start the sound or music file anywhere you choose. Should you have a need to immediately terminate a music file; you can use "mixer.stop ( )".

Have a look at Pygame's documentation for further details about what can be done with sound and music in Pygame.

CODING THE MAIN/GAME LOOP

In next lesson we will look at different coding styles including the most common Pygame style for organizing your code. Now our focus is on the "Main Loop" or "Game Loop." A primitive overview for organizing code would be to see them as follows:

1. Import your tools
2. Define stuff
3. Write the main loop/game loop

4. Exit peacefully

We discussed the mechanics of the first two on this list in previous chapters. Now it is time to take a look at our game loop. You will notice that our finished code is not exactly in a perfect or proper format or style. We skipped over some of these traditions to emphasize the meaning of the code in accordance with the lessons in this course.

You will find some things can be moved to many different locations in your algorithm without much of an effect on the way it runs. However, the precise locations of some parts of your code are vital for your program to work properly.

Challenge*: <u>Make at least two copies</u> of the complete game code from this lesson and move stuff around in one of them to see what happens. What can be moved? Where? What can't be moved? Why?*

<u>Take a look at our game loop:</u>

```
while not done: #Just another way of setting up while true"

        if not channel.get_busy():
                channel = music.play()
        for event in pygame.event.get():
                if event.type == pygame.KEYDOWN:
                        if event.key == pygame.K_SPACE:
                                if shots < 3:
                                        plasma = Laser()
                                        sprite_list.append(plasma)
                                        plasma.x = ship.x
                                        plasma.y = ship.y
                                        shots+=1
                                        asteroid = Asteroids(random.randint(1,screenW-500),0)

                        if event.key == pygame.K_LEFT:
                                ship.x_speed = -2
                        if event.key == pygame.K_RIGHT:
                                ship.x_speed = 2
                        if event.key == pygame.K_UP:
                                ship.y_speed = -1
                        if event.key == pygame.K_DOWN:
                                ship.y_speed = 1

                if event.type == pygame.KEYUP:
                        if event.key == pygame.K_LEFT:
                                ship.x_speed = 0
                        if event.key == pygame.K_RIGHT:
                                ship.x_speed = 0
                        if event.key == pygame.K_UP:
                                ship.y_speed = 0
```

```
                    if event.key == pygame.K_DOWN:
                            ship.y_speed = 0


            if event.type == pygame.QUIT:
                    done = True
            if done is True:
                    break
        draw_frame(sprite_list,0)

        update_sprites()


print ("SCORE:")
print (score)
print ("TIME:")
print (time.time()-start,"\n")
pygame.quit()
end = None
while end != "n":
    end = input("Type \"y\" to play again; or \"n\" to run away. ")
    if end == "n":

        print("Space Chicken!")
        break
        pygame.quit()
    if end == "y":
        print("Then close this window and re-run the game.")
        break
        pygame.quit()   #shuts down the Pygame module (opposite of initializing)
        sys.exit()
```

As you can see, if we did our preliminary work, the actual main game loop is not very complicated.

PUTTING IT ALL TOGETHER

Finally, the moment we have all been waiting for; **the complete**, *(well semi-complete),* **game!** It would be better not to just copy and paste this code. You should practice typing it out and finding your errors. You will find many of your errors will be typing, indentation, omissions and other common mistakes that can only be reduced through practice. If you really, really can't get it right and don't know why; you can load the .py version provided with this book to confirm that this code really does work on your computer.

```
import pygame
import time
import random
```

```
import sys

pygame.init()
pygame.font.init()
pygame.display.set_caption('Asteroid Shoot')


start = time.time()
font = pygame.font.Font(pygame.font.get_default_font(),10)
screen = pygame.display.set_mode((640, 480))

collision = False
screenW = 540
screenH = 480

pygame.mixer.init()
laser = pygame.mixer.Sound("data/laser.wav")
boom = pygame.mixer.Sound("data/boom.wav")
music = pygame.mixer.Sound("data/music.wav")
done = False
pos = (0,0)
toggle = 0
shots = 0
score = 0

#Defining color variables
black = [ 0, 0, 0]
white = [255,255,255]
purple = [215, 0, 215]
red = [255, 0, 0]

asteroid_image = ["data/asteroid.png"]
explosion = ["data/explosion.png"]

class Sprite:
        def __init__(self,image_path="data/asteroid.png"):
                self.direction = 1

                self.x = 0
                self.y = 0
                self.image = pygame.image.load(image_path)
                self.width = 30
                self.height = 30
        def update(self):
                        if self.x < 0:
                                self.direction = 1
                        elif self.x > screenW:
```

```
                    self.direction = -1
                if self.y < screenH:
                    self.x += 1
                    self.y += 1

class Asteroids(Sprite):
        def __init__(self,x,y):
                Sprite.__init__(self,asteroid_image[random.randrange(0,len(asteroid_image))])
                self.x = x
                self.y = y

                sprite_list.append(self)
                self.asteroid=True

class Rectangle:
        def __init__(self,x,y,width,height):
                self.left = x
                self.top = y
                self.bottom = y+height
                self.right = x+width
def rectangular_intersection(rect1,rect2):
        return not (rect1.right < rect2.left or rect1.left > rect2.right or rect1.bottom <
rect2.top or rect1.top > rect2.bottom)
        #rect.left refers to the integer value of the x coordinate on the left side of the
rectangle; .right to the right side;
        #.top to the y coordinate at the top; and .bottom to the y coordinate at the bottom
of the rectangle.


class Spaceship(Sprite):

        def __init__(self):
                Sprite.__init__(self,"data/spaceship.png")
                self.x = screenW/2
                self.y = screenH-130
                self.x_speed = 0
                self.y_speed = 0
        def update(self):
                self.x = self.x+self.x_speed
                self.y = self.y+self.y_speed
                if self.x < 0:
                        self.x -= self.x_speed
                if self.x > screenW-30:
                        self.x -= self.x_speed
                for sprite in sprite_list:
                        if sprite != self and not hasattr(sprite,"plasma"):
                                self_rectangle                                              =
```

```
Rectangle(self.x,self.y,self.width,self.height)
                                other_rectangle                                    =
Rectangle(sprite.x,sprite.y,sprite.width,sprite.height)
                                if
rectangular_intersection(self_rectangle,other_rectangle)and collision == False:
                                                global done
                                                done=True

class Laser(Sprite):
        def __init__(self):
                Sprite.__init__(self,"data/plasmaball.png")
                self.plasma = True
                laser.play()
        def update(self):
                global shots, score
                kill_list = []
                self_rectangle = Rectangle(self.x,self.y,self.width,self.height)
                for sprite in sprite_list:
                        if hasattr(sprite,"asteroid"):
                                other_rectangle                                    =
Rectangle(sprite.x,sprite.y,sprite.width,sprite.height)
                                if rectangular_intersection(self_rectangle,other_rectangle):
                                        kill_list.append(sprite)
                                        boom.play()
                                        if self not in kill_list:
                                                kill_list.append(self)
                                                shots -= 1
                                if rectangular_intersection(self_rectangle,other_rectangle):
                                        kill_list.append(sprite)
                                        if self not in kill_list:
                                                kill_list.append(self)
                                                shots -= 1
                if self.y < 0:
                        kill_list.append(self)
                        shots -= 1
                for sprite in kill_list:
                        if sprite in sprite_list:
                                sprite_list.remove(sprite)
                                if hasattr(sprite,"asteroid"):
                                        score+=50
                self.y -= 1


# Make empty lists
StarGroupOne = []
StarGroupTwo = []
```

```
screen_width = 640

# Loop 70 times and add a star in a random x,y position
for i in range(70):
    x = random.randrange(0,640)
    y = random.randrange(0,640)
    StarGroupOne.append([x,y])
    StarGroupTwo.append([x,y])

#Loop until the user closes the window.
done = False

#This creates a timer to control how often you want the screen to update.
clock = pygame.time.Clock()

def draw_stars():
    screen.fill(black)

    # Process each star in the list.
    for i in range(len(StarGroupOne)):
        # Draw the stars
        pygame.draw.circle(screen, purple, StarGroupOne[i], 2)
        pygame.draw.circle(screen, white, StarGroupTwo[i], 2)
                # Move the stars down one pixel ata time.
        StarGroupOne[i][1] += 1
        StarGroupTwo[i][1] += 1

        # If the star has moved off the bottom of the screen
        if StarGroupOne[i][1] > 640:
            # Reset it just above the top
            y=random.randrange(-70,-10)
            StarGroupOne[i][1] = y
            # Give stars a new x position
            x=random.randrange(0,640)
            StarGroupOne[i][0] = x
        if StarGroupTwo[i][1] > 640:
            # Reset it just above the top
            y=random.randrange(-70,-10)
            StarGroupTwo[i][1] = y
            # Give it a new x position
            x=random.randrange(0,640)
            StarGroupTwo[i][0] = x


#Function for time and score display
def draw_frame(alist,toggle):
        global score
```

```
        global start
        draw_stars()

        #Current time - starting time to get time elapsed
        timer = time.time()-start
        timefont = font.render(str(timer),True,(white))

        #Score indicator font and color for the word "score"
        scoreword = font.render("SCORE",True,(red))
        #Position on the screen to blit it.
        screen.blit(scoreword,(570,screenH-50))

        #Score indicator font and color for the numbers
        scorenumber = font.render(str(score),True,(white))
        #Position on the screen to blit it.
        screen.blit(scorenumber,(570,screenH-40))

        #Font color, and position for the word "time"
        timeword = font.render("TIME",True,(red))
        screen.blit(timeword,(570,screenH-30))

        #Time indicator font and colors for numbers
        screen.blit(timefont,(570,screenH-20))

        for sprite in alist:
                position = (sprite.x,sprite.y)
                screen.blit(sprite.image,position)
        pygame.display.flip()


def update_sprites():
        global toggle,lastupdate
        toggle=(toggle+500)
        if random.randint(1,600) == 1:
                asteroid = Asteroids(1,300)
        for sprite in sprite_list:
                sprite.update()
sprite_list = []
for x in range(1):
        Asteroids(random.randint(1,300),0)


ship = Spaceship()
sprite_list.append(ship)
music.play()
channel = music.play()
lastupdate = time.time()
```

```
while not done: #Just another way of setting up while true"

        if not channel.get_busy():
                channel = music.play()
        for event in pygame.event.get():
                if event.type == pygame.KEYDOWN:
                        if event.key == pygame.K_SPACE:
                                if shots < 3:
                                        plasma = Laser()
                                        sprite_list.append(plasma)
                                        plasma.x = ship.x
                                        plasma.y = ship.y
                                        shots+=1
                                        asteroid = Asteroids(random.randint(1,screenW-500),0)

                        if event.key == pygame.K_LEFT:
                                ship.x_speed = -2
                        if event.key == pygame.K_RIGHT:
                                ship.x_speed = 2
                        if event.key == pygame.K_UP:
                                ship.y_speed = -1
                        if event.key == pygame.K_DOWN:
                                ship.y_speed = 1

                if event.type == pygame.KEYUP:
                        if event.key == pygame.K_LEFT:
                                ship.x_speed = 0
                        if event.key == pygame.K_RIGHT:
                                ship.x_speed = 0
                        if event.key == pygame.K_UP:
                                ship.y_speed = 0
                        if event.key == pygame.K_DOWN:
                                ship.y_speed = 0


                if event.type == pygame.QUIT:
                        done = True
                if done is True:
                        break
        draw_frame(sprite_list,0)

        update_sprites()


print ("SCORE:")
print (score)
```

```
print ("TIME:")
print (time.time()-start,"\n")
pygame.quit()
end = None
while end != "n":
    end = input("Type \"y\" to play again; or \"n\" to run away. ")
    if end == "n":

        print("Space Chicken!")
        break
        pygame.quit()
    if end == "y":
        print("Then close this window and re-run the game.")
        break
        pygame.quit()    #shuts down the Pygame module (opposite of initializing)
        sys.exit()
```

That's all there is to it!!! Hey, don't complain; you're a programmer now. If you understand most of this, you are doing good; if not go back to reviewing and pondering. Don't stress on it if you don't get every detail yet; you will understand in time. The more times you type, read, and try various algorithms, the faster you will understand.

Space Cruise Alpha version 0.9.0 is ready for self/internal testing, evaluation and modification. Remember, Beta is the next level where you will freeze the game and release it on your friends and Beta testers for further evaluation and feedback. I will leave the game in your capable hands at this point.

For the sake of teaching you how to package and distribute your work, we will not finish or refine every detail of the game for you. This will push you to finish it yourself and give you some freedom to alter the game according to your own preferences.

Let's pretend that the game is finished to the version 1.0.0 level and we don't want to add any more modifications.

Of course, in reality you would want to:

1. Fix the "bug" where the ship can fly off the bottom of the screen.
2. Add graphic explosions rather than "blackouts"
3. Add a GUI for displaying high scores, entering player names, and a "play again?" interface.
4. Add an introduction and ending video clip.
5. Add more levels with increasing difficulty.
6. Clean up unnecessary code
7. Find better ways to write the code
8. Adding error code
9. Code a proper exit at the end of the game

You will have a better idea of how to reorganize and rewrite your code after the next lesson. We will take a look at code writing styles, organization, and error handling.

Remember, this game code was *not* written in the most efficient way. It is left unfinished with bugs to challenge those who feel this course is a little too easy or are ready for independent growth. Much of your software career will be fixing bugs and altering code. Practice makes perfect. Make back-up copies and play with the code. Change certain parts of the code to see what they do. Delete some parts; add some parts; change the order; and monkey around until you increase your understanding.

We can't perfect our game and release our Beta version to the general public without an install exe. We could, but most people would not appreciate it. We have to make it easy to install and evaluate to get useful feedback. So, after learning more about coding with style, we will have a look at creating and exe installation file.

REVIEW

Quiz 18:

18.1 Answer the following questions:

1. What are the three kinds of sound files that can be used in Pygame?

   a. ___________
   b. ___________
   c. ___________

2. What does this code; `pygame.mixer.init()` do?

3. What is another name for the "**Game Loop**."

4. What are the four primary groups of code when organizing your game?

   a. __________
   b. __________
   c. __________
   d. __________

5. What else could you do to improve this game?

Quiz 18 Answer Key:

18.1 Answer the following questions:

1. What are the three kinds of sound files that can be used in Pygame?

   a. Mp3
   b. WAV
   c. OGG

2. What does this code; **pygame.mixer.init()** do?

   It loads and initializes Pygame's sound and music mixer.

3. What is another name for the "**Game Loop**."

   The "Main Loop."

4. What are the four primary groups of code when organizing your game?

   a. *Import your tools*
   b. *Define stuff*
   c. *Write the main loop*
   d. *Exit the game*

5. What else could you do to improve this game?

Any of the following:

10. *Fix the "bug" where the ship can fly off the bottom of the screen.*
11. *Add graphic explosions*
12. *Add a GUI for displaying high scores, entering player names, and a "play again?" interface.*
13. *Add an introduction and ending video clip.*
14. *Add more levels with increasing difficulty.*
15. *Clean up unnecessary code*
16. *Find better ways to write the code*
17. *Adding error code*

Lesson 19: Programming With Style

- **PYTHON STYLE**
- **PYSCRIPTER STYLE**
- **PYGAME STYLE**

PYTHON STYLE

"Coding With Style" was covered in Lesson Nine where you were introduced to the details of writing readable code. In this brief lesson we look at the bigger picture; How should you organize your blocks of code? Back in the old days, (of lesson 9), you didn't know how to write enough code to worry about organizing it. We will explore a few organizational styles and set you free to choose your own. First, let's take a look at the conventional organization in Python :

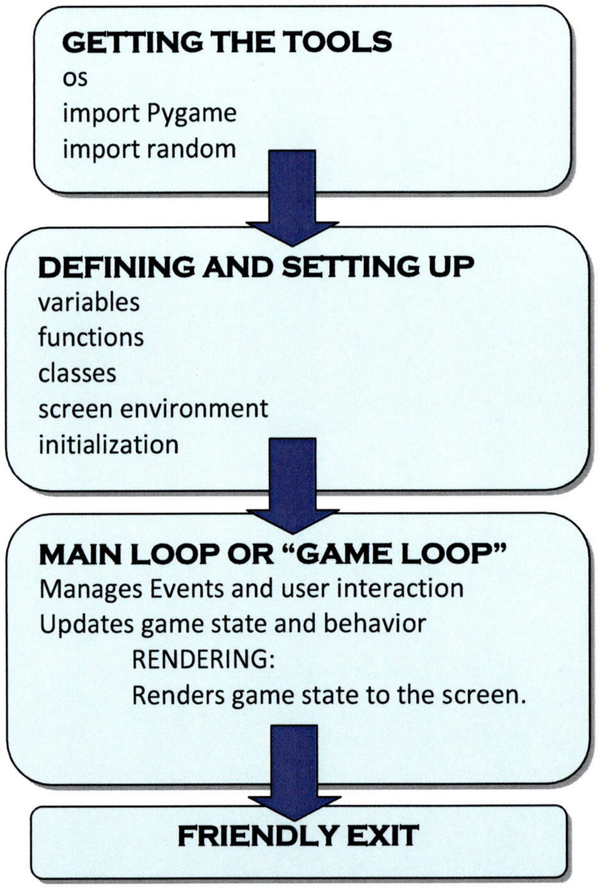

PYSCRIPTER STYLE

Whether you use PyScripter or not, you should look at the standard style it presents when you begin a new file. This information is generally included at the top of your code:

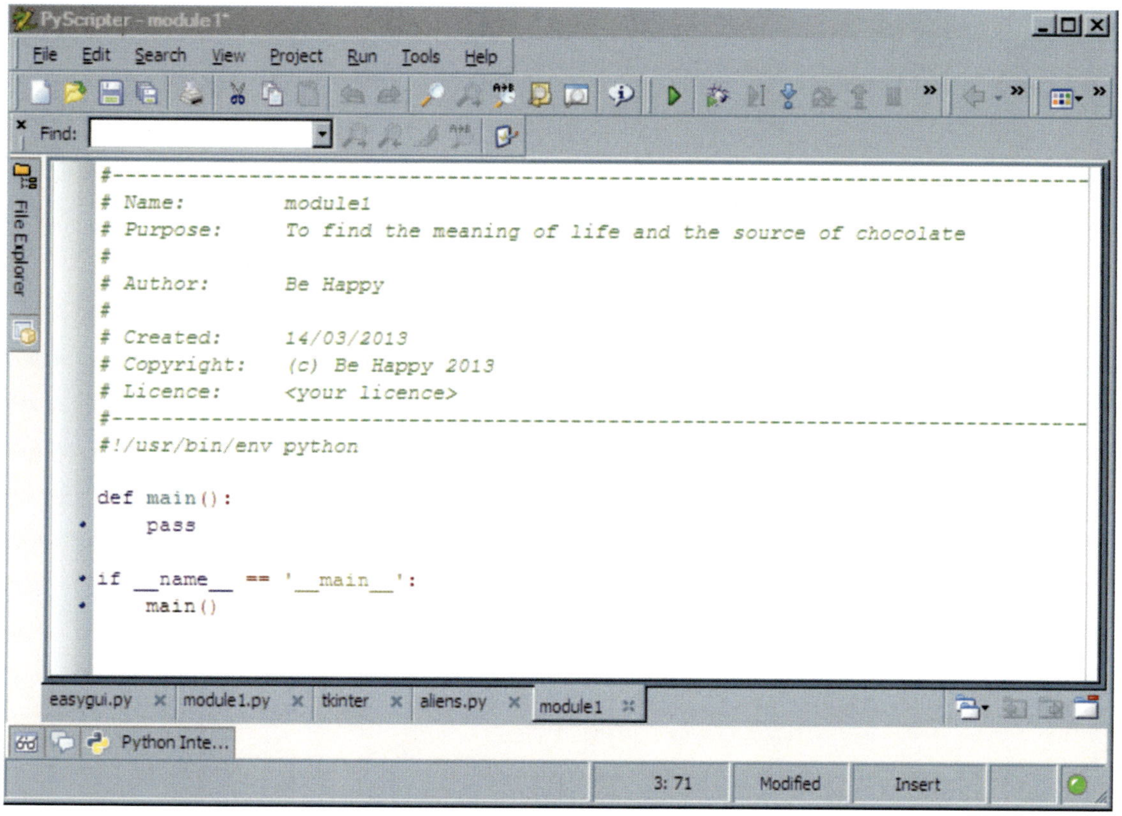

We will return to look at the kind of things you may want to include when we cover packaging and licensing shortly. Be patient! For now; look at the things Pygame puts at the top of your module for you to include. Pygame assumes a basic format for your module set-up. We purposely avoided these conventions to simplify your code and help you focus on the main points of each lesson. However, now it is a good idea to start looking at professionally written, complete, open source code of different kinds of programs and develop a consistent and easy to read style in all that you do.

You should review the "Coding With Style" section of Chapter 9 to start programming your brain and fingers to follow a standard syntax style as well as a consistent organization style for your programs.

**Reminder: PyScripter includes the forever useful Python manuals under "help."*

PyGame Style

You can see here that the general organization of code is similar. Some of the names have been changed to protect the innocent, but organization follows the same pattern. You will find reading and writing code much more convenient if you develop a consistent style similar to some conventional organization.

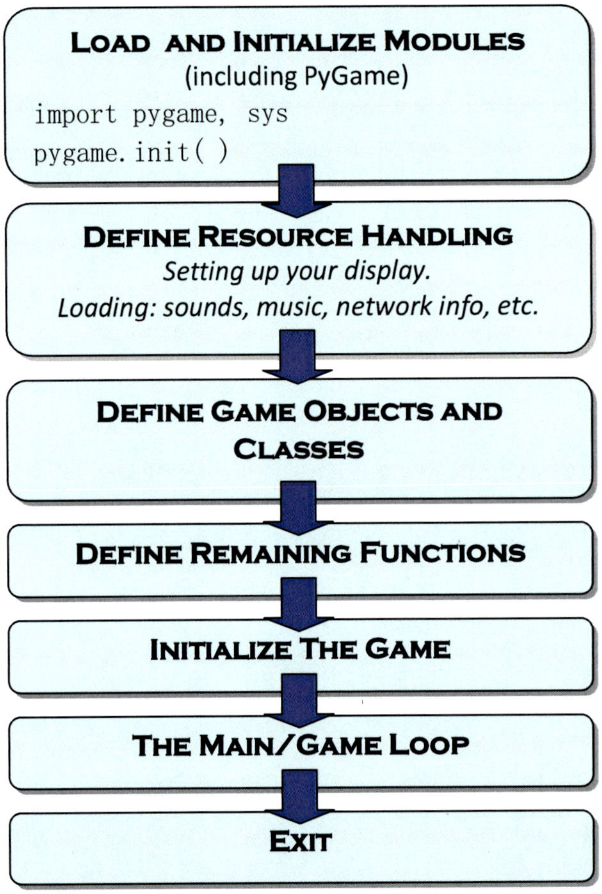

<u>Useful Tip:</u>

To save some typing when calling the Pygame modules functions, we can use the following statement:

```
from pygame.locals import*
```

If we include this statement we don't need to type the name of the module and the name of the function to call it. All we need to do is type the name of the function:

Type this:	***Instead of this:***
`thefunction( )`	`modulename.thefunction( )`

Quiz 19: ***Surprise!*** *There is no quiz for this brief lesson. Don't cry; we will make up for it soon. It would be good practice to look at the algorithms of open source software to study various styles.*

Lesson 20: Finishing Touches

- **ERROR HANDLING REVISITED**
- **MAKING AN INSTALLATION PACKAGE**
- **MAKING YOUR VERY OWN ICON**
- **FREEZING SCRIPT INTO AN EXECUTABLE**
- **CHOOSING A LICENSE**
- **TURNING YOUR EXE INTO AN INSTALLATION**
- **ON YOUR OWN: CHALLENGES**

Error Handling Revisited

Error Handling Revisited

Error handling *is adding code to deal with errors before they happen.* Our game lacks error checking code. Without error handling code our game will freeze or lock up when something goes wrong. We should include lines of code to tell the program what to do in the event of a particular error. Of course, we have to try to anticipate some of the possible things that could go wrong when our software is loading or running. We should consider possible problems that could arise by running the software in different environments, different machines, and under various circumstances.

We have three choices when considering the addition of error checking code:

1. We can get fanatical and write error code for every possible problem.
2. We could write code to catch the most common errors.
3. We could just take a chance and not add any extra code, (not generally recommended).

The amount and type of error checking code that you include will depend upon many factors:

- What kind of program are you writing?
- How vital is error checking to the program?
- What kinds of machines and operating systems will use the program?
- What are the errors you want to provide code solutions for?

Example:

When you load python it automatically loads many of the most used modules. However, there are some modules that are not automatically imported. You may want to check for possible errors in loading Pygame. *What if the fonts from the Pygame module are not available?*

After the import statements at the beginning of your code you might add:

```
if not Pygame.font: print  “Warning! Fonts are disabled!”
```

You can add code to anticipate any possible loading failure such as fonts, sound modules, music mixer, etc. and provide an error message or alternative action.

Remember also that you can use the try...except block or suite to find errors, (see lesson 12).

Looking at your code, ask yourself: *What could yourself say?*

Error handling can become complex and could be a book in itself. For your current level of programming, you should start to explore this vast new world. You can learn by trial and error and by examining similar code other people have written. Don’t forget to check online blogs and forums for good, *(and bad)* advice. Always keep in mind that some people, *(without lives of their own),* love to post comments and information on things they know nothing about. Don’t believe everything you read. Yet, always keep your eyes open for that true expert who is happy to help you. With this advice, let’s move on to the more exciting topic of “*Making an installation package.*”

Making an Installation Package

"How do I pack and distribute my game for people to test or install?" Making an exe and installation file is generally the best way to get your game out there. However, if you have algorithms of modules, classes, or other stuff you want to circulate, you may want to create a "*distribution package*." We will cover those in the next lesson.

First, we will need to organize the code, assets, and files properly before packing them and creating an install file. You will also need to choose a way to create the exe.

So, let's imagine that we now freeze our game and call it the "Beta release version 0.9.0" just for fun. We could let it graduate to version 1.0.0 when we release the revised first version. We could also use 0.9.1 for a first and 0.9.2 for a second Beta release if we expect to be doing more than one Beta release. Some companies' use 0.9a and 0.9b, *(refer to lesson thirteen under "Software Versioning" for more options.)*

Example:
Loading images: If you call "pygame.image.load()" and get "couldn't open..." make sure you have saved your py module in the same folder as your image files. Also double check your file extension and name.

The easiest way to make an exe and installation file is to get some software to assist you. You could write a script entirely in Python or find one to modify online, but for the sake of keeping things simple, we will discuss the easy way. You can pay money for some software with lots of bells and whistles; or you could try some of the free or open source versions that can get the job done. Be sure to check the license requirements. Some of them allow you to use their software for personal use or free distribution; but not commercial distributions.

Making Your Very Own Icon

You may skip this if you don't want an icon but icons are easy to make with the right tools. You could also do a search to find icons that are already made and available for your use, *(check licensing requirements and use restrictions).* One of the easiest ways to create a simple icon is to use Devious Code Works free program, http://www.deviouscodeworks.co.uk/imagicon.

Just download the program and follow the instructions. You basically create a png file within the acceptable size parameters, (like 64x64 pixels), open the program, then drag and drop your image into it. You can make your .png file in Gimp, Photo Shop, Corel or any of your favorite graphics programs. Save your image to the desktop, start imagicon, then drag and drop your image to imgagicon. Wow! You have an icon! *If you are seriously lazy, (shame on you), or failed to get an icon program, you can use the icon provided with this course.*

Freeze python Script Into an Executable

Now we will imagine that our script is complete and we want to create an install exe. As mentioned in previous lessons, we must "freeze" our Python script before creating the exe file.

The Hard way:

The easy way:

We will be using a free set of scripts and modules called cx_freeze which is available at http://cx-freeze.sourceforge.net/ to freeze our Python script. You can freeze your script a number of different ways, but to keep things as simple as possible we will do it this way.

Steps to an Easy Executable:

1. Download the correct cx_Freeze version according to your system and the version of Python you are using. *(I used the one for 3.2 Windows 32 bit for my configuration.)*

2. Install to the C:\Python32 folder, *(or wherever you have installed Python).*

3. Create a setup.py file:

   Open a new untitled window in Python's IDLE. Copy the following code:

```
from C:\Python32\scripts\cx_freeze import setup, Executable

Setup(
  name = "Asteroid_Fight ",
  version = "0.9.0",
  description = " Arcade Style Game",
  executables = [Executable("Asteroid_Fight.py")],
  )
```

Save as "setup.py" without the parenthesis.

4. Move ....files........ Alpha0.9.0.py, the data folder,(containing game assets), and setup.py to C:\Pthon32\Scripts *(or your appropriate directory).*

5. Change the file name of "Alpha0.9.0.py" to "Asteroid_Fight.py" without the parenthesis.

6. Open Asteroid_Fight.py in IDLE and add the following code just below "import Pygame":

```
import pygame._view
```

   (This addition is necessary due to a bug that causes cxFreeze to not always see parts of Pygame when creating the exe)

7. Another bug fix is required when using cxFreeze and Pygame. It seems when they are together, they don't always find the default font Pygame font. So, we must specify a very common font, *(Arial).* To change it replace our current line of code defining "font = ..." to:

```
font = pygame.font.SysFont("arial" , 10)
```

8. Open the command prompt. In Windows XP, go to the "Start" menu; click on "Run;" type in "cmd"; and "cd\" and hit enter to go to C:\.

9. Type; "cd Python32\Scripts" without the parenthesis and hit enter.

10. Type: "C:\Python32\Scripts\cxfreeze Asteroid_Fight.py" hit enter.

11. Copy data folder, (with assets), to the newly created "dist" folder.

12. The game should now run from this exe! If not, check your code or make changes according to the location of your files and according to your operating system.

**Additional notes: You data folder should contain the following files: asteroid.png, boom.wav, explosion.gif, Asteroid_Fight.ico, laser.wav, music.wav, plasmaball.png,and the spaceship.png.* Bug fixes will often be necessary when you start combining software to achieve an objective. You will also find that your environmental variables, such as your version of Windows, Linux, or other operating systems may change some things and you may have to tweak your code. The location of files and directories will also alter things. If you have another operating environment other than I used for this lesson, you may have to research the specific changes required online.

You should also note that if you add a GUI to your game, you will have to add some additional code to your setup.py file to get it to work with cxFreeze. This code will vary depending upon the type of operating systems and the GUI that you chose to create. Refer to their documentation for further help.

Choosing a License

Choosing a license can be confusing. Unless you are a lawyer, it is best not to write your own. You could end up with some really bad surprises and good lessons on how not to write a license.

Due to limitations on space and on the human attention span, I will not include word per word copies of each type of license. You must go online to find and copy the text for the license you choose to use and read the details. This is also not a comprehensive list of all license types and changes to them are always being made. We will just have a quickly boring glance at some common types. To be deeply bored you will have to go online to see the actual license and their requirements. (I suggest grabbing and coffee, tea, or other caffeinated beverage while listening to some heart-pounding wake up music before you start reading entire licensing information). Always read the find print when using or applying a license.

*Liability waiver: this information in no way constitutes legal advice and is for reference purposes only. The author, publisher, distributors, cooks, janitors, mailmen, and other entities that provided or contributed to this information are released from all forms of responsibility and liability that may result from the direct or indirect use of this information. By continuing to read or use any of the information herein provided, the reader implies agreement to these terms.

Yeah I know, you feel like you are taking an eye examination. Code released with ***no license*** is automatically copyrighted. This means the developer owns all the rights to the code and must be asked for permission to use it. The problem is that the author could change his mind in the future about anyone using his code if no license requirements or explicit agreement has been applied to it. So, if the author's true intent is to allow the public to use his code he must declare a license type or that he is releasing into the public domain. The type most "headache free" for beginning software developers would be the often difficult to find "*public domain*" code.

Before we begin we get too deep we will have to look at some terminology:

*A **viral license** type is one that requires the passing on of the same license type when using or altering the code.*

***Public domain** refers to works that are in essence "owned by the public." Licensing restrictions don't apply. You can sell and freely utilize public domain code.*

***Proprietary or Closed Source** software is when the owner of the copyright holds exclusive rights. The owner can dictate rights for distribution, modification, use, reverse engineering, and inspection of the source code. The source code is generally not freely available.*

***Explicit** refers to clearly expressed in detail, leaving nothing implied.*

Copyleft** is a fairly new term that is a play on the word "copyright." It means that the code is freely available for modification and distribution so long as modifications and extensions are released under the same license. They may require attribution to the author(s). The GNU General Public License is a good example. Copyleft **usually requires all derivative works to be released under the original license.

***Copyfree** only requires that the original work and direct modifications maintain the original license.*

The following two charts cover some primary considerations for choosing a license. These charts are only general guides to give you a brief and incomplete overview of the some of the main license types. With all of the following examples, carefully read the actual, updated license text before choosing one. Details will also vary depending upon the version of each license choose. (Each license name is hyperlinked to associated web sites. A list of the URL's is at the end of this lesson for those who have the printed copy of this course. If any of these URL's change, do a search to get the most recent URL's.

**Note: Copyright laws can vary depending upon your country or region, check local laws to be safe or consult a lawyer who specializes in software licensing if you have the money.*

Licensing Chart 1:

License	GPL v3.0	BSD	Zlib.net	Apache v2.0
May use for ***Commercial Works***	***Yes*** Must release all source code under GPL license.	***Yes***	***Yes***	***Yes***
May make ***Derivative Works***	***Yes*** Generally must release entire source code (see site for details).	***Yes***	***Yes***	***Yes***
Attribution	***Yes*** Within the **source code** and the **distribution.**	***Yes*** Included in source code and documentation	***Yes*** Authorship must not be misrepresented. License must not be removed from source distributions.	***Yes*** Within source code, and maybe in your distribution.
Viral	***Yes***	***No***	***No***	***No***
Extensions and Bug Fixes ***Must*** *be Released as Public Domain*	***Yes***	***No***	***No***	***No***
May Be Used in ***Proprietary*** *(closed source)* ***Software***	***No***	***Yes***	***Yes***	***Yes***
Debatable	**Copyleft.** **Not Copyfree.** **Some code linking requirements.** Disliked in commercial software circles due to viral aspects.	**Not Copyleft.** **Not Copyfree.** **Code linking required.** Not GPL compatible.	**Not Copyleft.** **Not Copyfree.** **Code linking required.** GPL compatible.	**Not Copyleft.** **Not Copyfree.** **Code linking required.** GPL compatible.
Generally Good	You can sell it as in selling copies, distribution services, etc. *(You can not sell the rights to use the license).	Virtually no limitations other than attribution. Includes legal disclaimer for liability.	Provides a general "as-is" clause of no warranty and wide range permissions with few restrictions.	Much like BSD but goes into greater detail about attribution and attribution rights.

Licensing Chart 2:

License	Mozilla Public (MPL)	Eclipse Public	LGPL v3.0	Public Domain
*May use for **Commercial Works***	***Yes***	***Yes***	***Yes***	***Yes***
*May make **Derivative Works***	***Yes*** Check specifics	***Yes***	***Yes*** Must allow reverse engineering for modification and debugging.	***Yes***
Attribution	***Varies*** Check specifics	***Varies*** Check specifics	***Yes*** In source code and distribution	***No***
Viral	***No***	***No***	***Not really*** Any derivative must be released under PGPL, but all source code need not always be released. See site.	***No***
*Extensions and Bug Fixes **Must** be Released as Public Domain*	***Yes***	***Yes***	***Varies*** Check specifics	***No***
*May Be Used in **Proprietary** (closed source) **Software***	***Yes*** Licenses can be combined	***Yes***	***Yes***	***Yes***
Debatable	Copyleft is limited, not Copyfree GPL compatible.	Limited Copyleft, not Copyfree. Not GNU or GPL compliant.	Copyleft, not Copyfree.	This is not a license but a legal declaration donating it to the public without restrictions; and sometimes to release the developer(s) from associated legal responsibilities and consequences.
Generally Good	A hybrid that allows mixing with proprietary software and other licenses.	Business friendly. Allows developers to choose their own license on derivative works.	Generally used to license libraries, allowing other terms to be applied to the software.	Can be used or sold freely in any form.

**Note: The terms "good" or "bad" are relative to your specific goals. In the context of this course we are viewing from the perspective of a software developer who wants to get paid for his work. However, I also believe in the necessity for some software and code to be released freely into public domain and as other variations of "free" software.*

We must consider both sides of the coin when thinking of proprietary software licensing. If we allow use and alteration of our code we could have the assistance of many other software developers to improve the code, expand its use, or join us in large projects. This will come at a cost and with further dangers of other people making most or all of the profit from our hard work. For closed source software, we may have some added security, better commercial opportunities, yet limited input from other developers. Be careful when combining licenses because generally, the more complex the licensing mix, the less businesses will be interested in it.

From the view of "*freedom*," in software development you have to clearly understand what their particular idea of "freedom" is. There is a continual debate about whether BSD or GNU licensing is better. Freedom comes with limitations as does licensing agreements. You must define what "freedoms" you need when using other people's work and what "freedoms" you want to grant to people using your work. If you want to grant total freedom, the easiest way is to just write a statement releasing it to the public domain.

Looking for Approval?

There are a number of organizations that choose to "approve" or recognize various types of licensing. Their criteria for approval will depend upon their philosophical goals. An online license generator can be found at; http://www.binpress.com/license/generator

Approval for open source software licensing can be discovered at:

- FSF, (Free Software Foundation), http://www.fsf.org
- OSI, (Open Source Initiative, http://www.opensource.org
- Copyfree, http://www.copyfree.org
- Debian, http://www.debian.org
- Fedora Project, http://www.fedoraproject.org

What about closed source software?

The moment you create the software in a physical form it has some copyright protection. You should display the date, copyright symbol © and owner of the copyright. See the US Copyright Office, (http://www.copyright.gov) for details on how to prove your copyright date in case of trouble. For details and explicit requirements or permissions you should consult a lawyer.

Once you have chosen an appropriate license, copy and past it from the relevant web site into a text file to save it. You will need this when creating your installation.

Turning your Exe Into An Installation file

Now, we will turn this "build" folder containing our exe and data into a normal installation file complete with the desktop icon we created earlier. *(If you did not get an icon, you can still create an installation, but it would make you feel better if you did).*

1. First, let's download "InstallCreator."
2. Run it and use the Wizard.
3. Browse to your C:\Python32\Scripts\dist\ or relative folder. Click next.
4. Select language and enter the game's name, "Asteroid Fight" or something else.
5. Click next, screen size for installation and next.
6. Continue through the wizard selecting your preferences.
7. When you get to the "shell" and the question; "please enter below the name of the file for which you want to create an icon in the Start menu..." Browse to your exe file and select it.
8. Enter; "Asteroid Fight" for the name of the icon.
9. Check the, "create desktop icon" and browse to it in the data folder to select it.
10. Finish selecting the other options in the wizard.
11. Choose a location to save and name the installation something different like; "Asteroid_Fight 0.9.1"

You did it!!!

Ok, this didn't happen in IDLE. We just learned that something new can happen in the compiled version. We have to slow things down so the screen will not vanish before we can read it. All we have to do is add the following code:

```
pause = pygame.time.wait(4000)
```

Can you guess where? ***Drum roll ....(crash cymbal)!!!***

The (4000) figure was chosen because this value is measured in milliseconds. There are other ways to do this in Pygame and Python but this way usually takes the least memory. I chose to place it before the "break" in two suites of code in the final "while" statement. I placed if just after the "print( )" statement in each block of code to allow a pause long enough to read what is printed. You can change the time or add this code wherever you feel a need for a pause. Ahhhg! But now these changes mean you have to save the new version of code, freeze it again, and package it again into a new installation file! That's ok, you need practice. You will be doing this kind of thing a lot so you may as well start getting used to it now. Every time you make changes to the code you will repeat this process.

You can also make an executable installation file for Windows within Python using ***bdist wininst*** command. This command would be entered from a DOS Window after the appropriate files have been set up to create a distribution package. We will talk about how to make a generic source distribution package shortly. However, using bdist winist is a bit more complex so you would have to consult the Python documentation to use it. This course chose the more simple way outlined above to create an installation exe. Other methods require additional information and parameters. You would have to specify that Python be included in the distribution, check compatibility of all packaged dependencies, accurately specify the paths and directories of all files involved, etc.

Now you are free to improve the game, add a GUI, video intro, exit, fix the bugs, or whatever you want to do with it. You can play with the game as it is to Beta test it and get some new ideas; or you could take on the following challenges before creating your own Beta version for testing.

***Rather than a quiz for this lesson you are now presented with real life challenges:**

ON YOUR OWN: CHALLENGES

MINI CHALLENGE

Go back to those primitive games in Lesson 5 now that you understand classes, functions, and methods to re-code them properly. Decide what you think the most common errors could be and add some error handling code. Now that you know more about Python you will see just how inefficient the old examples really are! In writing code you should generally not have to type the same line of code more than once. We did a lot of useless writing in the first lessons because you needed more tools like; functions, classes, etc. before you could write the code properly. I also wanted to avoid overloading you with too much information.

Now, the poorly written code should bother you enough to motivate you into fixing and improving those algorithms.
If not, tell your therapist you grew up without a conscious due to some childhood trauma. Maybe it was the unfairness of the entire world getting more peanuts in their chocolate bars that you did; which resulted in a total lack of guilt when you indulge in chocolate with extra peanuts. Of course, this behavior eventually spilled over into your programming.

These are referred to as "Challenges" because no answers will be provided. (You are growing up now).

** Hint: \n is for breaking text into new lines. Only one print statement is required for each group of text.*

If you feel you the Mini Challenge is too easy; move on to *the Super Challenge*!
(That would be this one.)

The Super Challenge!

For your final and greatest challenge; improve and complete the game! If you understand the lessons well and are ready for the ultimate challenge you can take our game to the next level. No solutions will be provided, time to get thrown out of the nest and learn to fly! If you feel you are not ready; re-do, and re-read the previous lessons in this course or set up a development team, (online or face to face), to help you make the game according to your preferences.

Unsolved problems:

- Our spaceship can fly off the screen.
- Our asteroids could be more accurate or come from different directions.
- The code to create an explosion after impact is missing.
- To restart the game we must re- run the code manually.
- Find and fix other errors in the code.

Unwritten code:

- We don't have a GUI for interaction with the player, especially at the beginning and end of the game.
- We don't have a video or animated introduction or ending.
- We don't have a high scores display.
- You could write more levels for this game.
- You could add joystick functionality instead of just arrow keys, *(you would have to research this problem in Python and Pygame's documentation or online).*
- We did not write error handling code. *Predict and write solutions for possible problems when running the game in different environments. How exhaustive should you be, so your code does not go on forever?*

Optimized code:

- Are there better ways to shorten the code this game or at least parts of it?
- Is there unnecessary code that can be deleted?
- How can you optimize the code to run faster and use less memory? (See one suggestion below).

That one suggestion:

In line 4 of the generic sprite class code, I mentioned that the self.image = pygame.image.load("my_image.png").convert() way to load an image was not always the best way. Since we will be using many instances of the asteroid image we will use another way to load these images.

With the previous statement for loading our images, every sprite copy will load the image from your original image file. This will take much more time and memory than doing it this way:

```
class Asteroids(pygame.sprite.Sprite):
    image = None

    def __init__(self):
        pygame.sprite.Sprite.__init__(self)

        if Asteroids.image is None:
            Asteroids.image = pygame.image.load("asteroid2.png")

        self.image = asteroid.image
```

This will load the copy from original image only the first time; after that the copy in memory is used again to apply to all other instances. Notice that as we begin to write the Asteroids class, we capitalized and used the plural word "Asteroids" for the name of the class, but the name of the image file is "asteroid.png" *(be careful).*

Ok, good luck on the game. Next we will take a look at creating your own packages for distribution. By the way, here is that URL list I promised in case you go the printed version of this course:

Software Licensing URL List:

GPL v3.0 http://www.gnu.org/licenses/gpl.html
BSD http://www.bsdnewsletter.com/bsd/license.html
**Note: BSD licenses come in a variety of flavors, as with all licensing choices, it is best to do some up to date research on the various types.*
Zlib http://www.zlib.net
Apache v2.0 http://www.apache.org/licenses/
Mozilla (MPL) http://www.mozilla.org/MPL
Eclipse Public http://www.eclipse.org
LGPL v.3.0 http://www.gnu.org/copyleft/lessser.html
Public Domain (no license or copyright) http://directory.fsf.org/wiki/License:CCO

Lesson 21: Now What?

- INTRO TO PACKAGES AND 3RD PARTY MODULES
- HOW TO MAKE DISTRIBUTION PACKAGES
- HOW TO INSTALL PACKAGES AND MODULES
- WHERE TO GET PACKAGES AND MODULES
- WHERE TO GO FROM HERE

INTRO TO PACKAGES AND 3RD PARTY MODULES

Don't forget that the standard library in Python has many modules that you may want to use. Refer to earlier lessons for the details. There are many 3rd party modules available on the internet. Modules are available targeting specific purposes such as; math, science, graphics, games, etc. The first place to start would be to check at Python.org.

Keywords to search or browse for: *Python 3x, packages, modules, 3rd party modules, 3rd party packages, distributions, etc.*

When choosing modules and packages; be careful to find out the exact details of the license requirements. If you are including code with specific license requirements like GPL, you must make sure that it is allowed to use it in a commercial manner. If you want to use a number of modules within your application, you may be faced with having an application under multiple licenses. This can get complex and software written in this way is often avoided by commercial organizations. *Some things to keep in mind:*

- If your software will be for personal or internal use only, you have a lot of freedom and many choices for modules and packages that you can use.

- If your software will be released for free or as open source, you have some limitations depending upon the modules and packages you will be using. Research them carefully.

- If your software will be sold, you are severely limited by restrictions and requirements of the modules and packages you can use. This will limit the number and kinds of modules you can chose from for your application, unless you plan to invest some money for the appropriate licensing rights.

1. So, we first come back to the questions;

- **Who will use this software?**
- **Will it be a commercial product?**

2. Next, we start searching modules and packages based on **license type** and the **needs** the module will fulfill for our application.

We will discuss where to get 3rd party modules and packages later. For now, let's have a look at how to make them and how to install them when you do find them.

How to Make Distribution Packages

Now that you are a software developer; with great power comes greater responsibility. Of course that also means; with little power comes little responsibility. Since we have only a little Python power at this point, we only have little responsibilities. The least a developer is responsible for when he has created some useful code is to make:

- *A Source Distribution*
- *A Setup script/file.*

Optional stuff, (yet highly recommended):

- *A setup configuration file*
- *Create **binary distributions**, (generally referring to exe installation files and packages for different operating systems).*
- *Create additional information files like Readme, License, etc.*

Distribution Packages *are groups of modules, "packaged" together.* Python comes armed with "***distutiils***." *This is a framework that; assists you in packaging your stuff, has installation tools for the users, and formats metadata to allow search engines to snoop through, find, and categorize packages.* Distutils also integrates well with Pypi.

The way to package things changed with Python 3.3 so we will be using the 3.3 version for this lesson. Module packaging software exists to help you with packaging, but at the time of this writing most of them are not compatible with Python 3.2 and up. In the future, they will catch up to the changes in Python and you will have more choices. For now, we will just use Python 3.3. Packaging can also get fairly complex depending upon the bells and whistles you need. This tutorial will only cover a very basic and generic package. You can also specify many options when creating packages. You can specify the specific handling of Libraries, other modules, conditional options, graphic files, sound files, directories, installation options, etc. Refer to the latest online Python documentation and Python sites to learn about your specific needs or the additional parameters you want to use.

You should also be aware of three terms when discussing packages and modules:

1. ***Pure Python Module*** *– refers to modules written entirely in Python*
2. ***Extension Modules*** *– referring to the module being written in C\C++ for Python 3.3, (additional low-level languages will be added in time).*
3. ***Package*** *– A group of modules put into one module.*

Creating a distribution package is another way to share your code or to get modules and packages written by others. Generally you will want to prepare the following files:

Your module ("**.py**" extension)
README ("**.txt**" extension; for information and installation instructions)
setup ("**.py**" extension; for metadata)
Manifest ("**.in**" extension; only necessary for you to create when additional code files, music, images, or other assets are to be part of your final package).

Note: If your module is only one .py file with no additional directories or files; then Python will create a Manifest automatically. To keep things simple, our example will let Python create the Manifest file.

Manifest files *contain commands to help maintain the directory structure of your package.* Shortly, you will run the command to create a "***source distribution***" of your package. Since we are not creating a Manifest file, you will see a warning that informs you that no manifest template was found so the existing files will be used to automatically create one. Just ignore the warning and let Python take care of it.

Let's walk through the steps to **making your own simple distribution package:**

1. Create your module with a "**.py**" extension. *(You must deselect "hide known file types" in folder options in Windows to change file extensions).*
We will just use a slight variation of our first game script to practice with. Create the following module and save it as "*Eggs.py*":

```
#My first program
print('How many eggs can you eat?')
amount=input()
print('Wow! You can really eat ' +amount, 'eggs?!')
exit( )
```

Note: the "exit( )" was added to intentionally raise an exception to close exit and close the window.

2. Create a `setup.py` file to include information or "****metadata,***" distribution package. You may include the following information in your setup file:

In case you forgot; ***metadata*** is often defined as *"data about data,"* but it is more accurately *"information about data"* because it may include structural information, data, and other information.

setup.py file *(watch the punctuation; single quotes can also be used)*

```
from distutils.core import setup

setup(
    name            = "Eggs",
    version         = "1.0.0",
    py_modules      = [ "Eggs" ],
    author          = "me",
    authors_email   = "myemail@email.com",
    URL             = "www.toonzcat.com",
    description     = "A simple module for taking over the world",
  )
```

This line of code imports Python's setup function from the distribution utilities module.

This line associates your metadata with the arguments in the setup function.

Everything between parentheses becomes the setup function's argument names.

Setup.py has required arguments, (these are not optional!), if omitted will cause errors or a crash:

- **name-** *Not yours, but the name of the package.*
- **version-** *Version number.*
- **author-** *Your name, (even if you have multiple authors to list, don't change " author" to "authors" or you will cause an error).*
- **author_email-** *Your email address, of course.*
- **URL-** *If you have a web page for this project, list it here. If not, then list the web page at Pypi or another location that hosts your package for download.*

To keep things simple in the creation of your first package, we will discuss the optional arguments later.

3. Create your README.txt file to include any special installation information, contact information, or other details you want to include about the package. You can create this in any simple text program such as Notepad.
4. Move the ***README.txt, Eggs.py, setup.py*** files to the Python33 root directory, (were you find the python.exe file). *(If we created a Manifest.in file we would also move it to Python's root directory).* If you did a default installation in Windows the path would be; C:\Python33\ and there will already be a README.txt file for the Python version. You can rename or delete this one before moving yours to this folder.

5. Open a terminal window. *Huh?* Click the Start menu in Windows. Type in "cmd" without the quotes and hit "ok" or the enter key. Poof! A DOS terminal window magically appears! *(How to open a terminal window may vary depending up on your operating system, just so a search online if you don't know how to do it.)*
6. Make sure you are in the correct directory. Use ***cd..*** to go back for example; if you are in C:\mydocs; type ***cd...*** to go to C:\, if not, repeat ***cd..*** and hit the *enter key* until you see ***C:***
7. Go to the directory that contains the python exe you will be using, ie: *C:\Python33* by typing; ***cd \ Python33***
   Hopefully you have arrived. If not; check online for os specific instructions.
8. Type the command: ***python setup.py sdist*** to make your source distribution.
9. You will see a warning about the "*Manifest*," don't worry about it, we didn't make one for this distribution so Python will do it for us.
10. By default in Windows, you will now find a new folder called "***dist***" that contains your distribution in the form of a zip file. Other file formats are available and can be specified. *(See Python documentation).*

As you probably noticed; Python automatically checks the details of your distribution when you tell it to create a distribution package. Python will tell you if you missed a required parameter or there are other common problems with your package. If it is not a vital omission or error, Python will still create the distribution file.

For complex packages you may need to consult the documentation at Python.org and PyPi to set up Manifest file commands, __init__.py file, and other stuff that meets your specific needs.

Optional Classifier Arguments

As mentioned earlier, you can also add a number of optional, yet important, arguments. We added a ***"short description,"*** *(one line);* but in a real package for release we should probably add "***classifiers***" and a "***long description,***" *(multiple lines of text).*

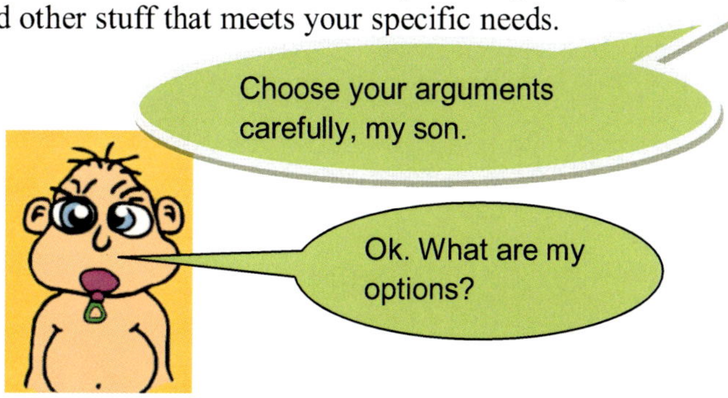

It would also be helpful to point out that our package is for Python 3 or later. ***Classifiers*** *are the keywords and information that will be used by other programmers when searching for specific packages.* You can browse through the classifiers at Pypi to get some ideas on how to classify your package. Many people will also search according to the type of license you have applied to your package. So, in other words, you will not be shot if you don't include the following arguments, but they are highly recommended for most packages, *Wow! in this case having more arguments can be a good thing!*

Arguments:	Format:
Description	description = 'info here'
Programming Language	Programming Language :: Python Programming Language :: Python :: 3
License Type	License :: GNU
Development Stage or Status	Development Status :: Alpha
Operating System	Operating System :: OS Independent
Intended Audience	Intended Audience :: Game Developers
Topical Classifiers *(one by one if multiple)*	Topic :: Game Development :: Libraries :: Modules Topic :: High Scores :: Game Modules

If you choose to use multiple classifiers, (strongly recommended), use the following format:

```
from distutils.core import setup

setup(
     name            = "my_distribution",
     version         = "1.0.0",
     py_modules      = [ "my_distribution" ],
     author          = "me",
     authors_email   = "myemail@email.com",
     URL             = "www.toonzcat.com",
     description     = "a simple module for taking over the world",
     classifiers     = [
         "Programming Language :: Python",
         "Programming Language :: Python :: 3",
         "Development Status :: Alpha",
         "License :: GNU"
              ],
    )
```

Note: If you are creating a distribution for systems other than Windows, it can get very complicated. You will need to do some internet research on your specific operating system. You may need to visit forums that discuss the specific questions and problems you will face.

Sharing Your Packages And Modules

The best way to share your packages and to get feedback on them is to upload them to Pypi. You will have to go through the registration process and become a member. Don't worry, it's free. Just go to their website and read the instructions on how to register and post your files. You can also find other code collecting sites and join Python communities.

HOW TO INSTALL PACKAGES AND MODULES

To install Python packages and modules you can use various approaches. The most convenient is if the developer created and installation package for you operating system. Generally, installation instructions are provided by the developer or all you need to do is run the "setup.py" file and everything will be done for you. If not, most packages and modules are just files that need to be placed in the same directory as the file that imports them. If an installation package is not provided, download the ***source distribution*** and unpack it. It may be a zip or tar file. Check the readme file for additional instructions, but generally it will just tell you to run the setup.py file from the command prompt within the same folder you unpacked the other files to. Once you have it all set up you can then just use the import command in your Python code to import the module into your program.

You would import the module this way:

```
import thedirectoryname.modulename
```

Of course, our directory or folder must be in Python's path or be a subdirectory within our program's directory for it to be found.

To import the package/module we just made this would become:

```
import dist.Eggs.py
```

Now that you have imported the module, you would call a function from within it this way:

```
modulename.function_name()
```

WHERE TO GET PACKAGES AND MODULES

Introducing **PyPI**:

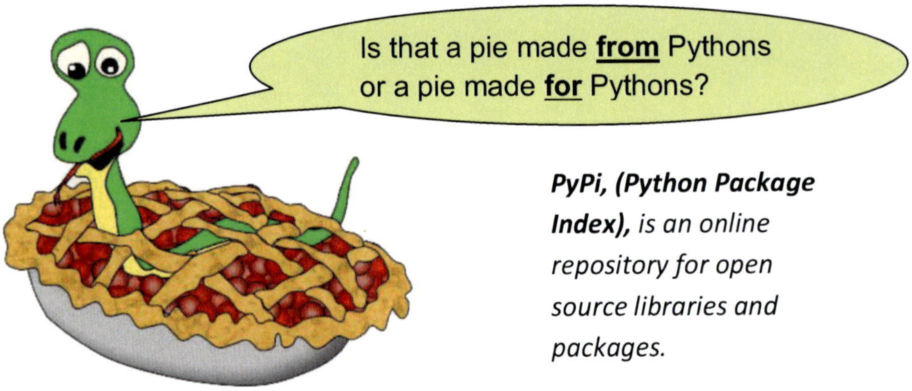

PyPi, (Python Package Index), *is an online repository for open source libraries and packages.*

www.toonzcat.com , 2013

Vistit PyPi at: http://pypi.python.org/pypi?%3Aaction=browse
Alternatively: http://pypi.python.org

You will find many modules and packages listed according to categories:

- **Topic**
- **Environment**
- **Framework**
- **Development Status**
- **Intended Audience**
- **License**
- **Natural Language**
- **Operating System**
- **Programming Language**

Browsing these categories and sub-categories can give you more ideas for keywords to choose for use in search engines if you don't find the modules you are looking for here. Make sure you are choosing modules and packages that are compatible with your current version of Python or change your version of Python to match the modules you will use. Keep in mind that major changes were made to Python 3x and it is not backwards compatible. To use earlier versions of Python you will have to study the differences and changes that were made. If you want to avoid confusion, just stick with Python 3x and compatible modules. Write the module if you can't find it. This also saves you the trouble of complying with various license requirements.

Other Useful Packages and Modules:

Be sure to check the compatibility of packages and modules with the version of Python you want to use for your application. Many of the sites listed in this course are only compatible with older versions of Python, (2.x). They are listed anyway, because many of most will eventually be updated to become compatible with Python 3x or later. Check the sites for version information and news on updates.

SEE INDEX B; "FINDING MORE PYTHONS" FOR AN ALPHABETICAL LIST OF MANY USEFUL PYTHON MODULES AND PACKAGES.

WHERE TO GO FROM HERE

As in the days of the Vikings, to teach a child to swim; the father threw his son from the ship into the ocean and screamed; "swim!" In nature some birds throw the baby bird from the nest and, (in bird language), screams; "fly!" In the programming world you are now being thrown out of the nest as I yell; "Code!" As I mentioned; there is a possibility of an intermediate book on Python in the future depending upon how much money I make from this one. My family complains if I stop feeding them for a few days. So, if you want me to write a second course; get your local universities, high schools, friends, neighbors, and arch enemies, to buy this course or make a donation. Encourage them to buy many copies and find creative uses for them like heating their homes with their fireplaces, using this for campfires or barbeques, as a toilet paper alternative, coasters for hot food, making paper airplanes, door stops, colorful paper for the bottom of bird cages, etc. Use your imagination.

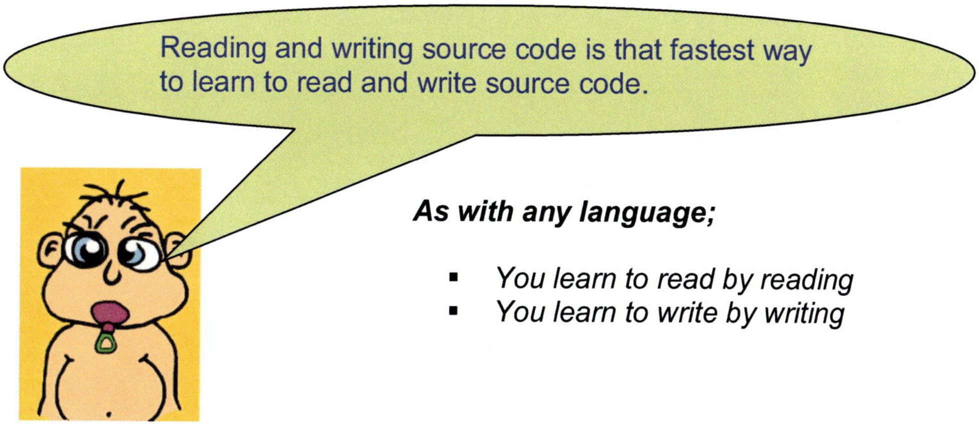

As with any language;

- *You learn to read by reading*
- *You learn to write by writing*

Being able to borrow and study other people's code can drastically speed up your ability to learn programming. Open source communities are dedicated to helping you rather than limiting you, (in theory). But, before borrowing code, make sure you have a clear understanding of the license restrictions of the code and the required assets. IF YOU ARE REALLY LOST; REPEAT ALL THE LESSSONS. IF NOT; REPEAT THE LESSONS YOU NEED UNTIL THEY ARE EASY TO REMEMBER AND DO.

Some Guidelines to Remember not to Forget:

- Practice, practice, practice, and after that practice.
- Go through the Python tutorials at Python.org and the documentation for everything you are using to do programming.
- When it gets too cryptic, search online for the meaning.
- Go through the Pygame tutorials that Pygame sites provide.
- Search available libraries to play with and study at http://pypi.python.org
- Join forums and communities on Python and Pygame programming. Join game making sites to post your games and get feedback. You can also study other people's games and the reactions to them.
- Read and analyze other people's code. Read and analyze other people's code. Read and...you know.
- Talk so many people into buying this course that the author makes enough money to make it worth his time to ditch other projects and write an intermediate course.
- Get some rich person to donate enough money to make the author feel guilty if he doesn't write an intermediate course.
- Get many not so rich people to pool their resources and donate enough money to make the author feel guilty if he doesn't write an intermediate course.
- Forget about the author of this course and read every Python book you can find.
- Check You-Tube and www.toonzcat.com for video tutorials on Python.
- View and join other people's projects, search Python projects on www.sourceforge.net
- Start a group project of you own.
- Regularly visit http://www.toonzcat.com to see if the author adds more free stuff, tutorials, code, or other useful things for programmers, graphic artists, and game makers.
- If you downloaded the pirated version of this course and found it was helpful, please feel guilty enough to make a donation at http://www.toonzcat.com

Now that you are a programmer it is time to say; "Goodbye." I will miss me. If you feel you are ready for it, take the "*Final Beginner's Test*." If not, return to repeat the areas of this course you don't understand. When you finish the test, evaluate your weaknesses and repeat the appropriate lessons. Did I mention...repeat...?

Now, jump out of the nest and...

VOCABULARY

Binary distributions *generally refers to exe installation files and packages for different operating systems.*
Distribution Packages *are groups of modules, "packaged" together.*
Manifest files *contain commands to help maintain the directory structure of your package.*
Metadata is often defined as *"data about data,"* but it is more accurately *"information about data"* because it may include structural information, data, and other information.
Short descriptor *one line description*
Long descriptor *multiple lines of text*
Classifiers *are the keywords and information that will be used by other programmers when searching for specific packages.*

The true tests were the challenges presented to you and your ability to code good solutions and algorithms. But, as a programmer, you must start developing your vocabulary and ability to communicate with other "geeks." So, take the "Final Beginner's Test" so see if you need to review the lessons in this course.

THE FINAL BEGINERS TEST

I. Match the term with the best definition:

1. __ program	a) are sets of instructions that tell the computer what to do.
2. __ source code	b) an interactive interpreter
3. __ algorithms	c) is software, (an editor), that helps you to communicate with the computer.
4. __ Python shell	d) is just a group of code that goes together.
5. __ high level language	e) are the algorithms and source code packaged together to achieve your objective(s).
6. __ IDLE	f) is great for writing programs you can save and run later. It is generally used for the final product.
7. __ Block	g) is for testing and trying small ideas quickly.
8. __ programming	h) is a computer language that is closer to human language and easier for us to use
9. __ script mode	i) are used when the programmer wants more direct control over the machine he is using.
10. __ interactive mode	j) is the art and science of making the computer do what you want it to do by creating programs.
11. __ low level languages	k) includes all the algorithms or instructions written in a particular programming language
12. __ docstring	l) another name for modules or collections of related code.
13. __ suite	m) a template that will contain your methods, functions, and other data for that object.
14. __ dictionary	n) are spaces reserved for names assigned to objects or code blocks
15. __ Tkinter	o) the assignment of a name to an object.
16. __ class	p) another way to refer to namespace assignment
17. __ namespace	q) a document string to document information about a function or object
18. __ mapping	r) a way to organize and reference data in key-value pairs rather than by index numbers.
19. __ binding	s) a Python module for making graphical interfaces
20. __ libraries	t) name for indented and grouped code blocks in Python.
21. __ data structures	u) is the over-all appearance of the widget class.
22. __ concatenate	v) object is object code that allows you to loop through items one at a time, repeating until the desired result is achieved.
23. __ list comprehensions	w) an unordered collection of data of zero or more object references that are iterable and hashable
24. __ sequence	x) is an immutable or a frozen set of data.
25. __ iterable	y) objects have a _hash_( ) special method whose return value remains the same through the objects life.
26. __ iterator	z) is a data type that contains items in a specific order
27. __ set	aa) Lists, strings, and tuples
28. __ hashable	bb) applies an expression to every item on your list and out-puts a new list of the results.
29. __ frozen set	cc) is a construct that allows looping.
30. __ style (widget)	dd) means to “glue together” or to combine in a sequence.

II. *True or False?*

1. _____ Blocks of code are organized to help you control the order in which your code is executed.
2. _____ The # key indicates the start of a string in your code.
3. _____ The " or the ' keys indicate the beginning and end of a string.
4. _____ Variables are like little boxes you can put things in.
5. _____ The " key defines a variable.
6. _____ ! = means the computer is calling you foul names.
7. _____<, >, =, <=, >=, != are called comparison operators.
8. _____ The most common operators are; +, -, /, *.
9. _____ "and," "or," and "not" are illogical operators.
10. _____ A "simple condition" means you are not going to die.
11. _____ A "compound condition is a comparison using more than two values like: ***x < 10 and x>5***
12. _____ Boolean data types refers to data that is either true or false.
13. _____ Boolean expressions are also called "conditional expressions."
14. _____ "Delimiters" is just a fancy way to say "the quotation marks around a string."
15. _____ A Float is referring to code that is not working correctly.
16. _____ Floating point numbers refers to numbers with a decimal point.
17. _____ Identifiers are a type of software that checks your code for errors.
18. _____ Integers are complete numbers rather than parts of numbers like ½.
19. _____ A string is a sequence of characters, words, or sentences in quotation marks.
20. _____ The world is flat.
21. _____ The input() command tells the computer that the computer user will enter some data into the computer.
22. _____ An "elif"is what a little green man with the hiccups calls himself.
23. _____ An "if statement" is a statement based on a condition.
24. _____ A "loop" is when the computer goes back and repeats something in a cycle until something breaks it out of that cycle.
25. _____ A while statement tells the computer to continue looping while some condition is continuing to happen; usually while it is still true.
26. _____ Immutable means we can edit it.
27. _____ A list is a sequence of elements.
28. _____ Modules are programs that can be activated in Python and provide you with more tools and functions to get things done more easily.
29. _____ Mutable means we can't edit it.
30. _____ Nested means (placed), inside.
31. _____ A "slice" refers to part of an operation.
32. _____ A Tuple is like a list but can't be edited or changed in its original form.
33. _____ A function is a re-usable mini program inside of your program.
34. _____ A function call is the code you type to turn on a function.
35. _____A global statement tells Python to be able to use the function everywhere in the program.
36. _____ The scope or namespace is the region of influence.
37. _____ A key is used to translate our code.
38. _____ A key-value pair includes the key term and its associated value or definition.

39. _____ Debugging a program involves spraying it with poison.
40. _____ Exceptions are important or exceptional events.
41. _____ Attributes are extra characteristics or pieces of information.
42. _____ A descriptor is an object attribute that can not over-ride attribute behaviors.
43. _____ A weak reference is a way to clean the cache and free memory by not keeping objects "alive" beyond their current use.
44. _____ A constructor makes a new instance of an object.
45. _____ Methods are classes.
46. _____ Procedural functions have parameters and return values.
47. _____ Ordinary functions follow a mathematical model.
48. _____ Tuples, strings, and sets are all mutable.
49. _____ Functional or acceptance tests are always designed by the developer(s).
50. _____ Unit testing involves isolation of individual modules for testing.

III. *Short answers*

1. What are the three types of data that can be stored in a variable?
   a) b) c)
2. The : sign means ______ in Python.
3. The meaning of %s. ______________________
4. Give and example of an escape character ______.
5. What does "OOP" stand for? ______________.
6. What is the meaning of an "object?" ________.
7. A particular appearance of a class or object in your code is called an ________.
8. Functions that come packaged within Python are called ________.
9. Functions you make yourself are called _____________.
10. The __________ is the extra space around elements or widgets.
11. The __________ is the arrangement of elements.
12. _______ refers to the proper structure of the words, indentation, spelling, capitalization, sentences, spaces, punctuation, etc.
13. ________ error refers to a problem that shows up when you run the program.
14. A ____________ is when you expected it and wrote some code to tell Python what to do if or when it happens.
15. The transparency value is the ______ value.
16. ________ is data about data.
17. _________________ are groups of modules, "packaged" together.
18. __________________ refers to the method that various software developers use to keep track of changes during the lifecycle of their software.
19. ________________ is an *outline of the instructions or main events you want to happen.*
20. _______________ refer to when your code runs fine but does not do what you expected or wanted it to do.

Score _________ (of 100).

Answers and explanations are in Index A. If you did not do well, review the vocabulary in Index D and the relevant lessons.

Index A: Answer Key To Final Test

Section I

1. e 2. k 3. a 4. b 5. h 6. c 7. d 8. j 9. f 10. g 11. i
12. q 13. t 14. r 15. s 16. m 17. n 18. p 19. o 20. l
21. aa 22. dd 23. bb 24. z 25. v 26. cc 27. w 28. y 29. x 30. u

Section II

1. T
2. F (*the " or ' keys; # indicates a comment*)
3. T
4. T
5. F (*the = key*)
6. F (*this is the "not equal to" operator*)
7. T
8. T
9. F (*logical operators*)
10. F (*A **simple condition** is a comparison that only uses two values:* **9<19)**
11. T
12. T
13. T
14. T
15. F *("float" refers to numbers that are not whole numbers like decimals*)
16. T
17. F (*identifiers are names*)
18. T
19. T
20. F
21. T
22. F ("elif" refers to the conditional statement "else if...")
23. T
24. T
25. T
26. F (***Immutable*** *means we can't edit it.)*
27. T
28. T
29. F (***Mutable*** *means we can edit it.)*
30. T
31. F *(a slice is a subset of a list)*
32. T
33. T
34. T
35. T
36. T

37. F *(A "**key**" is the name we choose for an entry in our dictionary)*
38. T
39. F (***Debugging*** *is finding and solving problems in a program)*
40. T
41. T
42. F
43. T
44. T
45. F
46. F
47. T
48. F
49. F
50. T

Section II
1. a) integers b) strings c) floats
2. The : sign means "then" in Python.
3. %s is a placeholder *(see chapter 2)*
4. \ *(see chapter 2)*
5. Object Oriented Programming
6. Moveable chunks of code
7. Instance
8. Built-in functions
9. User-defined functions
10. padding
11. layout
12. Syntax
13. Run-time error
14. handled exception
15. alpha value
16. meta-data
17. Distribution packages
18. Versioning system
19. Level-one solution
20. Semantic errors

Index B: Finding More Pythons

**Also see Lesson 21, "Other Useful Packages and Modules." Also check Index x; "Other Resources."*

Beautiful Soup **screen scraping**, parsing HTML, navigate, search and modify parsing to extract exactly what you need. http://www.crummy.com/software/BeautifulSoup

BioPython, **molecular biology**,
http://www.biopython.org/

CPython, standard **Python implementation** **written in C**,
http://www.python.org/getit/

CLPython, **Python in Common Lisp**,
http://www.common-lisp.net/project/clpython

Cython, Python **to C compiler**
http://www.cython.org

dateutil is a **datetime module** for working with date ranges and dates. http://www.labix.org/python-datutil

Docutils **processes plain text files** into other useful formats. http://www.docutils/sourceforge.net

html5lib parser to meet **HTML5** specifications. http://www.pypi/python.org/pypi/html5lib

IronPython, Python **in C# for .NET**
http://www.ironpython.net

Gloss, added to Pygame creates fast running **graphics for games**, http://tuxradar.com/gloss

Jython, Python **in Java**,
http://www.jython.org

Matplotlib, **2D plotting** library,
http://matplotlib.org

MySQLdb **SQL** database connector for Python. http://www.sourceforge.net/projects/mysql-python

NumPy, **science, linear algebra,**
http://numpy.scipy.org/

Pexpect for **controlling and automating other programs**; automation, testing, and screen scraping
http://www.noah.org/wiki/Pexpect#Description_of_Pexpect

PHP, probably the fastest data base **abstraction library**,
http://adodb.sourceforge.net

py2exe converts Python **scripts to executables** for Windows that are able to run without requiring Python to be installed on the target machine.
http://www.py2exe.org

Pychart, charting
home.gna.org/pychart/

PyDaylight, Chemistry
http://www.dalkescientific.com/PyDaylight/

PyEvolve, Genetic algorithms.
http://www.pyevolve.sourceforge.net

PyGame, game creation,
http://www.pygame.org

PyGTK, Easy to create **multi-platform GUI's**

Pyjamas, Python to Java script compiler,
http://www.pyjs.org

PyKyra, game creation,
http://www.alobbs.com/pykyra

Pylab, Python project to make a **Matlab like program integrating Numpy, Scipy, and Matplotlib into one** easy to use program.
http://www.skypy.org

PyMedia, sound file manipulation
http://www.pymedia.org

PyObjC, bridge between **Python and Objective C** http://www.packages.python.org/pyobjc

PyPy, Python in Python, **faster Python**,
http://www.pypy.org

PySoy, 3D cloud game engine
http://www.pysoy.org

Python for Mobile Devices many mobile device tools for developers
http://www.awaretech.com/pymo.html

Python Imaging Library, (PIL) adds **image processing** capabilities to the Python interpreter
www.pythonware.com/products/pil

PythonWeb web programming in Python.
http://www.pythonweb.org

Rpy simple but powerful interface for R programming that can handle any **statistical** problems you can throw at it.
http://www.rpy.sourceforge.net

Sage, offering and **alternative to Mathematica**,
http://www.sagemath.org

Scikit machine learning in Python.
http://www.scikit-learn.org/stable

SciPy, scientific tools for Python,
http://www.skypy.org

Simpi, discrete event simulation
http://www.simply.sourceforge.net

StatPy statistics and many **science** application links http://www.astro.cornell.edu/staff/loredo/statpy/

VPython, 3-D and animations,
http://www.vpython.org

wxPython, cross-platform **GUI toolkit, widget creation**, open source code/free,
http:/ / www. wxpython. org

xlrd a very useful module for **extracting data from Excel** spreadsheets.
http://www.pypi.python.org/pypi/xlrd

Index C: Other Resources

2-D Plotting, http://databits.Iternet.edu/node/75
3D graphics engine http://www.ogre3D.org
3-D Modules http://www.vrplumber.com/py3d.py
494 Projects tagged "**Python Modules**" http://www.freshmeat.net/tags/Python-modules
Code snippets, video tutorials, game making graphics and resources: http://www.toonzcat.com
Computer Graphics: http://cgkit.sourceforge.net/
Data tables, by Google, http://code.google.com/apis/visualization/documentation/dev/gviz_api_lib.html
Educational materials and resources for programming and web site development: http://openbookproject.net//pyBiblio
http://www.parellelpython.com
http://videocapture.sourceforge.net/
Finance, http://quantlib.org/index.shtml
Fluid, physics, http://www.elsa.onera.fr/index.html
Graphics, http://cgkit.sourceforge.net/
Graphics and Gaming: http://www.pythonorgre.com
Graphs, http:/zovril.com/2009/05/26/graphy-a-chart-library-for-python/
Imaging Library, http://www.pythonware.com/products/pil/index.htm
http://www.pythonsource.com
Imaging Library and XML, http:/ / www. pythonwar.com
Many, http://www.dmoz.org/computers/programming/languages/python/modules
Molecular Graphics, http://mgltools.scripps.edu/
Neural Networks, http://leenissen.dk/fann/
Networking Engine, http:/ / twistedmatrix.com
Pygame Cookbook (code to use) http://www.pygame.org
tkinter: http://www.ferg.org/thinking_in_tkinter/index.html
http://www.python.org
Web framework: http://www.djangoproject.com/
Web site development, **database**, and search: http://www.zope.org/
Widget construction kit, http://www.effbot.org/zone/wck.htm
XML, PDF creation, Vector Graphics, text, http://www.reportlab.com/software/opensource/

Index D: Dictionary of Terms

Algorithms *are sets of instructions that tell the computer what to do.*
Alpha value *is the transparency value. Zero would be invisible* while *255 would no transparency*
Assert *allows you to insert debugging code into your program*
Assignment *is just referring to an instruction that "assigns" a meaning or relationship of one thing to another.*
Attributes *are extra characteristics or pieces of information.*
Binary distributions *generally refers to exe installation files and packages for different operating systems.*
Binding *the assignment of a name to an object.*
Blitting *is making a surface object with a copy of the image appear on the screen.*
Block *is just a group of code that goes together.*
Boolean *data type is referring to two possible values;* ***True or False****.*
Break *breaks out of a block of code even if the while statement remains true*
Built-in functions *are functions that come within Python.*
Class *a template that will contain your methods*
Classifiers *are the keywords and information that will be used by other programmers when searching for specific packages.*
Comparison operators *are for comparing things, (<, >, ==, !=, etc.).*
Compound condition *is a comparison using more than two values, (x < 10 and x>5)*
Concatenate *means to "glue together" or to combine in a sequence.*
Conditional expressions *(also called Boolean expressions), are based on the condition that something is either true or false.*
Constructor *makes a new instance of an object*
Python to skip the remaining statements in the current loop block and jump to the next loop block.
Controllers *are any of the devices we use to control things in a game*
Coordinates/*location of a particular pixel is referred to by using a pair of numbers, separated by commas, within a set of parenthesis, (0,0).*
Data structures *Lists, strings, and tuples.*
Debugging *finding and solving problems in a program*
Delimiters *quotation marks to tell the computer we are entering a string.*
Descriptor *an object attribute that can over*
Dictionary *a way to organize and reference data in key*
Distribution Packages *are groups of modules*
Docstring *a document string to document information about a function or object*
Elements *parts of a widget like; label elements*
Else *statement offers a choice in a while loop...do this or else.....do...*
Escape *character tells Python to stop or continue to read the code through the eyes of*

Python
Exceptions *are important or exceptional events*
Expression *any combination of values, (numbers), that can evaluated into annother single value, (number).*
Flip *updates the entire screen and images to objects on the screen.*
Float *non-whole numbers like decimals..*
Floating point numbers *numbers with a decimal point*
For...in *looping statement to find if something is in a list*
Frozen set *is an immutable or a frozen set of data.*
Function *a re-usable mini program inside of your program like the "random" function*
Function call *the code you type to turn on a function.*
Functional or acceptance tests *are user acceptance tests often designed by users*
Global statement *tells Python to be able to use the function everywhere in the program*
Handled *exception is when you expected it and wrote some code to tell Python what to do if or when it happens.*
Hashable *objects have a* _hash_( ) *special method whose return value remains the same through the objects life.*
High level language *is a computer language that is closer to human language and easier for us to use than low level or machine languages.*
Identifiers *are names*
IDLE *is software, (an editor), that helps you to communicate with the computer.*
If *is a conditional statement/statement based on a condition; if a statement is true do...*
Immutable *means we can't edit it.*
Index *refers to the elements within the square brackets of a list.*
Instance *this particular appearance of a class or object in your code.*
Integer *a complete number as opposed to part of a number like ½*
Interactive mode *is for testing and trying small ideas quickly.*
Is *similar to the == operator*
Iterable *object is object code that allows you to loop through items one at a time, repeating until the desired result is achieved.*
Iterator *is a construct that allows looping*
Key *the name we chose for our dictionary entry*
Key-value pair *a key and its associated value*
Lambda *is a variation on the def statement with other functionality*
Layout *the arrangement of elements*
Level one solution is an *outline of the instructions or main events you want to happen.*
Libraries *another name for modules or collections of related code.*
List *a sequence of elements*
List comprehensions *applies an expression to every item on your list and out*
Logical operators *the words "**and, or,**" and "**not**"*
Long descriptor *multiple lines of text*
Loop *when the computer goes back and repeats something in a cycle until something breaks it out of that cycle.*
Low level languages *are used when the programmer wants more direct control over the*

machine he is using.
***Manifest files** contain commands to help maintain the directory structure of your package.*
***Mapping** another way to refer to namespace assignment and dictionaries*
***Metadata** is often defined as "data about data*
***Methods** are functions that are made to be used exclusively within a particular class or object. Methods belong to a particular object or class.*
***Modules** are programs that can be activated in Python and provide you with more tools and functions to get things done more easily. They are moveable groups of code..*
***Mutable** means we can edit it.*
***Namespace** are spaces reserved for names assigned to objects or code blocks.*
***Nested**, (placed), inside*
***Not** works like the English not and makes something the opposite meaning*
***Objects** are moveable chunks of code.*
***OOP** stands for Object Oriented Programming.*
***Operators** do something, like add, multiply, divide, subtract, or compare.*
***Ordinary functions** are the common type of functions that follow a mathematical model and return a value using the return statement.*
***Padding** the extra space around some elements or widgets.*
***Pass** acts as a neutral place holder in some statements*
***Placeholder** (%s) a symbol in our code that indicates a blank value*
***Procedural functions** have no parameters.* This kind of function *doesn't use the return* statement *and doesn't return a value.*
***Programming** is the art and science of making the computer do what you want it to do by creating programs.*
***Programs** are algorithms and source code packaged together to achieve your objective(s).*
***Pygame** is a Python extension library wrapped around the SDL library.*
***Python Shell** is an interactive interpreter.*
rect *variable* *represents the rectangular dimensions of an image or sprite*
***Return** returns a value from a function that can be assigned to another function*
***Runtime error** is when a problem shows up when you run the code. It will generally cause an exception or crash your program.*
***Scope or Namespace** region of influence*
***Script Mode** is great for writing programs you can save and run later. It is generally used for the final product.*
***SDL** library, (Simple Direct Media Layer), is a cross*
***Semantic errors** refer to when your code runs fine but does not do what you expected or wanted it to do.*
***Sequence** is a data type that contains items in a specific order.*
***Set** an unordered collection of data of zero or more object references that are iterable and hashable.*
***Short descriptor** one line description*
***Simple condition** is a comparison that only uses two values, (9<10)*

Slice *a subset of a list*
Source code *is all the algorithms, statements, and instructions that we used in a program.*
Sprite *a picture, or an image that can be animated. Sprites are the objects, characters, explosions, and things that usually move around in your game.*
String *a sequence of characters, words, or sentences in quotation marks.*
Statement *can be instructions that evaluate into a single value or a expressed fact.*
Style *is the over-all appearance of the widget class.*
Suites *are another name for indented and grouped code blocks in Python*
Surface *the space a sprite or image will occupy on the screen*
Syntax *refers to the proper structure of the words*
Theme *a set of widget styles grouped together*
Tkinter *a Python module for making graphical interfaces*
Try, except, and finally *can be used for testing error messages.*
Tuple *like a list but can't be edited or changed in its original form.*
Un-handled exception is what Python generally spits out to tell you *something happened but nothing was done about it.*
Unit testing *involves isolating individual modules for testing.*
User-defined functions *are functions you make yourself.*
Value *the details or definition for a dictionary entry/key*
Variables *are like little like boxes or containers to put different things in.*
Versioning system *refers to the method that various software developers use to keep track of changes during the lifecycle of their software.*
Weak reference *a way to clean up the cache and free memory by not keeping objects "alive" beyond their current use.*
While statement *tells the computer to continue looping while some condition is continuing to happen; usually while it is still true.*
While *while true repeatedly run this block of code*
Widget class *is the type of widget such as; a canvas*
With *statement has to do with writing new classes.*
Yield *has to do with execution flow control and "freezing.*

Index E: Beginner's Cheat Sheet

Common Python syntax colors:

Keywords orange
Strings green
Comments red
Definitions blue
Misc. Words black

Comparison Operators

> for greater than
< for less than
<= less than or equal to
>= greater than or equal to
= = equal to
! = not equal to

Keywords

```
and     continue except    global   lambda     pass     while
as      def      False     if       None      raise with
assert    del      finally    import   nonlocal  return yield
break elif    for      in       not      True
class else    from     is       or       try
```

something = input()
something = (int(input("number"))
print()
while something:
Lists and strings use [ ] mutable
Tuples use ( ) immutable
Mydictionary[ ]
entries= {'key': value}
sets{ } mutable

 # indicates text
\\ escape characters
\n for new line
''' docstrings'''
" " or ' ' for strings
%s position of placeholder
% assignment of placeholder value

mystring= "I eat %s."
food1 = 'apples'
print(mystring % food1)

Functions

```
def name(parameters):
      "docstring"
      suite, or code block
      return [expression]
```

```
nameOfModule.functionName(arguments)
```

```
>>>class    NameofMyClass:
    def __init__(self, txtstring):
    self.txt=txtstring
```

Index F: Files for This Course

You can download the working files, (FilesAndAssets.rar), for this course at www.toonzcat.com

star_field.py
Space_cruise.py
plasmaball.png
Eyes.gif
explosion.gif
spaceship.png
setup.py
Asteroid_Fight.py
Alpha.py

For data folder:
asteroid.png
boom.wav
explosion.gif
laser.wav
music.wav
plasmaball.png
spaceship.png
Asteroid_Fight.ico

Made in the USA
Monee, IL
17 August 2025

23612951R00174